ENDORSEMENTS

"A linguistic smorgasbord. Witty. Charming. An easy read."
Roger Rapske (Author)

"Insightful. Contextual. Deeply perceptive."
Roger Rapske (Student)

"Honestly blunt about the historical religious perspective concerning the parables of Jesus, the author challenges you to give your head a significant shake. His provocative understanding will rattle your theological cage."
Roger Rapske (Theologian)

"These insights will motivate you to spread your wings to experience the abundance and liberty of God's love for you!"
Roger Rapske (Dreamer)

"Is there only so much love for a father to dole out to his children? Say it ain't so! These parables prove God has plenty of love to go around." Roger Rapske (Father)

"The revelations of these parables substantiate the memorable doctrine of life espoused by the insightful Dr. Laura Schlessinger, 'Now, go do the right thing!' It's high time we adopt the mandate to get beyond just knowing what we ought to do, and actually just do it!" Roger Rapske, (Amateur Psychologist)

"Take a peek out the window and get a positive grip on life."
Roger Rapske (Mentor)

"Out from cloistered walls you're about to discover a magnificent view of a heaven of possibilities."
Roger Rapske, (Possibility Thinker)

MORE

THAN JUST

A PIECE OF SKY

Also by

Roger Rapske,
B.Th.

BUT...
an unauthorized autobiography of the Apostle Paul

MORE

THAN JUST

A PIECE OF SKY

Roger Rapske
B.Th.

Trafford Publishing
Victoria
British Columbia
Canada

DEDICATION

To my precious grandchildren:

Ryan & Keira

Love 'em to life!

They love me back 'cause, well, they just do!

I'm their grandpa and that's all they care.

Child-like acceptance.

Is there anything better?

FOREWORD

Coming up with a meaningful, imaginative, and provocative title for a book is a daunting task. The possibilities are staggering to consider. Although I had a number of terrific titles along the way, I left my decision to the very end of the writing process. I believe my choice captures a philosophy of living which Donna, and I aspire to.

As we travel together through our journey of life, on paths built upon a strong tradition and heritage of family and religious training, we've always had a sense in our hearts that there was something more. We've always been well aware there's an obvious sense of security attached to familiarity, just as the tranquility of a comfort zone has definite appeal.

And yet, the magnetic draw of possibilities beyond the confines of our sandbox is very attractive and tempting. The lure of "what's next" is an ever-present reality that challenges our desire for stability. Itchy feet? Maybe that's it. Is it that it's against the grain? Out in left field? Take you're pick. Donna and I have felt it.

We've had many discussions about our apparent problem and resolve it by being more than happy with our progression to expand our horizons. I'm not just talking about where we live, what we drive, or where we work. The spirit of adventure has also hit us hard between the eyes concerning our beliefs. Our theology has been shaken to its core.

Perhaps you've heard the glorious voice of Barbra Streisand sing an inspiring piece of work entitled "A Piece of Sky." To me it's the signature song in that marvelous movie called "Yentl." It's actually a declaration about the "more" in life many of us crave. Find the words and read the challenging expressions of a poet on a search.

Sometimes it's safer to keep our feet planted on the ground in spite of the fact dangers lurk close by. Memories often tug at our shirtsleeve to prevent the urge to step off the curbs of life. But, who has bewitched us into thinking that we're only entitled to a piece of sky?

Who has quashed our vision to dare?

FORWORD

Indeed, the more we learn the more we find out we don't really know. The more we read comes the realization more has been written for us to enjoy. The more we travel the more we need to update the GPS to navigate roads of discovery. Therein lies our quest to flap the wings of adventure and soar to heights beyond our wildest imaginations.

I'm convinced most of the religious training of the past and present has wittingly and tragically allowed pilgrims to see a mere piece of the sky through stained glass peep holes in our spiritual structures. It isn't until we step outside that we catch a glimpse of the immense scope of the heart of God for all. Out from cloistered walls you're about to discover you're no longer gazing at just a piece of sky, you're getting a magnificent view of a heaven of possibilities.

The parables you're about to read are laced with the reality there's much more to sink our teeth into than we've come to believe in. The parables are a colossal collection of illustrations of God's desire and blessing for His creation. The parables are a revelation of the very heart of God, a strong depiction of His limitless love, His amazing grace, and His mercy beyond compare. The parables are a recording of God's intention and invitation for His children to enjoy the abundance and liberty in the Kingdom of God He desires for us.

"Papa, I can hear ya, I can see ya, I can feel ya."

"Hey, papa, just watch me fly!"

Dare with me to spread your wings and soar...

ACKNOWLEDGEMENTS

Who in this world accomplishes anything without the great contribution of others who inspire the genius of creativity, who share the lessons of wisdom and experience, and, who challenge and inspire growth beyond the shadow of contentment? I'm not afraid to admit my indebtedness to many folks who have inspired me, shared with me, and challenged me in the process of completing this particular endeavor.

In 1972 a "you're so beautiful to me" bride came walking down the aisle and said "I do" when my pastor dad asked her if she really wanted to marry the twenty year old character standing beside her, with little more than the glint in his eye. Fortunately for me, Donna said she was up for the challenge. On that day we started our magical journey of discovery together, and after some thirty-seven years we're still growing strong. Beyond all the possessions we've been so blessed to receive and create, we share the treasure of our amazing children and precious grandchildren who spoil us with their love. "Thanks" is hardly sufficient to express my appreciation to Donna and our family for allowing me the time and space for my "authoring" pursuits. This project is, in large part, a legacy to them of my heart and my understanding of God's gift to all of us.

In 1976, Donna and I made the decision to leave burgeoning careers in the automotive industry and go back to school so I could to train to become a pastor. One of the few things we took with us back to North American Baptist College in Edmonton, Alberta, including our infant son Richard of course, was a very special book my father had given to me. The indispensable, invaluable tool was a very unique Bible edited by Edward Reese based upon the dating of Frank R. Klassen, a Christian layman from southern California, who developed a most interesting way of accounting for Biblical dates. I'm indebted to both these gentlemen I've never met for their marvelous work, and for the privilege of having such a framework to guide me in my on-going search for understanding.

ACKNOWLEDGEMENTS

Foremost among a vast assortment of Biblical scholars is a real gem named William Barclay, whose works containing social and historical context of Biblical times are a must for any student of scripture. I'm deeply indebted to him for the treasure of his writings.

I enjoy a rich heritage of religious training. Although the number of preachers and teachers who've made a dent in my armor of knowledge are too numerous to mention I'd be remiss if I didn't honor my favorite professor, Dr. Richard Paetzel. I credit him with shaping my curiosity with the parables as well as the apostle Paul's writings. Perhaps, if he actually has the chance to read my contributions to the literary world, he'd think he failed miserably in his attempt to educate and equip me. Au contraire, for I credit him with the inspiration to search, acknowledging with great respect his life and testimony, for he is the consummate example of one who not only knows what he believes, he lived it in front of all he taught. I applaud him.

I also give a big thumbs-up to all the wonderful inspirational, positive thinking preachers like Dr. Robert Schuller, and some of the other strange ducks out there like Mike Williams, who have the nerve and audacity to think and teach outside the box, somewhat like me!

Thanks to my best friend Paul Tymos for his heart and acceptance of all the heresy we've adopted together. Thanks as well to Tim Driedger, an inspirational mentor, one of those special, special folk in my circle of friendship who challenges me to be the best I aspire to be. I must also throw a big high five to my dear Uncle Eddie Unger, who has welcomed Donna and I with open arms into the fold of black sheep, knowing without a shadow of doubt we graze together upon the multitude fields of abundance and liberty God has blessed us with.

To Matt Hunckler and all the folks at Trafford I express my great gratitude. My sincere thanks to Jean Lawrence for her genuine kindness to guide me as I fearfully dared to move into the technical manipulations required for publication of this effort.

CONTENTS

CONTENTS

CONTENTS

CONTENTS

CONTENTS

INTRODUCTION

Matthew, Mark, and Luke. Three authors who had different writing styles, different recollections, and different audiences.

And then there's little ol' me. I'm certainly different. I'm not even afraid to admit my perspective will be at odds with some, o.k., with most, and the audience of my elocution will no doubt react much like the audience of the apostle Paul on Mar's Hill a few years back. Some will dig it, some will dig it literally (bury it), and some will not care one way or another.

Given the theological position I've arrived at I'd be lying to you if I didn't tell you I haven't considered the strong possibility many folks, especially those of a religious persuasion, will take serious umbrage (get their noses out of joint) with my understanding and interpretations. I doubt very much Matt, Mark, or Luke would have dared to put quill to papyrus if they thought for a nano-second their words would be labeled as infallible and inerrant by a large portion of the religious world for centuries to come.

Well, let there be no miscalculation. I claim not even the remotest aspiration of infallibility, for my inspiration and purpose in writing about my journey of discovery never involved the concept of inerrancy. Nor do I proclaim some kind of mystic understanding up to, or beyond, the level of my education and experience. I'm not a scholar, rather, I consider myself a student on a quest for understanding of God's kingdom, not afraid to question, and unabashedly unapologetic for thinking outside the proverbial box of acceptablility.

I'm also not promoting some new kind of gospel. The good news of Jesus is paramount, and there's nothing I could add to what has already been accomplished by His activity in heaven and on earth. My purpose in sharing my thoughts is to challenge you to give your head a shake, to stimulate you to think outside the sandbox of understanding you're accustomed to hangin' out in.

The common approach for each parable will be to share the parable in my own modern lingo translation; highlight the traditional interpretation of the parable from classes I took in Bible school and from the many different commentaries at my disposal; and then share an understanding I have come to discover and appreciate concerning the kingdom of God.

INTRODUCTION

I have specifically chosen not to dwell on the traditional interpretations that are included in most of the parables, rather, I simply throw them out there for you to gag on and leave it at that. Seriously, it would be well within my prerogative as the author to squash their viewpoints like an unwanted mosquito. That would lead to a very negative perspective and you'd only come away of thinking I'm pretty ticked off with the industry of religion and their bent to the system of self-righteousness. While all of this is true I'd prefer to dwell on the positive, liberating perspective of a new and living way I've chosen to pursue, leaving the wailing and bashing for others to debate. If you read carefully, there ought to be no disguising the vast ocean of difference between what I once believed and propagated, and what I now understand and hang my hat on.

I will not deny what you're about to read is probably very different from what you've ever been exposed to. I don't think you'll hear this kind of stuff from your average pulpit on any given Sunday. I happen to have come to an understanding God did "much more" than I ever dreamed He had before, more convinced of God's unwavering passion for His creation. I'm blessed to dwell in a place of satisfying peace, joy, and liberation I trust you too will discover and enjoy. It is my pleasure and honor to share this viewpoint with you.

As you'll soon see, I'm a firm believer in context. The earthly "ministry" of Jesus is said to have lasted approximately three years, time well spent packing in a whole whack of stuff. Was He consistent in His teaching? Did He alter His strategy along the way?

My research and study has convinced me Jesus was faithfully consistent in His understanding and teaching throughout His ministry. His goal in life and death was to enlighten the world with an accurate portrayal of the kingdom of God from the perspective of One who'd been there, done that. He did so with logic, with clarity, with authority, with irony, and most assuredly, with a wonderful sense of humor most folks don't even recognize.

The Jews called it "charaz."

In our lingo? "Stringing beads."

Any rabbi worth his salt understands the relatively short attention span of any audience. An accomplished tactician moves to educate with a stealth determination to disseminate information, entice response, and keep 'em comin' back for more. I'd consider Jesus to be a master bead stringer, one of the few in history who'd have been at the pinnacle of the art of communicating of any era.

INTRODUCTION

Although often confusing, Jesus employed the imaginative use of the parable as the chief tool in His bag of goodies. He bent some ears. He slapped a wrist or two. He also told more than a few to mind their p's and q's, and indeed, provoked a whole lot of head shakin'. Never did He offer His lessons from behind a pulpit with audiences neatly stacked in fashionable padded pews with bleeping microphone in hand and hi-tech, glossy, power point presentation at the ready.

In the Greek synoptics of Matthew, Mark, and John's writings the word "parabole" is employed 48 times. Simply put it means to "stand alongside." It's used to express a resemblance or likeness of a thing. I'm not sure if someone received a government grant to study it or not, but one industrious person actually counted the number of words Jesus spoke. Apparently more than 1/3 of His recorded words are contained in His parables.

The object of His affection and revelation concerned the kingdom of God. With pinpoint accuracy He has left a legacy of instruction for all to ponder. No audience is worthy of a different methodology. The conclusive active mind of a Jew was no different to Him than the argumentative, philosophical bent of a Gentile. Color, wealth, age, fame, social standing, nor religiosity is immune from the revelation of God's loving grace and mercy.

It's been said a parable is "an earthly story with a heavenly message." I prefer to think of the parables of Jesus as "heavenly stories with an earthly message."

The life of Jesus surely must be considered a model "parable" of the character of God, and, in the end, His death and resurrection became the ultimate parable of God's passion for His own. He unilaterally set in motion the plan to save us "all," yes, I mean everybody (past, present, future), from the righteous judgment we so richly deserved, and completed it by setting us "all" on a sure foundation of tranquility, liberty, and abundance we had no business even contemplating.

Grace. Mercy. Peace.

Wow!

Let's get on with it...

1. **CHEERS !**

THE PARABLE OF THE WINESKINS
Mark 2:18-22; Luke 5:36-39

The first four chapters of Luke's recollections introduce the greatest mover and shaker of all history. The revelation of God's will and purpose for His creation is embodied in none other than His son- Jesus. A cast of characters including the likes of Mary, Joseph, Elizabeth, Zacharias, angels, shepherds, wise men, Simeon, farm animals, and many other things like stars and manger beds play their part in the birth and early earthly life of Jesus (Luke 1:1-2:52).

And just preceding Jesus came John, the baptizer dude. Now there was a pot stirrer if you'd ever see one. He set the stage in his day for One who'd truly turn the world upside down, including the world of some devilish character during a wilderness time-out (Luke 3:1-4:17).

We can also thank Luke for recording perhaps the most definitive explanation of the purpose of Jesus' coming to this earth on God's behalf. Jesus was speaking in Nazareth in the synagogue, a place where the prophet Isaiah's writings were well known, when He revealed the culmination of the prophecies concerning Himself, including the acknowledgment folks probably wouldn't buy into the program. How prophetic indeed!

With literary license, as the author of this book, I've taken the liberty to employ my own translations rather than rely on the traditional scriptural sources like the King James Version, the Revised Standard Edition, the New International Version, or any of the others out there for public consumption. I strongly recommend you take my versions with a grain of contemporary salt while you study alongside with your favorite version.

So, take a read of my version of Luke's account...
"The Spirit of God is upon me."
Why?
"Because God has anointed me.
Why?
- So I can preach the good news to the poor.
- To heal the brokenhearted.
- To preach deliverance to the captive.
- To restore sight to the blind.

- To liberate the afflicted.
- To preach the acceptable year of God!

Listen up, 'cause your ears are hearing the fulfillment of this prophecy (Luke 4:18-21)!

Folks were astounded, not to mention shocked, by the ability of a loser from Bethlehem to heal, His proficiency to preach, His extensive command of scriptures, His nerve to associate with the other side, and His apparent gall to actually extend forgiveness to those who needed it. Fishermen Jim and John (Zeb's kids) and partner Pete couldn't fathom how much fish they caught after the great fisher of all told them where to cast their nets (Luke 4:22-5:1-26).

Well, we're just about at what's quite possibly the first parable Jesus offered up from His arsenal of teaching tools. It's at least one of the first on record. Let me set the scene and paraphrase the transcript.

Publicans, sinners, scribes and Pharisees were among the audience. Those who thought they were righteous couldn't figure out why Jesus would hang out with folks whom they thought weren't righteous (Luke 5:27-30).

Jesus: "If you're not sick you don't need a doctor. If you're sick you do. Hey, I didn't come to heal the healthy. I did, however, come to rescue the sick" (Luke 5:31,32).

Smart Dude: "Alrighty then, how come John's disciples fast and pray, how come the Pharisee's disciples fast and pray, and yet, your disciples party on" (Luke 5:33)?

Jesus: "Hey, could you tell the guests to stop partying while a brand new husband and wife are whooping it up with them? Not! Hey, the party will be over soon enough when the groom starts playing house with his new wife for good" (Luke 5:34,35).

What a vivid illustration!

A married couple back in the day didn't just fly off to some all-inclusive resort or to some state of the art, floating hotel for a sweet time of frolicking on their own. Au contraire! They stayed home and threw a weeklong bash for friends and family. Not only did they stay in their finest duds for the affair, they often wore crowns symbolizing their honored status. The groom and bride were literally king and queen of the domain for a week, and what they said went.

Guess what folks who shared their company were called?

"Children of the bride chamber!"

Beauty!

5

And the audience wondered why Jesus' buddies were having such a good time. Jesus simply told them the children of the bride chamber were just doin' what they were supposed to do! Party on!

Obviously, what Jesus was proclaiming was going against the grain, the religious establishment grain. Why should Jesus be allowed to get away with apparently sticking His nose up at the party line? Who does He think He is anyway?

It's at this point Jesus smells a rat.

Perceptive beyond compare, Jesus lays on them a parable, stringing beads designed with fashionable clarity to explain the reason He'd come.

In my lingo, of course, here's chapter 5:33-39.

"Nobody would try to repair a worn out old pair of jeans with a patch of material taken from a new pair of jeans. Why? If you did you'd not only wreck the new pair of jeans, you'd also make the old repaired jeans virtually worthless 'cause the new and the old materials just wouldn't get along together."

"Furthermore, nobody would dare put brand new, unfermented wine into old, hard, dry, skinned leather vessels. Why? 'Cause the fermentation process of new wine gives off a gas which would simply burst the old containers, not only destroying them, but, spilling out and wasting the good stuff all over the place as well. Look, new wine must be put into new vessels of skin which have a certain elasticity to them allowing the vessel to deal with the pressure of fermentation, thereby preserving both the wine and the vessel."

"Let me throw this in for good measure. Nobody who's enjoyed an old vintage would suddenly choose to dabble in some new wine. It's no secret old wine tastes better than brand new wine."

Folks, the true nature of the kingdom of God simply isn't compatible with old forms of religiosity sanctioned by the likes of the Law and other legalistic forms of righteous seeking endeavors. In Jesus the world was given a new and living way, an energizing revelation of the kingdom of God.

Thinking out of the box isn't a bad thing. New methodologies may well be needed, if for no other reason than sometimes simply doing something differently. Churches and businesses alike have an extreme distaste to go where no man has tread. Pity!

When God decided to place the creatures of His likeness onto this beautiful planet He surely recognized humans as special-the very children of God. Somewhere along the way "we" (oh, let's blame it on the snake) came up with the notion we weren't fit to be His children. A plan was hatched, sanctioned by God as a result of our pleading, to allow us to get back into His good books we assumed we'd been erased from. A phenomenal set of laws, rules, and regulations were established.

The bottom-line? Do good-get good. Do bad-get bad.

Did the system work? I've come to the understanding God came to the conclusion it simply wasn't working. I don't think any less of God 'cause He caved in to the nauseating pressure of folks who thought they could "do" their own way into His good books. Thousands of years went by with feeble results. Sure, some attained to righteousness through faith and works, however, the vast majority were abysmal failures at achieving justification in the eyes of God.

What to do?

God calculated, with absolute simple logic I might add, patching up an "old" system wouldn't suffice. The ability or possibility of restoring His creation into the kind of kingdom He desired from the beginning would take some drastic action, action that only He could take.

And here we've arrived at a parable with two novel concepts that were completely familiar to His audience to explain the concept.

1. Attempting to repair a tattered old pair of jeans up with a chunk of jean material cut out of a perfectly brand new pair of jeans would make most tailors cringe.
2. No vintner worth his cork would ever think of putting brand new wine into some worn out old vessels.

If it doesn't work in the garment industry, if it wouldn't work in wine industry, why in the world would one think mixing new with old could work with getting folks righteous enough to live in the kingdom of God, forever?

No, if the reality of God's will for His creation would actually come to fruition He'd have to come up with a new system all together.

7

Enter Jesus, the One who'd come to proclaim, to heal, to deliver.

Who needed to be rescued?

Those who've already attained to righteousness and health? NOT!

He'd come to redeem those for whom righteousness and health were but a distant dream! There was nothing wrong with the heart of God. There was nothing wrong with the will of God for His creation. He thought folks would want to be His children 'cause they were. Who knew they'd be so stupid to think they were disenfranchised, or, that they'd want to work to become His kids? It seems like they wanted a system so they'd know who was in and who was out.

Dumb or/and dumber!

Enter verse 39. Even Jesus was no dummy when it comes to judging wines. I'm no wine expert by any stretch of the imagination, however, after visiting a winery last summer with our dear friends Jim and Peggy, I'm savvy enough to know there's a mighty good reason they store wine in those big round kegs for years in temperature controlled cellars for years before it's bottled. Old wine is still the best. In fact, like a fabulous woman like my wife, wine gets even better with age.

Was Jesus implying God's love was old and mature enough to win the best-in-show ribbon? Perhaps you could draw this inference, however, I'm content to think Jesus was making a simple comment about His preference for old wine. Old is a good thing when it comes to wine.

It's important to remember Jesus, in His parable, wasn't calling into question the quality of the wine. He was commenting on patching up something old with something new, or storing something new in something old. Mixing old and new doesn't cut it in the sewing room, or in the wine cellar.

A plan recorded in the Old Testament was hatched to give folks what they wanted. Did it work? No. Was it ever going to work? No. Patch up the process? God knew better, becoming all too aware of the reality everyone was falling way short of the target.

The fact remains folks needed a reality check. The old systems couldn't understand the new and living way about to unfold before their very eyes. The old systems weren't going to be compatible with the new order about to be implemented.

Consequently, if folks were going to return to the abundant life in the kingdom of God, the process was going to have to be taken out of their hands and He'd have to inject some new blood into the equation.

No foolin'!

New wine. New bottle.

I'm sad to conclude most today aren't yet about to pop the cork on the best vintage goin,' the crop bottled on the cross, bottled the day Jesus was talkin' 'bout when He told folks they were witness to a new and living way, a fresh revelation of the heart of God for all!

For "all."

Jesus didn't tell this parable to discourage you from becoming unequally yoked. It's not even about you giving up your "old" ways so you can really get into a "new" way of living. Hey, it's not even some kind of negative approach to getting you out of one playground into another. Nor is it about having garage sales to exorcise collectibles.

I've got good news for y'all.

The parable is about the kingdom of God. It's all about what God has done to make the "all-inclusive" nature of His love, mercy, and grace applicable to one and all. Jesus came to fulfill a prophecy that this world would require a new and living way. He came to heal, to restore, and to liberate. Mission accomplished!

What now?

Hey, you're a "child of the bride chamber!"

Party is on dudes! Enjoy!

Cheers!

2. TOOTHPICKS & 4 x 4's !

THE PARABLE OF THE SLIVER
Luke 6:39-49

Jesus was clearly becoming more than just a sliver in the eye of some of the religious leaders and Pharisees. The toothpick was becoming more the size of a nagging 4 x 4 fence post. They were ticked 'cause Jesus and the boys had some corn on the cob on a Sunday (Luke 6:1-2).

Oh for stupid!

What was Jesus' response?

"Hey, you chaps know the good book well enough to be fully aware Davey, back in the day, snuck some grub meant for only the pristine palates of the priesthood. Why shouldn't I be able to stick my hand in the cookie jar on Sunday too, after all, the Son of man is Lord of the Sabbath" (Luke 6:3-5).

Wwwhhhhoooooooooah!

Did Jesus just call Himself the Son of man? Guess so! To top it off, He had the incredible nerve to do some doctoring, namely, hand reconstruction. Yes, on a holy day! Why'd He always pick that day to do all the neat stuff? Well, Jesus was definitely going way overboard now. They, the religious establishment that is, were choked. Something must be done about this dufus-Jesus.

Oh, Oh. Now He's gone and healed a whole whack of folks of all kinds of diseases (Luke 6:6-19). What's got in to Him anyway?

He gave a sermon way up on a mountain, spread some happiness around, dished out some woes, and issued some words of encouragement and exhortation (Luke 6:20-38).

And then Jesus spoke a parable. In my version...

"Can a blind person lead another blind person? Isn't it logical they'd both fall off the curb and land up in the gutter? Any disciple isn't smarter than the master, however, if you're ever going to be perfect you're gonna have to be like your master" (Luke 6:39,40).

Let the truth of Jesus' parable sink in for a moment. Blind leading blind folks generally don't work. I wonder if Jesus wasn't really throwing out a little upper right jab at the religious industry.

The left hook took a poke at those who had a more lofty view and opinion of themselves than perhaps was warranted. Any disciple isn't smarter than the master. Kids aren't smarter than their parents. Students aren't smarter than their teachers.

However, here's a truth you can't shake.

The only way to become as good as your parent is to become, like wow man, a parent. The only way to become as smart as your teacher is to become, like wow man, a teacher. Dah. The only way you're ever going to be perfect as the master is if you become, like wow man, the master!

What an awesome challenge. What to do?

Well, I'm here to inform you there's nothing you could ever do to become like the master on your own!

You'll never have enough "faith."

You'll never "believe" enough.

You'll never have enough money to "buy" your perfection.

You'll never have enough time to get to as many church services as you think you might need to get your life turned around.

Nope, you're going to have to become like the master if you ever hope to become perfect, and there's only one way I know how this could ever happen. It's too bad it had to take a blood bath to make you perfect where it counts.

Oh, there's more Jesus had to say...

"How in the world can you spot the sliver in your buddy's eye when you can't even perceive you've got a log jam in your own eyes? Nor could you say to your buddy, 'Hey, let me help you take that sliver out of your eye' when you can't see well enough to pick up the tweezers."

"You hypocrite! First of all, get the beam out of your own eyes before you attempt to help your buddy get the sliver out of his."

"Listen, you won't get rotten fruit from a healthy tree just like you won't get beautiful, juicy fruit from a lifeless tree. You can tell an apple tree is an apple tree if you see apples growing on it. You can tell a pear tree is a pear tree if you see pears growing on it. You don't see men yanking figs off a thorny rose bush, or grapes off a mess of blackberry branches. Do ya? Not!"

11

"It's also a no-brainer to realize out of the heart of good folks comes an abundance of good words and actions. To the negative, it's also logical to acknowledge bad folks exhibit bad behavior. What comes out of your mouth is a pretty good indicator of what's in your heart."

"Why do you call me 'Master' and yet you don't accept what I'm telling you. Listen, I'll tell you what a person is like who truly understands what I'm saying."

"They're like the guy who decided to build a house. He brought in a donkey backhoe and dug out all the topsoil until he hit rock bottom. He then built his home on the solid foundation. When a flood came the torrent of water raged a losing battle against the house 'cause it was built upon a rock solid footing."

"And what's a person like who doesn't dig what I'm saying? Well, they're like the chump who went ahead and built the house on the topsoil. The floodwater simply scooped up the house and well, let's just say, the house took quite a beating" (Luke 6: 41-49).

There's a progression happening. In the context of the time Jesus was increasingly stirring the waters of understanding as He made His foray into the world of religiosity that seemed to smack Him at every turn. He was coming out of the proverbial theological closet in a way, and folks were starting to take notice.

Jesus was giving a revelation of the kingdom of God and His role in it. He was letting them in on the exciting prospects of paying attention to what He was saying, along with the disappointing results of preferring not to pay attention. The positive spins on how you establish a home, what you let come out of your mouth, and assorted other practical applications based upon the sermon-on-the-mount dialogue are inspirational indeed.

However I hope you'll come to see I'm putting a bit of a different spin on things. I'm convinced Jesus was trying to lay on folks a vision of the kingdom of God that He indeed shared with God. This parable is certainly a lesson concerning the kingdom of God.

The kingdom of God is made up of folks who "are" perfect. There aren't any imperfect members of the kingdom of God.

Folks, this is so important. I said there aren't any citizens of the kingdom of God who aren't perfect.

Did you get it?

Not of themselves, mind you.

No, they're perfected as a result of the work of the Son of man. Remember, the only way you're going to be perfect is if you're "like" the master. The only way you'd ever become "like" the master is if you're recognized as such.

And now, in the eyes of God, you are!

Wow! This is something you'll need to sink your chicklets into. It's good stuff. You've been made as whole as you're ever going to get! When God sees you He sees nothing less than Jesus!

And here's the itch. Most folks didn't get it then, and most folks don't get it today. Jesus unfortunately had to let it out of the bag that folks in the day we're stuck in the muck 'cause they had blind folks leading the blind. Sad. Look, according to Jesus, way too many waste time trying to pluck the toothpicks out of their brothers' and sisters' eyes when they can hardly see the trees for the forest because of the plank they've got stuck in their own.

Why do you think there have been so many wars goin' on around in our world, so much chaos in our lands, such dissatisfaction in our marriages, and such disillusionment in our churches? Folks can't seem to get it through their thick heads that apples come from apple trees, healthy fruit comes from trees which are alive and well, dead ones don't produce a thing, figs don't grow on rose bushes, nor do grapes appear from bramble bushes.

Duuuh!

Jesus was right on. Boy, did He ever hit the nail on the head. He laid it on the line describing two kinds of folks, one kind gets what He came to do, the other doesn't.

Those who have a handle on the truth He was proclaiming concerning the kingdom of God are livin' the life. An understanding of the heart and will of God for "all" is like having a home built on a solid foundation, strong enough to withstand any torrential flood that could possibly come against it.

Unfortunately, the same can't be said for those who don't dig it. They'll find themselves tossed and turned by every sniff of wind. Every time there's a new wave of that-or-this that comes along a flood of enormous change causes nothing but needless challenges to one's sense of belonging and purpose. Folks, without the firm foundation of understanding, don't know what to believe any more.

What a shame!

13

Yes folks, you're being set up. There's much more to come. You're going to learn much more about the kingdom of God as we proceed. There's some mighty fine good stuff comin' down the pike.

Where's the tweezers?

Hang on!

3. TWO P's at a BAR-B !

THE PARABLE OF THE TWO DEBTORS
Luke 7:31-50

The first ten verses of chapter 7 describe the healing of a Roman centurion's slave in the city of Capernaum. Shortly thereafter Jesus, His disciples, and no doubt an entire contingent of hangers-on, arrived in a little town called Nain. Verses 11 to 17 then inform us how Jesus raised to life the son of a woman who'd already suffered the loss of her husband.

Two miraculous healing scenarios happen in 17 verses. Not bad! Is that a tough act to follow, or what? Not really. This is Jesus that Luke is writing about after all. In verses 18 through 23, Luke continues His recollections of some degree of communication that transpired between Jesus and John. Remember John? He's that Baptist dude. Verses 24 to 30 record Jesus' opinion of this great prophet of whom, I'd conclude, Jesus was pretty impressed with. He suggested there wasn't anyone born greater than John. Surely this is high praise if ever there was high praise.

Oh wait. Hang on a second. Hold the applause. Jesus had one little thing to add. Allow me to paraphrase.

"Keep in mind, however, a humble member of the kingdom of God is greater than John."

OOPS!

John, all of a sudden, is no greater than any other humble kingdomite. John baptized all kinds of folks, except of course, folks who should have known the significance of the baptism he performed.

Who'd that be?

I'd be referring to the Pharisees, the very ones who were supposed to be the experts in the Law. Religious leaders. Yep, they were a big time thorn in the butt, frustrating the heck out of folks for whom God had purposed a new and living way of life.

O.K. I'm going to pick the story up at verse 31. Many don't think the parable actually starts until verse 36, however, I think it's very helpful in the context of things. In my lingo...

Jesus,
"To what then should I liken folks of this
generation? What could I compare them to? Well, let's see.

15

They're like children sittin' down at the shopping center calling out to each other saying, 'Hey, we've struck up the band for you at your weddings, and you wouldn't even get up and dance for joy. Hey, we came to funerals to grieve with you, and you didn't even cry.'"

"Look, John the Baptist came along and he didn't even indulge himself with food or wine. What did folks say? 'Wow, what a wacko!' And now the Son of Man comes along eating and drinking and folks say, 'Lookie here, what a pig. Must be an alcoholic. He's even buddy-buddy with tax collectors and outcasts!'"

"Go figure! The reputation of wisdom is surely, and yet most unfortunately, entirely in the hands of those who think wisdom is their inheritance."

Then a Pharisees by the name of Simon decided to ask Jesus over for supper. Jesus graciously accepted the invitation and showed up at the appointed time. He took His place on the picnic blanket, and faster than you can say "pass the corned beef on pumpernickel," the meal was on.

One particularly curious woman managed to discover where Jesus was doin' dinner that evening. Small town rumor mill I suppose! This wasn't just any woman mind you. No. No. Well, perhaps we should take the high road and say she was simply a woman of ill repute. O.K. The lady was a tramp, a prostitute!

She decided to crash the party. She made sure she had on her best little going-out-on-the-town outfit, cute sandals, with matching purse. Into the purse went a most beautiful alabaster flask containing a very expensive perfume. Off she goes to pay her respects to someone she certainly thought worthy of getting to know a little better.

Somehow she managed to sneak into Simon's courtyard where the bar-b was happening, approaching Jesus from behind. She came 'round, knelt down in front of Him, and promptly started bawling her eyes out. Her tears flowed onto the feet of Jesus as He was sprawled out on the lawn mat. Taking no time to search for the handy wipes in her purse she decided to wipe His feet with her hair, following this up by anointing them with her perfume.

Now, the Pharisee host didn't know exactly what to make of this rather strange disturbance of the proceedings. I'll bet this is what he was thinkin.'

"Hey, if Jesus was truly a prophet He'd surely know who the woman was, and what's worse, He must know what kind of person was touching Him. Surely He'd realize she's not exactly a keeper."

Jesus must have surmised what Simon was thinking.

"Hey Simon, I want to tell you a little story."

And now we have, according to most commentaries, the parable. My version...

"Very well Master. Say on."

"Once upon a time...there was this banker who had two chaps indebted to him. He had loaned one fellow 500 bucks, and the other fellow only 50 bucks. The time came for the loans to be repaid and, low and behold, neither of the two could come up with the cash to repay their creditor. For some goofy reason the banker graciously decided to forgive both of them their debt."

"Now Simon, tell me, which one of these two characters d'ya think had a greater sense of appreciation of their banker and his graciousness towards them?"

"Well," Simon responded, "I'd think it'd be the one who'd had his 500 buck debt wiped out."

"Very perceptive!" Jesus replied.

Jesus looked down at the woman sprinkling perfume all over his feet and spoke to his host, "Simon, do you see this woman? I came into your home as your guest and you didn't even provide me with any water to wash my dusty feet. But this woman not only washed my feet with her tears, she wiped them clean with her beautiful hair. You didn't even greet me with a peck on the cheek, and yet, this woman hasn't stopped kissing my feet since I sat down. You didn't offer to soothe my parched head with oil while this kind soul has soothed my feet with her precious ointment."

"Look Simon, let me level with ya. The lady may not exactly be the cream of the crop in your eyes, perhaps a tramp in the opinion of others. Indeed, her deeds of indiscretion may be too numerous to mention, however, her sins are forgiven! She's just full of love."

"D'ya get it? Those who have the least forgiven seem to have the least amount of love to give."

Then Jesus directed His words to the woman who had given of her love to him.

"Sweet woman, I want you to know your sins are forgiven."

As they munched down the mountain of prime ribs, pickled potato salad, baked beans, and peaches 'n' cream corn on the cob some of the folks started a whispering campaign.

"Who the heck does this guy think he is anyway? How come He thinks He can forgive sins?"

Jesus acknowledged the woman once again.

"Alrighty then, your understanding has made you well. You can go home now. Take care, and go in peace."

Pharisees were experts at keeping the law, and not just the written, recorded law either. They were zealous to keep even the oral, traditional laws of the Talmud. Any who didn't maintain their strict view of the legal observances were frowned on with contempt. Simon, of course, was a Pharisee.

Perhaps he was super-aware of the trouble Jesus could become, so he invited Jesus over for supper to keep an eye on Him. Nah, somehow I doubt it. Perhaps he just wanted to get Jesus off by himself where he could try to get in a few digs without causing a disturbance. Nah, somehow I doubt it. Hey, maybe Simon just liked to hang around celebrities. Then again, maybe he was downright taken by Jesus and His message. Nah, somehow I doubt it.

Whatever the case, Simon must have been shaking his head with profound pride to have such an important guest in his home.

Then there was the woman. Talk about nerve. You've probably seen the commercials with the staid looking secretary with glasses and hair up in a bun. At the appropriate moment she loses the glasses, reaches her hand to the back of her head, releases the hair clip and voila, her hair explodes into this long, flowing mass of adornment to a now gorgeous looking specimen.

Well, this vision somehow reminds me of this particular parable woman. She must have been quite stunning, a real looker when she felt the liberty to let loose. In the time of Jesus, however, if a woman took her head out of its customary bun cover you'd have been staring directly at a prostitute. For a woman to unbind her hair in public was considered the height of immodesty.

And don't kid yourselves. Having some smellies around during a time when showers weren't exactly a common household feature wasn't that bad of an idea. It was quite common for women to wear a little vial of concentrated perfume around their necks. The alabaster containers weren't cheap either to say nothing of the perfume.

Some things never change. I can personally attest to the cost of not only the perfume, but also the container. The smell of "Angel" perfume on my beautiful wife is a real turn on, and Thierry Mugler was a marketing genius to put the perfume in those incredible star-shaped bottles we just "have to" collect. And do we have a collection!

Roads were more like hard pack dirt than pavement. Even roads made of bricks gave off their share of dust. Sandals were hardly a sufficient type of shoe to keep one's feet from getting a bit on the smelly, or dirty, side. It was common courtesy for any host to offer some water at the front door so the traipsing feet wouldn't mess up the carpet. It wasn't even an oddity to provide some olive oil or something similar so guests could comfort their parched foreheads.

Some folks probably even had servants to help out with the kind and gracious task of greeting their guests with purposeful, practical hospitality. And when a rabbi would come to visit, he even got a special peck on the cheek, perhaps both cheeks. Not to do so was a definite sign of disrespect.

Well, let's get into the traditional view of this parable with a view to understanding some of the common views and interpretations floating around the religious countryside. This is similar to the exercise we did as we studied each parable in one of my favorite classes at Bible school.

Central Truth:

One who is forgiven much will feel a greater sense of love and forgiveness towards others. The one thing that shuts us off from God is self-sufficiency.

Traditional Interpretations:

- The difference between Simon and the prostitute isn't the degree or measure of their sin, but that she realized more truly and deeply the reality of her sin. Simon, armed in self-complacency, wasn't even conscious of his need for forgiveness. The prostitute, on the other hand, was keenly aware of her need, and of her deliverance from sin.

- We love God because He first loved us.
- There's a definite link in the ratio of the measure of forgiveness received and the measure of subsequent love.
- The generosity of one's character is revealed in their spirit of hospitality.

Practical Applications:
- If one loves little it's because they have little sense of deliverance. Only when we're conscious of the degree of our forgiveness do we feel the wonder of being forgiven.
- It isn't the amount of sin but the awareness of sin that makes us appreciate the forgiveness of God.
- Our love for Jesus is no greater than our appreciation for pardon, which depends on our conviction of sin.
- This parable doesn't teach us to abound in sin so grace might more abound. This isn't a license to sin more so we can appreciate forgiveness all the more.
- Hospitality, generosity, and kindness are a reflection of a heart changed by the presence of God.
- If our heart is to love God a lot we must think much of what we owe to Him.
- Sins, like selfishness and pride, can wreck life for even those we meet in the privacy of our own homes.

Think about the context for a moment as opposed to just a few verses. Jesus was painting for us a picture of how people think and act. He set us up with an irreverent view of the wisdom of mankind. We think we're so smart. Wisdom, far too often, has become a detriment and impediment to action. Furthermore, we generally apply our wisdom to justify whatever we jolly want to do anyway.

"But wisdom is justified of all her children" (Luke 7:35, KJV).

"Ah well, wisdom's reputation is entirely in the hands of her children" (Luke 7:35, J.B. Phillips).

"The reputation of wisdom is surely, and yet most unfortunately, entirely in the hands of those who think wisdom is their inheritance" (Luke 7:35, my version).

What was Jesus getting at? I'm thinking Jesus understood the human condition very well indeed. The generation of folks He found Himself surrounded by couldn't make up its mind about anything.

They didn't know whether they should be happy or sad. They couldn't recognize a prophet if they saw one. Nor did they know how to recognize the Son of man in spite of the fact He walked among them.

How come?

Wisdom is in the eye of the beholder!

Wisdom is the tool by which priorities get assigned. It's the implement theologies and philosophies are established by. Generations come and go thinking they're the ones with the smarts.

Makes me think of a sad but true statement I read recently. "There are two classes of people, the righteous and the unrighteous. The classifying is done by the righteous."

Well, Jesus must have been saddened to witness the cloud of wisdom emanating from that particular generation. Just to prove His point Jesus issues a wonderful little parable. The folks who happened to be present at the little soiree probably left the event scratching their hairpieces, a sure sign Jesus was correct in His assessment of their wisdom.

The parable itself concerned someone of means who lends different amounts of money to two clients. When neither one of them could repay the loan the banker graciously wiped out both of them.

What good fortune.

Jesus then posed a question trying to ascertain who they thought would have more thankfulness, the chap behind door # 1 or #2.

Upon hearing it Jesus simply says, "Go figure.

You know, in my opinion, Jesus wasn't really telling Simon something he didn't know. The principle shouldn't have been anything new to Simon. "Simon, don't you get it? Those who have the least forgiven seem to have the least amount of love to give" (Roger's version vs. 47).

You see, Simon had deliberately chosen to focus on the reality that the chap who'd been forgiven the 500 bucks would, by any natural standard, be most thankful, and in response, be more giving than the chap forgiven the 50 bucks. No-brainer you'd think!

Well, not so fast on the trigger folks. Lost in the shuffle of human wisdom is the fact that, from the perspective of God's wisdom, the banker forgave the debt of both chaps. Five hundred bucks was the same as the fifty bucks to the lender.

Forgiveness wasn't allocated based upon the response to it by the two gentlemen who had their debts obliterated. Forgiveness was extended based upon grace and mercy. Both of them didn't get what they did deserve, and furthermore, both of them got what they didn't deserve!

Folks, the sad truism of this parable is that the concept of grace is understood more completely by folks who accept grace for what it is, a gift. The religious community, folks who should have known better, got their noses out of joint by affixing their wisdom to the concept that some they consider less than worthy could receive what they've received as a result of a fantastic gifting. Well, the unmerited, unjustified gift is nothing less that God's limitless and eternal love, forgiveness, and acceptance.

From their perspective Simon wasn't much of a sinner whereas the prostitute was a miserable loser. Simon didn't show the honor he perhaps should have to Jesus but he wasn't really a lose cannon or something, however the prostitute was able to show her love because she was a slut. They couldn't figure out the rationale of Jesus to forgive the sins of the prostitute after she threw herself all over Him, and yet, He didn't think it was necessary to say anything about the sin of their gracious host. The host was left to clean up the kitchen perplexed as all get out, and the prostitute left forgiven. What's up with that?

I doubt very much that Jesus considered the social butterfly as a tramp just waiting to be set free. Nor do I think Jesus looked down upon His host for not giving Him a peck on the cheek or oiling his feet. Jesus was very well aware that the proportion of His love ought not to be confused with their response to it.

Furthermore, as if all this duplicity staring them right between the blinkers wasn't enough, they were blown over with the whole terrifying prospect of authority. "Who does Jesus think He is?" "How come He thinks He has the right to forgive anyone's sin? That's blasphemous!"

Go figure.

Human understanding figures God came to save the poor wretched sinner. Lost in that notion is the reality God sent Jesus to save the whole world! Jesus didn't discriminate between good and bad. He didn't pick whites over blacks. He didn't favor the poor over the rich. Nor did He base His decision of whom He'd save upon what make of camel they drove, what color they white-washed their house, or which particular village they choose to live in.

The decision of God to forgive the sins of the whole world on the stripes and scars of His only begotten Son was based upon one thing, and one thing only, namely, the love of His heart! Folks were led to believe it's all about how they responded to the laws, rules, and regulations that bound them to political correctness. You can be as ambivalent about God's love as was Simon, or as unfamiliar with it as the prostitute was. Don't matter. God's love will never change.

This is precisely the point Jesus was trying to get Simon to understand. The woman understood the gift of forgiveness and left without a whimper. The snobs of superiority and political correctness were left to consume themselves wondering about authority and rights.

I don't know about you but I'm so thankful God took care of my debt. It makes little difference to me whether it was fifty cents worth or fifty gazillion dollars worth. Hey, it didn't even matter to God. He forgave my debt. All of it!

Why?

Because He wanted to! Because of His grace!

Grace showered upon me what I didn't deserve. His mercy prevented me from getting everything I did deserve.

Why?

Because He loved me, and knew in His heart I was worth every drop.

And now, with this completely different perspective, I have the great joy of understanding God provided His grace to everyone else too. I've been liberated from the folly of judging anyone else. I no longer am consumed with the notion someone else got what I didn't get, or that someone else didn't get what I got.

Talk about a mind-altering perspective.

4. AGRICULTURE 101 !

THE PARABLE OF THE SOWER
Matthew 13:1-23; Mark 4:1-25; Luke 8:1-21

Here's the scene from Matt's account.

Jesus decides to take a hike. Seeking peace and quiet He hits the beach to enjoy the tranquility of the warm air and gentle breeze off the water.

No such luck.

Like one of the many famous religious stars of the day, folks recognize the charismatic character and are attracted to Jesus like butter to popcorn. Some were zealous memorabilia hunters just waiting for His autograph to increase the value of their collectibles. Others were no more than avid curiosity seekers. To be sure, some wanted merely to hear words of wisdom from one recognized as a premiere teacher of the day, not to mention one of the most imposing crap disturbers of the religious community.

Witnessing the commotion amid the throng of beach bums caused a flurry of activity among a flotilla of recreational and commercial fishing boats just offshore. Not wanting to miss out on anything many of the mariners cranked their rudders and headed in to participate in the event.

Recognizing the value of a floating pulpit Jesus hopped aboard one of the anchored puddle jumpers to address the gathering. Speaking to them in parables Jesus began to illuminate the throngs with revelations concerning the nature and scope of the kingdom of God.

"Hey y'all, listen up!"

"The farmer went out into his field to plant his crop. As he scattered the seeds some of them fell along the pathway. Well, it certainly didn't take long for the birds to swoop down and devour the treat."

"Some of the scattered seed fell upon patches of rocky ground. The seeds sucked the life out of what little nutrients there were in the shallow covering of dirt and grew rapidly into a mere form of things to come. In turn, unfortunately, the blazing sun then scorched the life out of what little had become of the sprouts. Without roots to

provide stability and nourishment the plants simply
withered away."

"Some of the seeds the farmer scattered ended up in
soil overrun with baby thistles. As the thorny weeds grew
up side by side with the intended crop the fledgling seeds
were choked by the sheer veracity of the pesky neighbors."

"But, indeed, seed did fall into some good soil.
Some sections produced a yield of 100%, some 60%, and in
other areas the maturation rate was more like 30%."

"Now, if you've got ears to hear, listen to what I've
just told you."

If the records of this revelation ended here we'd be scratching
our heads the same way the disciples probably did. At the earliest
opportunity they were able to get Jesus to themselves for a few
moments when they not only questioned the teaching methodology of
Jesus, they required an explanation of the teaching 'cause they were
duly confounded by its meaning.

Jesus was keen to perceive their ears were primarily attached to
the heads for hearing, and not so much for understanding. It's true!
Just because something goes in doesn't necessarily mean it gets
processed!

Let's examine the response of Jesus to two questions. How
come you're talking to us in riddles? What you talkin' 'bout?

First, "why parables?"

"Because, the challenge for you chaps is to know and
understand the mysteries of the kingdom of God. The problem is that
all these wonderful folks haven't had the benefit of the same
instruction you've enjoyed from me."

"Look, I use parables for two reasons. First of all, those who
have some understanding can handle the message, and they'll gain an
even greater appreciation of the truths expressed in the parable.
Secondly, those who don't understand the mysteries of the kingdom of
God will become even more confused than they already are by what
they've been taught!"

"You've witnessed this yourselves. I can draw a simple picture
and some folks still won't get it. I could speak with the clarity and
authority of synagogue bells and some folks still wouldn't get the
drift."

"Don't look so perplexed. Remember what that Isaiah dude said a long time ago about God's frustration with folks who couldn't seem to take a hint."

"For stupid! You folks have heard all you want with your ears, and yet, you still don't comprehend a thing. Your eyes see what's right in front of you, and yet, you still don't perceive a thing! For this people's heart has grown cold, their ears are dull of hearing, and their eyelids have closed up shop. Wouldn't it be ironic if at any time folks would actually see what's right in front of their faces, if they'd actually listen to what their ears have heard, or if they'd actually understood with their heart the truth they've heard. My goodness gracious! Perhaps they might actually be converted from their ignorance to allow themselves to be healed by me" (Isaiah 6:9,10).

"Hear me out. Your eyes are truly blessed for they actually can see what's right in front of them. Your ears are truly blessed as well, for they actually hear the truth from the very source of truth. You've been blessed beyond compare. I'm tellin' ya, prophets and righteous men alike would loved to have seen the things you're getting to see. As insightful as they were, they never did get to see such things as you've seen. They'd have given one of their ears if their other ear would have been able to hear the very same things you've been privileged to hear, and yet, they never did get to hear them."

And then the response to the second question of, "what the heck did you just say?"

"So, listen up to the message of this parable of the sower. When anyone hears the truth about the kingdom of God, and understands it, they're left wide open for one to come with the wicked purpose of deceiving and misleading them away from the great truths planted in their heart."

"But, just like the soil lightly covering the stony base is the one who hears the word of truth and receives it initially with great enthusiasm. And yet, the depth of understanding is able to sustain them for only a short period of time, for when the truth of the kingdom of God begins to actually hit home, their comfort zone is slowly challenged to the point they truly become offended by the truth."

"The one who received the seed among the thistles has been blessed to hear the word of truth, and yet, the cares of this world and the deceitfulness of self-righteousness choke off the wealth of understanding contained in the word of truth, becoming unfulfilled, hopeless, and frustrated in their life."

"But, the one who receives the seed of truth concerning the kingdom of God, like the good ground received the seeds, is one who's heard the word of truth and has come to understand it in varying degrees. Some get it 100%, some get 60% of it, while others get about 30% of it."

Then Jesus threw in a few extra gems for those who cared to listen.

"Is a lamp brought out in to the living room just to be put under a latte table, or under a bed in the boudoir for that matter? NOT! Isn't it supposed to be set upon a lamp stand?"

"Listen here! There's nothing to hide as far as God is concerned. Everything will be made abundantly in due course. Neither is there anything to be kept secret, for the clear intention is that the truth concerning the kingdom of God will be fully revealed."

"If you got ears, use 'em!"

As if this weren't enough for the disciples to chew on, I'd like you to pay special notice of this solemn warning He gave them as He wrapped up their lesson of the day.

"Pay attention to what you've heard. Your life will be measured by the strength and depth of your understanding of truth. The more you understand, the more you will come to understand. The more you know, the more you will come to know. Those who get the picture, and yet, who don't do anything with their knowledge and understanding of the word of truth, well, let me just say they're big time losers!"

Ooftah!

I feel obliged to make a few comments since I've taken the liberty to share with you my own transliteration and lingo in combining the three New Testament accounts into this one version. You can read the separate accounts of Matthew, Mark, and Luke on your own. They've all recorded what they seemed to recollect of the actual events.

Are there differences? Sure. Don't be alarmed. Hey, even my dear wife and I through thirty-seven years together in the blissful state of matrimony don't always see eye to eye on certain things. If you think three of the twelve fellows who spent three years hoofin' it around Palestine with Jesus would agree on every detail you're a bit naive.

Did Jesus tell the parable down by the bay or from a bench in some city park? Was His audience a collection of farmers, fishermen, beach volleyball players and sunbathers, or city slickers? How come one author (Mark) can count from low to high (30-60-100%), another (Matthew) counts backwards (100-60-30%), while another (Luke) likes to deal with a whole meal deal (100%)?

It's obvious horticulture wasn't the specialty of any of our three diary keepers. Soil conditions, weather conditions, and other factors involved in the life and death of the seeds are somewhat different in each account.

I say, "WHATEVER!"

Then there's the audience.

Let's count among them the disciples. Luke informs us there were also a suitcase of women, including a group who'd been cured of a variety of mental and physical illnesses; Mary (Magdalene) out of whom went seven devils (curious information); Joanna-the wife of Chuz, a financial advisor and accountant to non other than Herod himself; Susanna; and many others who helped minister to the physical needs of Jesus out of their own ability.

And we shouldn't forget the mother and brothers of Jesus were present. Guess what Jesus replied when told His mom and brothers were in the crowd and that they wanted to see Him? He said, "My mom and brothers are ones who understand the word of God and live it."

Interesting eh!

Well, let me summarize what you've been told this parable means by pulpitizers (new word) and teachers who regurgitate the writings and thoughts of scholars whom they think have nailed it. At least these are the traditional main themes we gleaned during our study of this parable in Bible school.

AGRICULTURE 101 !   PARABLE OF SOWER

Did you get it? "Gleaned." Parable of the sower. "Gleaned."
O.K. O.K. I thought it was funny.

Central Theme:
There are different responses to the seed that is sown due to
the variety of soil conditions. However, in spite of the apparent waste
of some good seed, a harvest will indeed occur.

Traditional Interpretations:
- The outcome of the crop depends on the conditions of
  the soil-the heart and mind of individuals who respond
  to the implantation of the seed. The different soils
  represent the different states of hearts and minds of
  mankind. While the quality of the soils may be called
  into question, the quality of the seed may not.
- Surely the disciples must have been keenly aware of the
  meager effectiveness of the ministry they had struck out
  on, with Jesus as their fearless leader. So, the parable
  was spoken primarily to the disciples, with the purpose
  of encouraging them with the certainty of an ultimate
  harvest. The outward signs of the kingdom of God may
  not be recognizable as yet even though the inauguration
  of the kingdom of God has been set in motion.
- Allegorical view: seed=Word of God; birds=Satan;
  thorns=cares of the world, deceit of riches;
  soil=shallowness or depth of character; wayward
  ground=shut mind which won't respond; rocky
  ground=shallow faith and understanding; thorny
  ground=life overtaken with worldly interests; good
  ground=responsive heart yielding fruit galore

Practical Applications:
- Just plant the seeds! You aren't responsible for the
  harvest.
- Be patient! There will be a harvest.
- Be ready to hear the truth of God's Word and it'll
  produce a harvest of fruit in your life.
- Men can and do reject the seed (Word of God). Indeed,
  it can only be accepted by those whose hearts have
  been prepared to receive it.

29

In my humble opinion, more than just a few folks have missed the boat on this one. Get it? "Missed the boat." Jesus spoke the parable from a boat. O.K. I'll move on.

I can just imagine how frustrated Jesus must have been. Here He was trying to give folks a revelation of the kingdom of God and they couldn't see it for looking at it. He couldn't even tell a simple story without having to explain Himself. Some folks probably didn't get a whiff, some folks fell asleep, some folks were daydreaming about what, and, just as important and time consuming, where they're going to do lunch. To be sure, some folks actually dug the message of the parable of the sower. Get it? "Dug" the message. I know, I know. And, for those folks who did dig it, there must be the realization the fruit of their understanding certainly varied quite substantially.

The sad reality is those who claim to have ears to hear are as deaf as deaf can be. Is it any wonder Jesus felt some compassion and empathy with Isaiah? Isaiah was choked. He was frustrated beyond belief 'cause he was one who saw more than most folks did. His understanding and trust rested far beyond himself, and yet, when he looked out at the "chosen" people, he just couldn't believe what he was witnessing. Folks in his day didn't get it either. Everything they ever had need of was right in front of them. They had the eyes to see it and they couldn't see past their blinders. They had minds to comprehend, and yet, they didn't have a clue. Did they ever get it? Not in his lifetime.

The religious community, ones who "chose" to be soil # 4, or ones who thought they were the "chosen" ones to be soil # 4, seemed to claim a higher level of understanding. I wouldn't be surprised if Isaiah, if he could have poked his nose down into the situation would have concluded this group was still the most discouraging of all. What an indictment!

Jesus was compelled to speak in a way folks could understand Him. Did they? Not! We have here another parable that's an incredible revelation of this inability. Parables were employed to give a revelation of the mysteries of the kingdom of God, a revelation of the heart, character, and will of God for all.

Folks, the parable is not about you. Neither is it a slick, sexy seminary course named:
"Agricultural Studies 101-How to Grow a Great Crop!" or
"Horticulture 201-Soil Manipulation!"

AGRICULTURE 101 !   PARABLE OF SOWER

What was the first clue?

It's not called the parable of "the" sower for nothing. In the Greek it was not "a" sower who went out to sow, it was "the" sower who went out to sow. So, right from the beginning Jesus was letting us in on a wonderful truth. The parable is about the nature of "the" farmer, namely God.

When God set about to plant He didn't discriminate! There's not a dose of favoritism in His heart. The seeds of His love were dispatched to those many didn't think have a hope in Iraq, to the shallow and inept, to the self-indulgent, as well as to those who've been prepared to receive them. While many in the crowd were treading desperately in the water of confusion Jesus sat comfortably dangling his feet over the bow of the boat trying to help folks see the majesty of God's grace and mercy.

There are four nifty words in Mark's rendition Jesus used to identify those upon whom the seed fell.
- "And these are they by the way side where the word is sown..."
- "And these are they likewise which are sown on stony ground..."
- "And these are they which are sown among thorns..."
- "And these are they which are sown on good ground..."

You see, these are they: the stoned, the shallow, the thorny, or the fertile. You could be any one of these. No matter. The seed of God's love has touched your life. The point of the parable is that while some folks get it, many folks don't.

I once preached what I considered a masterfully crafted, not to mention exquisitely delivered, sermon drawn from the Mars Hill message given by Paul. What were my main points? There are three basic responses to the preaching of the gospel. You see, I was taught by my homiletics professor every good sermon is constructed on three points.
1. Some won't dig it at all.
2. Some folks will procrastinate about making a decision.
3. Some folks will get it.

I'm disappointed in myself that, while I probably said a few insightful things, I didn't really have a clue at the time about how accurate this understanding falls in line with the intent of the parable Jesus told from the boat docked in the bay.

31

Paul had been wandering around the ancient city of Athens noticing all the idols to various gods, including an auspicious statue erected to an "unknown" God. Paul had the great honor of declaring to folks who this unknown God was, and furthermore, what He had done for the whole world.

Don't believe me? Read it for yourselves (Acts 17:19-34). And pay attention to what God did. For the "whole world."

Universal. Unequivocal. Unashamed love.

I'm hear to tell you I'll feel ripped off if I come to find out Jesus came to die for only 30 % of the world. If God Almighty would be happy to settle for a 60 % yield then He can have it. I'll feel cheated if God, the loving, gracious, merciful God in whom I have placed my hope, merely sent Jesus to this world for only those who would "believe" in Him.

Jesus better had died for the whole world as far as I am concerned. How could God possibly have left my fate in my own hands?

"What about free will?" you ask.

Free will? Give your head a shake! It sure isn't anything I'd put my faith in!

In this parable none of the soils had any say in regards to which kind of soil they were, let alone a say about what kind of yield they'd deliver. Even soil # 4 apparently couldn't claim 100% across the board.

No, the point of the parable is this: "the" sower sowed.

The fact some don't get it doesn't negate the gift. It's unfortunate many are swayed away from this truth by the profoundly ignorant theologies of self-righteousness. It's sad so many lose out on the joy of God's abundance by getting choked up on the pleasures of this world. It's ironic that many who should know better miss out 'cause they've been convinced you don't get something for nothing.

Why did Jesus say those who had understanding would receive even more understanding, while those who didn't understand would lose even what understanding they did have?

Why indeed!

I can only speak for myself. I've been on a wonderful journey for 57 some odd years. Thirty-seven years have been spent with a wife I treasure more than anything we have come to possess together. We've lived in times when we barely scratched a few quarters out of the cookie jar to hit a 7-11 so we could share a slurpee. I said share "a" slurpee.

Ah, we've also lived in abundance. I'm blessed beyond my wildest dreams to have amazing children and fabulous grandchildren to boot. Together we woven a tapestry of life with our collective creative genius that surely is the envy of many folks we've come to know.

In addition, yes, beyond all of this, I've experienced in the past six years or so an incredible journey into a world of understanding I never could have imagined for most of my life. The more my eyes are opened the more I see, kind of like the poet who penned the song, "A Piece of Sky."

Like Paul of old, I've had a major league eye opening experience along the way. The mysteries of the kingdom of God are clearer to me now than ever before, including the years I spent studying to be a pastor, as well as the many years of committed service in a wide variety of positions in a number of church systems.

God has done more, no, "much more," than I ever thought He did. While the territorial doctrines of inerrancy, infallibility, and divine inspiration have little appeal to me now, I have a deeper appreciation for the Bible than I've ever had in my previous understanding. The insights I've gained from the studying and writing about the life of Paul have stunned me into an understanding I never thought was possible.

What am I saying?

The parable is an accurate description of reality. Understanding the heart of God has led to a greater depth of understanding about the mysteries of the kingdom of God. Unfortunately, many folks have lost their understanding of God's grace.

How?

They've had it plucked off by deceivers. They've had it choked off by the lust and perversion of self-righteousness. They've become over run by the pressures and conventions of daily life. Just as sure, there are many who've settled for under achievement in spite of a solid base of teaching and revelation. Sadly, many have been led down the proverbial garden path of thinking they hold the key to their eternal fate.

Well, according to Jesus, the mysteries of the kingdom of God have been revealed in Jesus, and in all He was to accomplish. Miracle of miracles, there's nothing left to be accomplished. Folks are more loved than they know. They're more saved than they've been led to believe.

Folks, fruit isn't a product of our doing.

The production of fruit isn't an obligation or responsibility we have to repay God, nor to gain His favor. Exhibiting the "fruit of the Spirit" was never something we were charged to do. Fruit is the nature of God. The "fruit of the Spirit" are qualities of God in Jesus!

And now, because when God looks at us He sees in us the beauty and purity of Jesus, we "are" the fruitfulness of God's loving grace, mercy, and peace.

So, the parable of "the" sower means something quite different to me than I previously understood. I feel much more comfortable placing the focus of this parable on the goodness of God rather than on the degree of my fertility or servitude. It speaks much more to me of God's blessing than of my role and responsibility in trying to attain His righteousness.

Why?

Because His righteousness has already been applied to me on the cross and from the empty tomb. The seed has been planted all right, in Jesus. For one and all, once, and for all time!

The harvest isn't something that God is waiting for, so what in the world are we waiting for? He reaped what He sowed when Jesus completed what He was sent to earth to accomplish, and then returned to His honor and majesty just waiting for us to join Him the moment we're done doin' what we're to do on planet earth.

And what are we here to do? We're here to make a difference! A message like this shouldn't be kept under wraps.

Hide it under a bushel?

NOT!

Keep the candle under the bed?

NOT!

What on earth good would that do? Set your light on the vast banquet table set for you where it'll do some good.

Can you dig it?

Well, you can if you've got ears to hear...

5. WHAT A FARMER !

THE PARABLE OF THE SEEDS
Mark 4:26-29

Here's my version:

> And Jesus said,
> "The kingdom of God is like a farmer who planted some seeds out in his field then continued on with his normal routine, sleeping at night and rising up during the day to work."
>
> "The seeds have a life too. They spring to life and mature even though the farmer doesn't fully understand all the genius intricacies of the scientific miracle which transpires to make it all happen."
>
> "You see, nature has a way of taking care of herself. In due season you simply see a glimpse of a blade of grass. Soon enough a cob take shape, eventually maturing into a masterful earful of corn."
>
> "But, when the crop's ready for harvest the farmer gets to it, his sickle is sharp, and his barns ready to be filled."

This particular teaching of Jesus really doesn't get much attention from scholars, perhaps because of it's singular treatment from Mark, or perhaps, because of it's brevity.

In the scheme of things it's sandwiched between a threesome of horticultural based parables: the sower, the tares, and the mustard seed.

However, we did study it in our parables class in Bible school and here's a brief synopsis of the traditional approach to understanding this teaching of Jesus as we studied it.

Central Truth:

The kingdom of God is like a growing crop in which there are times of activity and inactivity. The point isn't the gradualness of the growth of the seed, rather, the sureness and inevitability of its growth. The seed develops from stage to stage of its own volition.

Traditional Interpretations:

- There were some among Jesus' followers who advocated the use of violence as a means to an end. In response to this Jesus asserted the kingdom of God, its times and seasons, were in God's hands.
- Jesus was counseling His followers to persevere in faith.
- The harvest represents the completed order and nature of God's reign whether in the heart of a person, or, with the fulfillment of the reign of Jesus.
- Growth involves several observable stages that vary in length and characteristics.

Practical Applications:

- The work begun in us by the Spirit of God will continue until His purpose in us has been fulfilled.
- We must resist the temptation of expediency for immediate results but sow the seed for more permanent results. The parable is a summons to patience.
- While the process of growing Christians may appear to be slow, it's sure.
- Accept the sovereignty of God for the present as well as the future.

These are but a few of the titles thrown at Mark's recollection of this particular teaching of Jesus.
- "The parable of seeds growing secretly..."
- "The parable of seed growing by itself..."
- "The parable of the sickle..."
- "The parable of agricultural grace..."

Take another look at the opening words of Jesus. Did He say:
- The kingdom of God is like an ignorant farmer?
- The kingdom of God is like the seed?
- The kingdom of God is like the growing seasons?
- The kingdom of God is like the sickle?

Not! Jesus said the "kingdom of God is like a farmer."

I spent a few years of my growing up life in a farming town where my father was the pastor of a country bumpkin church. The thriving 4-block metropolis of Hilda nestled 40 miles northeast of my birthplace, Medicine Hat, Alberta.

Farming was all the rage back then in those parts as it is today, albeit on a slightly different scale. While most of the great farmer characters I knew hadn't even completed their high school education, I'd definitely not call any of them ignorant. While they might not have understood the complexities of the scientific marvel of seed reproduction, they knew how and when to plant, and they knew full well how and when to harvest.

Most of my farmer friends were hard workers. They even slept hard. I witnessed many of them take a Sunday afternoon nap on the floor beside the dinner table right after a fabulous meal of freshly baked bread, new potatoes rejoicing with a lake of home made gravy right dab in the middle of the mashing, unbelievably sweet vegetables, and the most awesome sausage right out of the farmer-sized smoker.

Wow! I just made myself hungry! These memories go back over 40 years, and my taste buds haven't forgotten a thing.

The farmers I knew couldn't affect the weather. They couldn't affect the length of the growing season. They couldn't even predict the quality of the crop in spite of the fact they had remarkable intuition. Oh yes, they did know how to read the agricultural bible, the farmer's almanac.

But what I remember most about them was their unrelenting ability and willingness to let God do what God does. They went about their lives and their business day after day, come rain or shine. They planted in season. They harvested in season. They took it a bit easier out of season.

You'd probably prefer to call what they had "faith." Perhaps you'd be right. It's uncompromising acceptance of God's will.

Well, life in the kingdom of God is like that!

I'm inclined to understand God has a much different perspective on things than we do 'cause He sees the whole picture. Jesus was trying to give His listeners, many of them of them with an agricultural bent, a different view from what they'd been taught. He told them they may not understand when corn gets its first breath of life, nor how exactly the maturation process proceeds from blade to ear to a full and ripe ear of corn, however, it none-the-less happens. The very fact that the kingdom of God happens without our interference is ample information that planting, feeding, and weeding our not even within the scope of our mandate on earth. While it may appear God is somewhat distant and uninvolved nothing could be further from the truth. He's got a pretty good handle on things.

Furthermore, Jesus was no less accurate or emphatic in describing the surety of a harvest. These folks weren't dumb either. When grapes were ready, they needed to be harvested. It was party on 'cause trampling all over the grapes to make the wine was a blast. No less pleasurable I'm sure was the sweet fulfillment of getting the entire harvest of grain into the barns in due season.

The object Jesus chose to help folks visualize the implementation of a harvest was a very common tool from the farm, namely, the sickle. Wow. Sharp. Stealth. I find it quite interesting this particular tool has been adopted in some circles as a Christian marker of global missionary endeavor. Even more interesting that the sickle became the predominant symbol of communism!

Could it possibly that the kingdom of God was initiated by His creative genius whereby the doctrine of "one-for-all, and all-for-one" would be the order of the eternity. What a concept! Let your noggins work that whole idea over a bit and you'll see why the "all-inclusive" nature of the kingdom of God makes so much sense to me.

I also think it's high time we enjoyed the revelation that it isn't our job to "sickle-ize" the world over and over again. Jesus made an amazing statement, one that we've conveniently glossed over because it just doesn't quite fit into our theological perspective. You see, we continue to be taught a harvest is a future event.

What did He say?

"...the harvest "is" come."

This parable is such an incredible revelation of the heart of God it isn't even funny, it's fabulous! If there ever were a picture of what the kingdom of God is like you'd be hard pressed to find a better one. The parable isn't a description of our role in the kingdom of God. It's all about God's role in bringing the whole kingdom together at His pleasure.

It's time we gave our heads a collective shake.

God's the farmer all right. Not only that, God established the farm. He established the perimeters of its operation. He planted the seed. When the seed bore the fruit it was to bear, it was harvested.

WOW!

While it may be absolutely contrary to what you've been taught in the past, give your brain a few moments to mull over this incredible question. How many harvests do you think there are going to be? I can't fathom the notion God would plant and harvest, plant and harvest, plant and harvest, and plant and harvest over and over again.

The thought of Jesus having to die on the cross over and over and over again is not only repugnant to me, it's incomprehensible.

Ain't gonna happen!

Don't believe me? Get into the writings of Paul. He concurs with Jesus. The harvest was ready, and God used the sickle all right. "Once," and for "all." If you still think there's a harvest yet to come I'm afraid you're either badly misinformed, misguided, or plain too caught up in a world of self-righteousness.

The parable isn't about you. It's not about how good a farmer you are. While not unimportant, it's not about the significance of your perseverance in faith. While not to be depreciated, it's not even about your trust and hope in God's ability to take care of His kingdom.

The harvest indeed represents the completed order and nature of God's reign. He's already gathered the harvest into the barns. It's a done deal!

Folks, please understand this parable is a wonderful teaching by Jesus concerning the nature of the kingdom of God. It's all about His sovereign will. It is a revelation of God's love, His grace, and His mercy towards His kingdom.

What a farmer indeed!

6. BASTARD WHEAT !

THE PARABLE OF THE TARES
Matthew 13:24-30; 36-43

Many of you have heard sermons preached on this little teaching of Jesus often called the "parable of the tares" however, many of you may not even know what a tare is.

Well, in Job (31:40) the word is used to describe some foul, stinking weed. Elsewhere in the Old Testament (Jonah 2:5) it may actually refer to a kind of seaweed, or, as a poisonous hemlock weed (Hosea 10:4). Sometimes a tare referred to a variety of useless grass having the appearance of barley. Apparently, a tare might even be described as a common grain field pest in Palestine called "corn cockle."

The word "tares" used by Jesus in this particular parable most likely referred to the bearded darnel (Lolium tremulentum). Ain't that cute? Say lolium tremulentum 10 times as fast as you can. In its early stages of growth one probably couldn't distinguish between the weed and the wheat. Unfortunately, before harvest, it was almost impossible to remove the weed without doing major damage to the crop if the infestation wasn't controlled from the outset.

In fact, farmers had such a hate-on for the darnel weed they had a nickname for it. "Bastard wheat!" That's right, bastard wheat.

Etymology lesson: The Greek word for the weed (ziznion) comes from the Hebrew (zunim), closely connected to "zanah," which means: "to commit fornication."

Popular tradition taught the bearded darnel originated at the time of wickedness preceding the great flood. Everything in creation, animate and inanimate alike, goofed up big time, committed fornication, bringing into creation lots of things completely contrary to nature.

Not only was the weed a pest, it also posed somewhat of a health hazard. Being slightly poisonous, digesting the narcotic, bitter, and unpleasant tasting weed could cause symptoms of dizziness and stomach aches.

Just think about the spiritual implications of this thought. Self-righteousness will make you dizzy all right! Get caught up in the frustration of trying to be good enough and your stomach will be in knots too!

"Hey, dude, pass me some of that weed" may not be as contemporary as we might think. I wouldn't be surprised if that darnel stuff lifted more than a few spirits higher than the proverbial kite back then.

Separating the pesky weed from the wheat was accomplished during the harvest. Large trays of grain were placed before women and children who had the unenviable task of plucking out the offensive weeds. Although similar in size and shape with the grain, the bearded darnel weed was distinguishable by its slate gray color.

Don't be overly amused or caught off guard by the notion some enemy might be responsible for infecting a nice guy's field. The declaration of "sharing the weed" and its inherent ill is no idle threat in many countries to this day. This offensive crime was actually forbidden in Roman times, with codified laws laying down appropriate forms of punishment. I dare say many could fall into the category of virus spreaders, many of them within the religious community alone.

Well, enough weed talk. Here's my rendition of Matt's account:

So Jesus hits 'em with another parable.

"The kingdom of heaven is like this farmer chap who went out and planted some good wheat seed into his field. The stealth, nighttime operation by an enemy of his was undertaken to plant a whack of that pesky bearded darnel weed on this farmer's field while he slept ever so soundly."

"But, in time, as the wheat developed and matured, so too did the weed. The farm hands were the first to notice what was going on so they went in to the farmer to confront him."

"Hey boss, what's up? Did you plant wheat this year or did you somehow get the bags of seeds mixed up? How come the field is weeping with weeds?"

"Go figure. All I can think of is some dirty rat must have wanted to pull one over on me!"

"Well, what do you want us to do? Should we go out and rip the weeds out?"

"Nah, let it go. If you start yanking the weeds you'll end up wrecking the wheat too. Just let the both plants grow up together and when it comes time to harvest I'll let the harvesters know they'll have to be careful to separate

the two. I'll tell 'em to cut and stack the weeds in bundles then burn the whole mess, and to gather the good wheat together into the granaries."

Well, Jesus goes on to tell folks the parable of the leaven (13:33). You see, Jesus taught in parables. In fact, He didn't even talk to folks without using a parable or two (13:34). Why? For one thing, prophets said He would. They said He'd use parables to reveal secrets that haven't been understood from the beginning of time (13:35).

After He finished the parable teaching Jesus told the crowd to get lost. Well, maybe He was a bit more tactful. Some time later the disciples came up to Jesus while He was relaxing in the home they'd been invited to stay at.

"What's up with the weed parable, eh?"
"Well, the farmer who planted the good seed is the Son of man, the field's the world, and the good seed are the children of the kingdom. But the weed seeds are the children of the wicked one, and the enemy who sowed them is the deceiver. The harvest is the end of the world, and the harvesters are the angels.

"Just as the weeds are gathered up and burned in a fire, so it will be in the end of this world. The Son of man will send His angels to gather out of His kingdom all things that offend and sin. They'll cast them all into a furnace of fire, and let me tell you, there'll be plenty of crying and gritting of teeth goin' on."

"After that righteousness will shine like the sun in the kingdom of their Father."

"Got ears? Then pay attention to what you've heard."

What's the traditional approach? Here's a brief synopsis of what you'd find if you did some research.

Central Theme:
Good and evil will grow and exist together until the harvest of all harvests down the road will reveal and separate the two. Patience is needed in leaving the judging to God.

Traditional Interpretations:

- sower=son of man; field=world; good seed=sons of kingdom; tares=sons of satan; ower of tares=satan; harvest=end of world; reapers=angels
- Jesus said what He said and we shouldn't try to overstate or over-allegorize it. If the central truths are evident without putting meaning into it, that should be sufficient.
- There's an evil one (Satan) present in this world trying to destroy the good.
- Weeds or not, there will be a harvest.

Practical Applications:

- It's possible the disciples were worried about the kind of folks Jesus was attracting.
- This parable taught the disciples to leave the judgment of the heart to God who looks not on the outward appearance, but on the inward.
- Be patient in your judgments 'cause some day God's judgment will inevitably come.
- Not all who follow Jesus are genuine.
- The church isn't a great exhibition hall for the display of perfect Christians, but an educational institution for the development of imperfect believers.
- The premature effort to get rid of bad may uproot good.
- Guard against being judgmental 'cause folks won't show their true colors 'til the end.

Let me tell you, I find this parable extremely fascinating. As I reflect on my previous understanding I'm not surprised I bought into the traditional approach hook, line, and stinker. This whole concept of a future harvest to root out evil once and for all makes perfect sense if you want to find rhyme and reason to the perversions of our day.

Knowing judgment was reserved for the future at least gives some breathing time to sow a little wild barley, so to speak, before it all comes crashing to an end. I secretly hoped God wouldn't come until I at least had a chance to live a long, healthy, happy, and productive life here on this world. If Jesus wouldn't show up 'til after I'm dead and gone, all-the-better!

However, I'm now convinced Jesus issued another revelation of the mysteries of the kingdom of God that very few folks have picked up on. It all boils down to a matter of timing, the timing of the harvest. Traditional understanding points to a future harvest. I believe Jesus was telling us the harvest was about to happen in His day. So, it's already happened as far as I'm concerned!

The Hebrew term could either be the end of the "world," or, the end of the "age." The cross ended one "age," and the resurrection invoked a completely "new age." The age of the coexistence of good and evil in the viewpoint of God came to a screeching halt on the fateful day over two thousand years ago now. Furthermore, the Law, the conveyer belt tool used to identify the difference between good and evil found itself no longer useful or necessary under the fire of God's passionate justice of grace and mercy.

Indulge me.

You might think Jesus' analogy, as recorded by Matthew, would really throw a monkey wrench into what I've come to understand. At first blush, and perhaps subsequent blushes, you might assume I'd prefer not to have the explanation Jesus provided for His parable.

Not! I quite appreciate His commentary.

I don't have a problem with understanding God and His Son created the farm. Hey, they own it and manage it. Furthermore, they came up with a plan to fill it up with their likeness and let 'er rip. I also appreciate the reality of a radical interruption of a deception that has been a royal pain in the butt for many a folk.

Deception. Dah. Has to be the devil. I wouldn't be surprised if the translators of the word were motivated to personalize a sinister perpetrator. The devil! Satan! Sounds scary. Why? It's the ultimate fear factor. Good versus evil. Good guy versus bad guy.

You may not know it but the word "devil" is the very same word as "slander," or "deceive." The uninformed and disenfranchised could understand the concept of fear even though they were uninformed and disenfranchised. Control. That's what it was all about. Reality and truth aren't altered by terminology. The fact remains the rightness of God's kingdom was interrupted by the lust and deception of the doctrine of human self-righteousness. Self-righteousness is a slanderous deception of enormous proportions.

I don't really care what you prefer. Call it what you may, the devil, Satan, deception, seduction, slander.

One illustrious comedian captivated the concept in his famous monologue proclaiming he wasn't the problem. Accepting responsibility wasn't the way to go. So he concluded "the devil made me do it!" Whatever. The deception of humankind's role in its eternal destiny is a perversion of truth.

It may look like truth. It may smell like truth. It may even feel like truth. Well, it's not! Those who proclaim it make it sound like it's the only way. "You've got to believe or it's a no go." "You must accept the gift or you won't get it."

Well, no matter how much the deception of self-righteousness tries to exemplify and imitate the righteousness of God it simply can't do it. It never could. It never will!

We've bastardized the teachings of Jesus, Paul, and others with the horrible, cancerous deception that we possess the power to gain the righteousness of God by what we believe, by the strength of our faith, or by the resolve of our good work. The consequences of the doctrine of self-righteousness maturing along side the gospel of God's limitless grace and mercy is exactly the same as the bastard wheat (tares) maturing right along with the good wheat in the farmer's field Jesus spoke about.

And then the harvest! In the parable the bad and good grew together until the harvest. The time came for both of them to show their true colors. The bad was wiped out, the other fulfilled its destiny. The harvest for all eternity took place at the end of the age all right. The fire of God's justice took its vengeance out upon all that was sinful. Weeping and gnashing of teeth hardly describes it.

It happened at the cross!

Out goes the old. In come the new. A new age began with the resurrection when the kingdom of God was forever and unalterably etched upon the entirety of God's creation.

Oh, what did Jesus say when He wrapped up His summary of the parable? He just happened to pick a beauty from good old Dan.

Read it and weep...for joy. "Then will righteousness shine forth as the sun in the kingdom of their Father" (Daniel 12:3).

When? At the end of the age, when the cross and resurrection introduced a whole new history in the making. That's when "then" occurred.

Folks, the sun of our Father's righteousness is brightly and warmly shining on His kingdom as you read.

Snag a ray, or a zillion of 'em!

7. I DIG IT !

<u>THE PARABLE OF THE HID TREASURE</u>
Matthew 13:44

We live in a day when we have innumerable sources of storing away our money. Banks, whether you like their methods or not, provide a service which most of us take for granted. Some folks, according to some of the latest commercials, even love paying the fees the banks dispense, if for no other reason, they get reminded just how much money they don't have. Quite funny. Lending institutions have spread their wings so much we can access our money from a cash dispenser on virtually every corner you find a mini market or gas station.

Things were a tad different two thousand years ago. Hey, most common folk didn't have an overabundance of disposable cash in the first place either, however, places to safely store their meager savings were virtually nonexistent. Safety deposit boxes and home safes weren't all the rage back then.

According to a rabbinical saying there was really only one safe place to protect your money or prized possessions, specifically, in the ground! The Jews, then and now, inhabit probably the most fought over chunk of land in the whole wide world. Josephus, that great history buff we've all come to know and appreciate, wrote about how Jewish folks would bury their precious possessions of gold and silver underground in hopes of protecting themselves during times of uncertainty and impending war. They left their homes with the hope they could return to reclaim their treasure.

"Finders keepers, losers weepers!"

Ever use this line? I've used it on more than one occasion, especially as a young pup when rights of ownership came into dispute. It might have been a stick of gum, a cherished baseball card, or a discarded Archie and Jughead comic book. My goodness, I should have used the "bury it in the backyard" trick. I'd be worth a small fortune today if I could get my hands on all those Mickey Mantle, Roger Maris, Whitey Ford, and Yogi Berra cards we used to play with like they'd never be appreciated for anything more than the great noise makers whacking against our rear bike tire spokes.

The good ol' Talmud also laid down the rule of law for Jews concerning items up for grabs. Loosely translated it went something like this:

"Whatever is found belongs to the finder. And what kinds of things must one cause to be proclaimed? Well, whatever is found belongs to the one who found it. If a man finds scattered fruit, scattered money...these belong to the finder."

Jesus, no doubt, was very familiar with the teachings, so He set about to give us His take on the rule. Matt records his version and I employ my translation skills.

> **"Again, the kingdom of God is like treasure hid in a field, which, when a man discovers it, is hidden again where he found it. Then, with great joy and knowledge of the value of the treasure, he goes and sells everything he has in order to purchase the field where he re-hid the treasure."**

It seems the guy who discovered the valuable buried treasure in this parable wasn't prepared to test the system. The discovery warranted some extraordinary precautions. He was shrewd enough to understand if something could go wrong it probably would. Now, I know Jesus didn't tell us his name, but I think his name was Murphy. Since he didn't find the treasure in his own back yard he felt it prudent to preserve the secrecy of his discovery. So, he shrewdly re-hid it. He then set in motion a plan to sell everything he had in order to acquire the land on which he had made the amazing find.

Once again we've been treated to an amazingly beautiful description of the kingdom of God. The traditional approach we studied in Bible school will serve to illustrate again the emphasis placed upon "our" role in the kingdom of God, a bill of goods that hardly comes close to the magnificent jewels in this little parable of Jesus.

Central Truth:

If we'd be willing to give up almost anything to secure an abundance of earthly treasure, how much more should we be willing to give up in order to attain an abundance of heavenly treasure?

Traditional Interpretations:

- The value of the kingdom of heaven is greater than anything else. The parable was intended to encourage the disciples that, even though they'd given up everything to follow Jesus, they'd receive even more back at some point in the future.

- There is true joy in sacrifice and a definite reward for genuine commitment.

Practical Applications:

- We must seize the great moments when they unexpectedly come if we are to possess the treasures found in the kingdom of God.
- Surrender must precede victory.
- The compensation will exceed the sacrifice.
- The man who found the precious treasure was doing his daily work, therefore, you'd better get to work!

My! My!

And for years I thought like this. Go figure. I'd like to propose a different perspective, a perspective that sheds light on an amazingly simple picture of the kingdom of God from One who helped paint it.

The treasure didn't suddenly become treasure because it was discovered! The treasure was a treasure all along. Neither did it increase in value after it was discovered. Although the treasure was technically his, based on established principles of religious law, the discoverer made provision to secure the treasure. When all the dots were dotted, and all the T's were crossed, a price was paid to ensure there'd be no dispute whatsoever concerning ownership of the treasure.

The value of the acquisition was not merely in the value of the land. It found its worth in the value of the treasure. What did Jesus say? He said, "The kingdom of God is like unto treasure hid in a field."

Now, He didn't say, "the kingdom of God is like a guy who gave up everything to buy some treasure." He didn't say "the kingdom of God is worth more than you could possibly imagine so don't just take the goods, buy the farm," nor, "the kingdom of God is worth the price of admission." Jesus didn't even say, "the kingdom of God is like 'wow man,' so get busy and find some treasure for yourselves to sink your teeth into."

NOT!

Folks, the kingdom of God is like a treasure.

I've always understood the treasure was Jesus because this is what I've been taught over and over again.

I always thought the parable was instruction for me to do something spectacular to secure my spiritual destiny. It was my great responsibility to do everything I could to secure the rights to Jesus.

Buy the farm too! If it meant the sacrifice of family, friends, future, and in fact, most earthly joys in order for me to be a productive member of the kingdom of God, then it was my obligation to do so.

In an understanding of a new and living way I recognize this viewpoint just doesn't make logical sense to me anymore. The parable isn't merely about me in the traditional sense! Like the man in the story, God was unwilling to leave any possibility of disputing the question of ownership in the future. Like the finder in the story, when the time was right, God sacrificed everything He was, and had, in order to acquire something of inestimable value.

Oh folks, this is absolutely incredible. What a turn around of understanding. Please, track with me now.

I am the treasure!

Yes, I'm the treasure God bought the farm for!

I'm the treasure that cost God the power and glory of His only precious Son!

I'm the treasure that cost the very life of Jesus!

I'm the treasure which Jesus became sin for!

Did you get that?

I'm not so much perplexed at how God could make me sinless, as incredible as this is. I dig the part how the grace and mercy of God has made it possible for me to be righteous in His sight. It might have been a mystery before, but now, I get it.

What I'm still trying to wrap my brain around is how Jesus could become sin in the first place! This just blows my mind. I don't know about you, but this whole concept freaks me out. Blood, sweat, and tears.

Why?

To ensure nobody could ever question to whom I belonged to again, Jesus became sin for me!

Why?

Because I'm worth it!

God knew I "was" worth the pain and suffering. Not only was my value to Him worth the sacrifice, He was happy to do it. It brought Him tremendous joy to do so.

WOW! ! !

Don't be misdirected to press the story to go where it ought not go. The story isn't about me giving up everything to gain the kingdom of God. The story isn't about my commitment and dedication. The story isn't about me paying a price I can hardly afford to acquire something I could never purchase in the first place.

What the story is about is God paying a price He could afford to pay for someone like me, one who continues to give Him so much joy it thrilled Him to pieces to do so! The story is all about the recognition of God of my inestimable value to Him!

The story isn't about me becoming someone God needs or wants. It's all about me being someone God loves!

Perspective and context.

Folks, I dig it!

8. BLING ! BLING !

<u>THE PARABLE OF THE PEARL OF GREAT PRICE</u>
Matthew 13:45,46

Here's another gem (get it? gem? pearl? oh, carry on) from the pen of
Matt. It's like Jesus wasn't getting through to His audience so He had
to hit them with the same idea using another analogy.

> **"Again, the kingdom of God is like a shrewd jeweler
> on a pearl hunt, who, when he found a pearl of great value,
> sold everything He had to buy it."**

Pearls have long been alluring jewels of choice, achieving great
value far beyond their genuine, natural beauty. The aesthetic joy of
simply holding or rolling a smooth pearl around in one's fingers is hard
to describe. What wouldn't most women give to have a beautiful
matching set of pearl necklace and ear rings?

Pearls weren't exactly a rare item on the world stock exchanges
in the time of Jesus. Pearls from the shores of the Red Sea, the Persian
Gulf, and even from far off places we know today as Great Britain and
India were traded commercially. The passion to acquire fine pearls for
investment purposes would no doubt require a fair amount of
disposable cash.

In this little parable Jesus told we've got a jeweler who
recognized quality when he saw it, and knew what it would cost him to
get it. He was on the lookout for a pearl and when he found it, gave up
whatever it took to acquire it.

The traditional approach has seen fit to concentrate on the
sacrifices we (the jeweler) must make in order to attain a sniff in the
kingdom of God (the pearl). Let's take a brief look at this analysis.

Central Truth:
The parable speaks of the necessity of sacrifice in order to
obtain an object of great value-the kingdom of God.

Traditional Interpretations:
- The kingdom of God, like a pearl, is the ultimate value
  of man's search.
- Second best must give way to the very best.

- There may indeed be other pearls out there, however, there's but one pearl with the greatest value.
- While men may search for the hidden treasure and come upon it quite unexpectedly, this particular merchant had spent his life searching for this priceless pearl.

Practical Applications:

- If you want the best (the kingdom of God) you're going to have to give up everything you have to get it, whether it may be money, comfort, or even family.
- No response can be made to the call of the kingdom of God that doesn't begin and end in complete surrender to God.
- There will be a certain amount of risk involved. The price for entry into the kingdom of heaven is the willingness to risk.

Whoooaah!

For years I've understood that a main objective for my life was to hunt down the seemingly elusive jewels of the kingdom God always intended me to have. I've come around to understand Jesus' view of the kingdom of God was vastly different from what I thought it was. In this little story He wasn't giving me a revelation of the pearl as much as He was giving me a revelation of the jeweler. He didn't tell folks, "The kingdom of God was like a pearl." Nor did He say, "The kingdom of God was like a pearl of great price."

What He did say was that "the kingdom of God is like a shrewd jeweler."

Different focus. It's about Him folks, not us!

Once again, the traditional approach made the success or failure of my search dependent on my responsibility. I won't dispute the fact sacrifice may be required in almost any endeavor to get something you're after. Hard work is commendable if not a downright critical element of success in any endeavor. Perhaps it's even true that there's a statistical correlation between the amount of sacrifice required and the value of the object being pursued. The higher the stakes the higher the required sacrifice. I'd be the last one to squash enthusiasm and effort. Very little in this life comes without some kind of cost.

While this may be true in the mortal, earthly dimension, this requirement of a sacrifice on my part is absolutely contrary to the revelation of the kingdom of God that Jesus has presented for us. In the eternal, heavenly dimension the very reason God had to send Jesus was my inability to sacrifice enough. The entire sacrificial system built around laws, rules, and regulations was not enough to get me righteous, let alone anyone else, let alone the whole world!

My traditional understanding of the comparison between a pearl of value and the invaluable kingdom of God is quite lame to me now. The notion I carried with me that other religions, philosophies, gods (pearls) out there could be at any comparative level to the kingdom of God (ultimate pearl) just doesn't do it for me any more. All you have to do is go to a bookstore or a library to discover the search for a higher meaning to life has captivated our culture. In my opinion, the challenge to search for truth through a maze of different truths until you actually stumble upon a "real" truth is a somewhat precarious challenge indeed.

Who's to say which truth is the real truth? Buddhists think they have it. Roman Catholics think they have real truth. Surely Pentecostals know what's true and what isn't. Then there are the Methodists, Hindus, Mormons, Unitarians, Lutherans, Anglicans, and oh yes, the Baptists among others. All of them profess knowledge of truth.

None of the above choices do it for me. Sorry. I prefer the wisdom and truth Jesus spoke about. He gave us a revelation of the kingdom of God that makes a whole lot more sense to me. The kingdom of God resembles a jeweler, a merchant of fine jewels.

Now, this cat in the parable seemed to have it all, or did he? If he had it all, why was he still looking for that one special pearl?

Here's the rub. God had majesty. He had power. He had infinite wisdom and knowledge. He had unspeakable authority. However, there was a pearl of worth He had His sight on!

ME!

Oh, do you remember the little chorus we sang so proudly as children in Sunday school? It went something like this:

Jesus loves the little children, all the children of the world,

Red and yellow, black and white, all are precious in His sight.

Yes, Jesus loves all the children of the world.

As a child this was very comforting to me. How could I lose with a God who loves me just because He does?

The carpet of my childlike understanding was all too soon ripped out from under me when, as a teenybopper, I was informed it would take my "belief" and then some to ensure I'd stay the apple of God's eye. He'd continue to love me all right, as long as I gave up most everything to continue the lifelong obligation to cover the insurance policy with a life of sacrifice.

Egads!

Do you know how many times I went forward in dedication and rededication services? Countless times. I remember the hell and brimstone meetings, the campfire sessions, and the fire and freedom services? Fear, guilt, and uncertainty were drilled into me every time an altar call was given.

No more!

I refuse to travel down that aisle again. The trip never ends. I prefer to take Jesus at His word. I'm confident He's given a different vision. It's a revelation of my Heavenly Father who deliberately chose to give up everything He had to get a pearl He deemed worthy of the price.

He's the jeweler who had an eye for the bling.

Fortunately for me I was a real gem!

Life isn't about me searching and sacrificing to discover the kingdom of God. No, life is now the wonderful trip enjoying the life I have because the jeweler of jewels gave up everything to purchase ME!

Bling! Bling!

That's me for sure!

9. I GET THE DRIFT !

<u>THE PARABLE OF THE DRAGNET</u>
Matthew 13:47-53

Here we go again. These folks really must have been a bunch of knuckleheads. Jesus is anxiously waiting for them to get a hit, so He lobs another slow curve in for them. Matt relates the parable repeating a theme Jesus has been trying to reinforce.

"Again, the kingdom of God is like...a net...cast into the sea to gather in whatever it can."

"When full the fishermen brought their net onto the shore where they sat down to sort out their catch. They placed the edible, acceptable fish into containers however they chucked the fish without scales or fins back into the water."

"So it will be at the consummation of the age. The angels will come forward and wickedness will be separated from the just. Evil will be cast into a furnace of fire and there will be wailing and gnashing of teeth."

Jesus said to them, "Do you get it? Do you understand all these things?"

The folks replied, "You bet, Lord."

Then He said to them, "Well then, every student instructed in the knowledge and understanding of the kingdom of God is like a guardian caretaker of a household who cherishes things both new and old."

And when Jesus finished relating a number of parables He took off.

Wow! Can you believe it?

Sitting on the edge of a boat on the Sea of Galilee Jesus comes up with a fish story almost too good to believe. The sad truth is most folks still don't.

Sport fishing probably hadn't reached the pinnacle of popularity back then like it has in some parts of the world today. Commercial fishing, however, was all the rage. There were primarily two ways of commercial fishing in Palestine-with a boat or without a boat. Nets were used in both methods.

Those fortunate to have a boat employed a technique known today as "seine" fishing. The trawling net (sagene) was essentially a large square net with cords at each corner. Weights placed along the bottom of the net caused it to hang like a curtain when placed into the water. Sometimes one end of the net was attached to a wharf or something secure on shore while the other end was attached to a boat. As the boat pulled away the net neatly formed a giant snare for all kinds of water creatures.

Another variation of seine net fishing was the two-boat method. Each boat, dragging one end of the net, would go in opposite directions forming a wide circle, allowing the net to be drawn into the shape of a cone. As the cone was gathered together it became a snare for some very confused prey. The challenge of getting the catch to shore was truly dependent on the size of the haul.

Those without a boat to row skillfully fished from shore. The net (amphiblestron) fishermen used was shaped like the top of a bell tent with a long cord fastened to the apex and a cord at the other end tied to the arm of the fisherman. The net was folded in such a way that it would, when thrown, expand to its greatest circumference. Beads of lead were strung around it so it would drop nicely to the waters' floor. A keen eye and patience were definite assets when assessing the correct timing to both throw and collect the mass of net with the hopeful abundance of useful catch.

While fishing was no doubt a pleasurable experience, it was also a lot of work. Perhaps this is why Jesus didn't have too much trouble recruiting a school of fishermen to follow Him. Just kidding.

The boats weren't exactly equipped like modern day seine boats. The net would usually be dragged onto the shore where a whole crowd of folks would gather to sort out the good from the bad. Read Leviticus 11:9-12 to discover which fish were ok and which weren't as far as the Jews were concerned. To sum it up, if you didn't have fins or scales you weren't a good little fishy. The slippery, consumable fish were usually placed into shipping containers filled with fresh water. Sometimes the fish were left alive to preserve their freshness for the public market.

A few years ago I had the wonderful opportunity to go out commercial seine fishing with a dear friend of ours off Prince Rupert on the north coast of British Columbia. Truth be told I'm not too sure if Bill actually thought I'd make a good fishing companion.

It's not like he could just drop me off on the beach somewhere if my stomach couldn't handle the constant bobbing motion, especially if the unpredictable weather would turn nasty. I accepted the invitation to join his normally one-man operation on the condition he would allow me to be the chief cook and bottle washer in the primitive little kitchen on board.

To this day I'll bet he'd love to have me along on another trip. He ate stuff he probably never would have cooked himself!

Anyway, what a blast! If memory serves me correctly we were out for three days and two nights. During the night Bill probably got to sleep for about an hour at a time, rising throughout the incredibly beautiful darkness to check on things. He let me sleep a bit more, although it was hard to do so cramped up in the little sleeper in the bowels of the bow.

The modus operandi?

The net was about 1/4 of a mile long! That's right. Floatation balls dotted the top of the net while weights buried the bottom of the net well down into the water. Bill would attach a big floater ball to the end of the net so we could tell where the tail would be, then let the rest of it all hang out. Sometimes he'd just leave the net attached to the boat and sometimes he'd attach another ball to the opposite end and let the net just drift in the water. Bill obviously knew which way the fish were traveling. He'd drive the boat like a racing car up and down one side of the outstretched net attempting to scare the prey right into the net.

Great fun!

At night the boat and net would simply drift with the current. Apparently we'd move up a channel as much as six or seven miles. Good thing there weren't too many boats out where we were, mind you, I guess they'd just drift the same as we were. Dah! Fishermen tend to be pretty territorial, each one thinking they had an inside scoop on where the fish would be.

Bill would generally leave the net out there for about two hours at a time. He'd crank up the giant wheel and the net would start the trip back onto the boat. We'd untangle the slimy, wiggling desperadoes, slipping their gills out of the net. With great excitement I'd watch the flopping salmon dance onto the deck of the boat. It was my job to see them find their way to a briny mixture of salted ice down in the hold. Slippery little...

Sometimes we got completely skunked. One time I think we had one fish in the whole net. Other times we had a whole whack of salmon. Some were downright small, some weren't too bad, and lots of them were just fabulous specimens of the water-based animal kingdom. Yes, we even caught a chunk of driftwood once in a while. And jellyfish! Talk about yuk. Gross. I sure didn't expect to see some of the stuff that got entangled in the net.

To say I had a lesson in a real live commercial fishing expedition would be an understatement. I can truly say this was the greatest experience I've ever had fishing. I can say this because I've probably only been fishing four or five times my whole life. I did have two other fishing experiences while I lived up in Prince Rupert, of which I could almost write a reality comedy TV series about. Suffice it to say it's a lot easier to laugh about those trips now.

Fisherman me? Not!

I can visualize the scene Jesus was describing. Jesus knew all about drifting but He wasn't sure His audience did. Well, I get the drift! Alrighty then, before I give you my understanding of this beautiful object lesson Jesus told, allow me to share with you the traditional drift.

Central Truth:

Just as the fishermen's net is indiscriminate in capturing its catch, so is the kingdom of God open to embrace every human kind. Also, just as the fishermen do their sorting after bringing the catch to shore, so too will the sorting of good and evil be accomplished at a future time.

Traditional Interpretations:

- Jesus was mostly likely shedding light on the meticulous discrimination of the religious establishment in contrast to the all-inclusiveness of the kingdom of God.
- While the net of acceptance is thrown out to encompass all, you can count on a time of separation of good and evil to occur in the future.

Practical Applications:

- The church (kingdom of God) is to embrace all.
- The church is comprised of a mixture of good and bad.

- The bad will be separated out when Jesus comes again. The selection process of determining good from bad will be based upon the responsive confessions of repentance and belief/faith.
- Bring in all you can. God will ultimately judge the catch.
- If the church were a place for only perfect people there wouldn't be a church.
- The process of selection is ongoing.

"So shall it be at the end of the world."

Most folks today read this statement in verse 49 and immediately find justification for believing in a future judgment. It almost seems logical. The world's still here so the end of the world hasn't happened. The end of the world hasn't happened yet, therefore, the separation of good and evil hasn't occurred yet.

"The end of the world" is actually a very poor translation, misleading at best. Now, I don't really want to get too deep into a word study since I'm no linguistic expert, however, humor me for a moment as I let you in on what I've found in my journey of discovery.

There are four different nouns used in the New Testament translated into the single term "end" or "ending." Each of these original words each has multiple possibilities of expression. I've noted some of the places where these terms are used.

1) Telos:
   a) The limit, either at which a person or thing ceases to be what he or it was up to that point, or at which previous activities were ceased (2 Corinthians 3:13; I Peter 4:7).
   b) The final issue or result of a state or process (Luke 1:33).
   c) A fulfillment (Luke 22:37).
   d) The utmost degree of an act, as the love of Jesus towards His disciples (John 13:1).
   e) The aim or purpose of a thing (I Timothy 1:5).
   f) The last in a succession or series (Revelations 1:8).

2) Sunteleia:
   a) Signifies a bringing to a completion or consummation of the various parts of a scheme (Matthew 13:39,40,49).

3) Peras: a limit, boundary of
   a) Space, chiefly in the plural "ends" (Matthew 12:42).
   b) The termination of something occurring in a period (Hebrews 6:16).
4) Ekbasis:
   a) A way out (I Corinthians 10:13).
   b) An issue (Hebrews 13:7).

The word used here in this particular parable is the second term, "sunteleia." It's a combination of "sun" with "teleo." It marks the consummation of the various parts of a scheme. The word doesn't denote a termination, but rather, the heading up of events to the appointed climax.

Now, as if this weren't enough, listen to this.

The term "aion" should not be translated as "the world," but a period or era in which events take place. In Hebrews 9:26 Paul (yes, I think he had his hand in writing Hebrews) used the term in the plural referring to the "consummation of the ages." It was at the heading up of all the various periods of time appointed by God in which Jesus was manifested.

To do what?

"To put away sin by the sacrifice of Himself."

Do you see where I'm going with this? First of all, a doctrine of a final futuristic judgment has been formed on a misunderstanding of terminology. It meant the consummation of a period of time as opposed to the actual ending of everything. Secondly, in the understanding of Paul, the consummation was the manifestation of Jesus, culminating in His sacrifice on the cross.

Now this is important. Don't miss this.

We're talkin' 'bout the cross. What was its purpose?

To put away sin!

How?

By the sacrifice of Himself!

Who spoke the parable? Jesus did. Did He speak the parable before or after the cross? Was it in the future for Him? Of course it was.

I'd like to let you in on something that continues to be a mystery for too many folks. The cross is not in our future! It's in the past. The sacrifice for the putting away of sin is a done deal. Folks, the end of the world Jesus was describing has already happened a couple thousand years ago!

Angels were in attendance. The wickedness of the world was heaped on the broken bones and the scarred tissue of the only One who could bear to accept the burden. No more would there ever be recognition of sin.

Why?

Evil was cast into a furnace of fire never to be recognized in the sight of God. The wailing and gnashing of teeth must have been horrific. I've yet to see the movie "the Passion of Christ." I hear it's an amazing portrayal of sacrifice and love. I'll bet it didn't even come close to depicting what really went on behind the heavenly scenes.

Let's back up a moment.

Timing is everything. I've describing the sorting and canning process. Let me talk briefly about the fishing.

This parable's been used by the religious community as a basis for fishing expeditions for centuries. The world is a sea of fish to be harvested and most missionary endeavor is based upon a perceived need to bring in a catch. The fishing fleet is the church, the nets are the tremendous number of excellent programs established to do good in our society, and the fisher-folk are the individual members. The ultimate process of sorting out the riff-raff from the genuinely acceptable is of course in the hands of God.

Fish fishing for fish sounds like a fishy idea to me.

I've got good news folks.!

The kingdom of God operates from a different premise. We're the fish all right, however, God sent Jesus on a fishing expedition. With a mighty swoop of His all-inclusive net the fisherman of fishermen did what was necessary to reel us all in. Then He built a cannery where He'd once and for all separate those who'd make it from those that wouldn't. The name of the cannery just happens to have two names posted high above the main gate of the kingdom: "cross" and "resurrection."

And here's the rest of the story.

Jesus then said those who get His drift will be like..."a housekeeper who cherishes both new and old."

Now when I think of a housekeeper I can think of no one who fits the description better than my incredible wife. Talk about someone who appreciates old things. Talk about someone who loves new things! That's my wife. My wife gets it. She gets it in this space we now occupy, furthermore, she gets it in the realm Jesus was referring to.

There's much we can learn from other schools of fish. Donna and I have truly enjoyed studying the faiths and traditions of other fish. History is a great teacher and the lessons we're taught by it should not be set aside lightly.

The new and living way Jesus informed us of is something else. It's new all right. Donna and I are hooked. It's liberating to the max. The greatest lesson is the scope of the kingdom of God, and what it took God to make it happen. I can understand how folks didn't quite get the picture Jesus was trying to paint for them 'cause the cross hadn't happened yet. Well, we've no excuse for us to miss the boat.

The kingdom of God is like what?

A net...all inclusive...all sorted out...canned for good...

Now there's a fish story if I've ever heard one!

10. THANKS, I'LL TAKE YOUR WIFE!

THE PARABLE OF THE UNMERCIFUL SERVANT
Matthew 18: 21-35

Ah, here's another of my dilly versions of this portion of Matt's letter.

Peter: "Jesus, how often should I forgive a brother who keeps ripping me off? Is seven times enough?"

Jesus: "Pete, 7 times simply doesn't cut it. Try 490 times, then see how you feel!"

Peter: "Are you serious?"

Jesus: "Look, Pete, let me tell you a little story which will give you another revelation of what the kingdom of God is like."

"It's like this. A certain king wanted to get his financial books in order. It seems quite a few folks were taking advantage of his lenient accounting practices. One chap, in fact, owed him about $12,000 and it was pretty obvious he didn't have the funds to repay the loan. In order to recoup his losses the king ordered a "for sale" sign to be placed on this debtor, one on his wife, one on each of his kids, and yes, a "for sale" sign on everything the dude owned."

"The conversation went something like this."

Debtor: "What? Are you serious? Look Mr. King Sir, I'll pay you back. I promise. Just give me a little more time to get my affairs in order and you'll get back everything I owe you. Please. Pretty please. With sugar on it."

King: "Oh, alrighty then. I think you really mean it. In fact, you've really impressed me with your sincerity. I'll tell you what I'm going to do. I'll wipe out your entire account. You don't owe me a thing any more. How'd ya like them apples?"

Debtor: "No foolin'? Gee, thanks King. You're the best. I'll never forget your kindness and generosity. Whoopee! Thanks again."

Jesus: "Well, Pete, this guy was a sharp cheddar. He figured he'd better examine his own financial books to see if anyone was taking advantage of him. Wouldn't you know, he discovered one of his buddies owed him $120, so he went over to his house where he proceeded to accost his friend."

Former Debtor to friend: "Hey Buckwheat, you owe me $120. I need it right now. Pay up or I'll strangle you right here on the spot!"

Friend: "You gotta be kidding bud. I don't have that kind of cash floating around in my petty cash stash. Who do you think I am? Hang tough. Please, I'm begging you, give me a bit of time, and I'll see what I can do."

Former Debtor to friend: "No way! I can't wait. It's month end and I want to get this thing cleared up right now. I'm going to small debts court tout suit, and they're going chuck you in the clink until you repay the loan."

Jesus: "A bunch of his friends got wind of this whole mess and weren't too pleased to say the very least. They knew what the King had done for him, and yet, he had refused to extend the same grace to one of his debtors. What'd they do? They went and ratted him out to the King who summarily had the sorry case brought before him."

King to former debtor: "You dufus! What's your problem? I not only gave you a break on what you owed me, I wiped out your entire balance. You cried wolf and I showed you nothing but grace and mercy. How come you couldn't have shown a little kindness to your buddy who owed you a few measly bucks? What's up with that? Man, you just tick me right off! Get out of here. Go directly to jail. Do not pass go! You pay me back every red cent you owe me! I just un-cancelled your debt!"

Jesus: "Pete, my heavenly Father will treat you the very same way if you don't forgive your brother when he wrongs you."

Ouch!

"He who begs forgiveness from his neighbor must not do so more than three times" (Rabbi Jose ben Hanina).

"If a man commits an offense once, they forgive him; if he commits an offense a second time, they forgive him; if he commits an offense a third time, they forgive him; the fourth time they do not forgive" (Rabbi Jose ben Jehuda).

Forgiveness is an interesting subject. Read Amos (1:3-13; 2:1-6) for some pointers. Forgive three times, after that, lights out. Rabbis figured out if God had a three-count rule on forgiveness so should they.

Likewise, Pete was no dummy. He knew how to count and he knew how to keep score score. His mission, and he decided to take it on this occasion, was to score some good old fashioned brownie points with Jesus, and to drop a few "na-na-nana-na-nas" on his teammates. Let's double it and add one for good measure. Three plus three plus one equals seven.

What was the question again?

"If someone screws me, if I forgive them seven times, am I ok to write him off on the eighth?"

Can you just imagine the size of Pete's head? I'll bet he expected Jesus to give him a big pat on the back for this bit of mathematic genius.

NOT!

"Let me use the calculator on your palm pilot Peter. Seventy times seven. Hmmm. 490 times! How does that grab you?"

Well, there's a dispute over this figure. One commentary guy would argue the correct translation is a mere 77 times. Others suggest the numerological approach implies an infinite calculation of 7 x 7 x 7 x 7 x 7 x 7, and so on and so on, infinitely on. In either case, 77, 490, or whatever is a long way from 7 on my scoreboard.

Before Pete could utter a comeback (he was probably choking and gasping for air) Jesus figured He'd better hit him between the eyes with a few more little tidbits of information concerning the kingdom of God he'd obviously not picked up on yet.

Some cultural notes may help you out at this point. You might not know what a "talent" is. Well, don't worry your little abacus machine 'cause nobody else seems to know either. I've tried to research the amount the servant had borrowed from the king as an amount in our present day currency. Commentaries suggest the amount outstanding was anywhere from $12,000 to $12,000,000. Yes, that's twelve million (that's illion with a "M") dollars. And the amount of money owed by the buddy? Something less than $1 to $120. In any case, most agree the loan was approximately 1/600,000 of the amount owed to the king.

Get this. The first debtor had borrowed 10,000 talents from the king.

Incredible! The total revenue of the province which included Idumaea, Judaea, and Samaria was only 600 talents, while a wealthy province like Galilee was a mere 300 talents.

What was the king thinking? Or perhaps, what kind of goods (or dirty pictures) did this dude have on the king?

Rules of engagement for the settling of accounts were well established. It wasn't unheard of for a lender to literally grab the throat of a debtor and drag him before the bench. "No pay up, o.k., I take yo' wife. No pay up, I take your kids. Nah, on second thought, keep the kids, I take wife! Anything else you got worth anything, well, me take."

I have yet to figure out how in the world you could get an imprisoned man to repay a debt while bound in stock and chains. Anyway, let's take a look at the traditional ways of understanding this parable.

Central Truth:

The outflow of God's mercy towards us must coincide with the outflow of our mercy towards others. We can't know the forgiveness of God until we've shown forgiveness to others.

Traditional Interpretations:

- The enormity of the debt describes the bankruptcy of the human condition while the generous forgiveness of the king illustrates the generosity of a gracious and merciful heavenly Father.
- It's a man's unforgiving spirit that bars the door against him. The wrath of the king against the unmerciful debtor is descriptive of the righteous indignation and justice of God towards those who refuse to acknowledge the example of forgiveness.

Practical Applications:

- Laid upon the Christian is the privilege of being forgiven as well as the duty to forgive.
- No life is open to God that bitterly nurses resentment and bitterness.
- We can't demand standards of others we aren't prepared to fulfill ourselves.
- Wrongs committed against us are nothing close to the wrongs we've done to God.

Context. Here we go again. Read almost every commentary on this parable (21-35) and you'll find no mention of what actually precedes or follows this discussion between Jesus and Peter. I challenge you to go back and read at least from the start of chapter 18.

The chapter begins with a discussion of the nature of the greatest in the kingdom of heaven, the humility of little children. It continues on to challenge those who cause offense to the simplicity of understanding. Then comes the amazing promise that the Son of man is come to save the lost (11). Of course, any shepherd would leave 99 sheep to save the 1 who took off, and would be tickled pink when he found it (13).

And d'you know what? Grab hold of this one.

The will of your Father in heaven is that not even 1 will perish (14)!

This is followed by a discussion concerning disputes between friends and a course of action to resolve them. Then comes an incredible passage that implies the government of heaven is bound by the governance of humans. If two or three folks agree on something, especially since the Father is in the midst of two or three who affirm God's name, then it will happen.

It's at this point Pete interjects with his insightful question to Jesus concerning his role as a gracious, merciful forgiver. Now, before I tackle the wise instruction of Jesus concerning the kingdom of God, I want to go backwards for a moment because I don't think the parable Jesus told is based simply on Pete's question, but rather, on the entire teaching of this chapter.

Most scholars have a great deal of trouble with passages such as Matthew 18. It seems to be riddled with inconsistencies. How is it possible God could be so merciful not to allow even one of children to become lost and immediately after lay out the possibility heaven could be bound by the actions of mankind? Then there's the talk of cutting out your eyes or whacking off your hands or feet. What's up with that? And eventually we get to this master/servant story where the moral of the story seems to be "forgive or else!"

One very popular scholar almost implies Matt was into the sauce a bit too much the day he wrote his account. He suggests Jesus couldn't really have said these words. In addition, he suggests it doesn't take a rocket scientist to figure out that two or three people agreeing on something is nothing close to a guarantee their agreement in prayer will surely come to pass.

You know what, I didn't say that but I agree with him for the most part. If God was truly expected to make decisions based upon the agreements of folks He'd be left scratching his head so often He'd be balder than a bowling ball by now!

Well, let me say I'm no longer befuddled by problem passages. Why? What's made the difference for me? I've come to understand context. What do I mean?

I've gained a tremendous amount of clarity from my study of Paul's writings. The consistency and logic of Paul's systematic theology was based upon his understanding of a significant concept which modern scholars have by and large failed to comprehend. Like Paul, I've come to understand that there have been two systems at play in history of humankind. The two systems collided at the focal point of all history, the cross!

The first system ended at the cross. The second system began at the cross. The first was called the system of the "law." The second is called the system of "grace." Until the cross folks were bound by the system of laws, rules, and regulations in the futile attempt at achieving the righteous acceptance of God. It really was up to us. Our fate was literally in our own hands.

Do good-get good. Do bad-get bad.

After the cross folks are bound by the system of God's grace. His grace ensured we'd all get what we could never deserve on our own merit, namely, abundant life. His mercy ensured we'd never get what we did truly deserve, namely, eternal damnation.

Do good-get good. Do bad-get good!

Wow! What a difference. Hey, all it took was the cross. The cross has made all the difference in the world!

By now you're probably wondering what's all this got to do with the parable. Alrighty then, let's get back to it.

When did Jesus teach these things recorded for us by Matthew? This teaching was before the cross, right? Right! You see, I'm not faced with the embarrassing task of explaining away passages I think present a problem of interpretation. I don't have to make excuses for what Jesus taught. I have no problem with what He taught. In fact, the parables are all the more special to me than ever before because I actually see how His teachings fit into the scheme of the plan of God. I understand them in the "context" of their offering.

I'm convinced what Jesus taught was the absolute truth. What He revealed was the complete impossibility of human endeavor to attain the righteousness of God.

He constantly drew pictures of our inability. The standards of God's expectations made our acceptability, based on belief, faith, works, good looks, talent, wealth, fame, etc., a virtual failure in every sense of the word.

No one would make it off the planet if we had to measure up to the standard Jesus set. There isn't enough money in the whole wide world to purchase His grace. There aren't enough good deeds done in the whole world to initiate His mercy. No amount of belief could make Him accept you for who you are. You could have a mountain range of faith and you couldn't come close to His love.

So, when you start to recognize the context, the teachings of Jesus aren't difficult to understand at all. Pete, unfortunately, hadn't clued in yet. He was obsessed with the idea of what "he" had to do. He was still bound by laws, rules, and regulations, even if he was being very overly generous in his sense of justice.

Jesus promptly put Pete in his place, not by putting him down, but by showing him the impossibility of living up to the standards of God's justice under the system of the law. Jesus wasn't satisfied with 3 times of forgiveness set down by Jewish Rabbis anymore than he was with the 7 times Pete offered. Hey, 490 times was more like it, and that still wouldn't cut it.

Now, just think about this for a moment.

Can you even imagine someone doing something to you that really ticks you off 490 times? To tell the truth, I don't think I could actually get in 3 forgivenesses. If someone offended me 490 times and I'd have to forgive each and every time, then I'm afraid getting to heaven would surely be impossible for me.

Wait, there's more Jesus wants you to know.

Here's the picture again.

A certain king loaned some civilian 10,000 talents.

Think on that for a moment.

For some crazy reason this certain "wise" king lent out more money, without collateral no less, than whole countries had in their lock up cells in Fort Mesopotamia.

Now who in their right mind would do this?

I sure wouldn't!

Well, the king decides prudently that he wants his money back so he holds court to get it back. He hauls the servant in on the regal purple carpet and tells him the score. I'm not too sure why the servant needed this much money, nor are we told what he did with it, in spite of the fact he could have started a new country, or at the very least, funded the Olympic games.

What to do? The king then informs the servant he's taking his wife, kids, and property until he pays back the loan. The distraught servant starts to throw a pity party. The "poor me" syndrome kicked into high gear. He begs for more time. He must have made quite an impression. The king caves. No, the king really caves in. Not only does he give the servant more time, he wipes out the account. Did you get that? He wiped the slate clean! I'm blown away. This servant borrowed 10,000 talents. Now he doesn't even owe 1 talent back!

Simply amazing!

The story Jesus told Peter doesn't end here. The heart of the servant is now exposed. A buddy of his had borrowed 100 pence. I don't know how much a "pence" is but it sure doesn't sound anything like 10,000 talents. I still can't figure out what the servant did with the 10,000 talents that he'd needed the 100 pence back for. In any case, his buddy was granted no mercy. Instead, the servant grabbed his buddy and hauled his sweaty neck off to court, had him incarcerated, and then promptly took his wife, kids, and property to repay the debt.

As an aside, I wonder what their wives looked like. Perhaps the buddy had one sexy mama and this was one way of getting his hands on her. Oh, just kidding!

The story continues...

The servant had some fellow servant buddies who were well apprised of the goings on. They finked on the servant to the king. The king was now royally ticked.

Get it? "Royally" ticked! I'm so funny.

Anyway, he hauled the servant's neck onto the royal purple carpet again, took his good looking wife, his kids, his property, and then had him chucked in the soup coup. Show no mercy-get no mercy. You naughty servant you.

What was Pete supposed to get out of this story? He'd face the same fate as the servant from the heavenly Father if he didn't forgive a brother (or sister I'm sure) every single time they committed an offense against him! I guess 490 times isn't really enough. All of a sudden we have an opened ended number.

Are you starting to see how impossible the system of laws, rules, and regulations are?

If Peter really understood the difference between the system of law and the system of grace to come he probably would have nailed Jesus' hands to the cross himself!

God had given humankind everything, certainly more than 10,000 talents worth. We couldn't even handle it. Throughout the centuries folks begged and begged God to give more time, more chances to pay Him back. He actually caved in by allowing us a system of laws to govern our acceptability. Hey, we even screwed that up.

The impossibility of the task under the "law" was a certainty. Our eternal fate was sealed by our own actions. We see this in verse 18 as well as in verse 35. Loose, and it will be loosed. Bind, and it will be bound. Forgive, and it will be forgiven. Don't forgive, and it won't be forgiven.

I don't know what you're feeling right now, but I'm so grateful for the cross. I didn't stand a chance without the cross. I could never have measured up. I actually doubt anyone could. Think of the most revered person you know of from any of the disciplines of life: politics, entertainment, religion, or science. If they didn't forgive just one time, they wouldn't have been able to make it into the good book either. Scary, eh?

Are you starting to get a glimpse of what the cross means? I sure hope so. This is a wonderful chapter, even if Matthew didn't really understand the full scope of what he was recording for our benefit. Jesus was bound to teach folks the dangers of inappropriate behavior because, at the time, He taught folks who were under the system of laws. While He could point to a better time ahead, it was still to come until He had completed His task here on earth.

What were the final words Jesus uttered on the cross?

"It is finished!"

He did not say, "It will be finished." He didn't even say, "I'll wrap this whole thing up when I come back later."

Folks, the old system of the law was wrapped up on the cross. The new system of grace was introduced on the cross. And are we ever blessed because of it. We never again should worry about our eternal destiny.

Oh, don't misunderstand me. I'm not trying to say for one moment that extending forgiveness to one another when wronged is a worthless exercise.

I never said that. In fact, understanding how secure your eternal destiny is under the system of grace will make it all the easier, exciting, and rewarding to live as if you were still under the law. It's all a matter of perspective.

You know what? In my old understanding I wouldn't have been able to forgive someone three times. Now that I understand the kingdom of heaven in a new and living way, I have no problem forgiving someone four hundred and ninety times. Why wouldn't I?

Talk about a different perspective. I don't "have" to forgive. I just do it because I can, and because I was forgiven!

Confession?

Well, I confess I only want the wife I have, and hey, I'm not even sorry about that!

And you can't take my wife either!

11. PUT IT ON MY TAB !

THE PARABLE OF THE GOOD SAMARITAN
Luke 10:25-37

We can thank Luke alone for what is probably one of the best known of all the parables Jesus told. No doubt there have been more sermons preached on this particular parable than all the other ones combined. It's been diced and spliced in so many ways, and yet, the basic message of inspiration and motivation to be a "good" Samaritan is usually the bottom line.

Please don't be alarmed but I'm about to put a different spin on this one than any you've probably ever heard before. You're about to find out the identity of the really "good" Sam! By now you know I'm a little bit bent on context, so, let me set the scene for the parable.

Verses 57 through 62 of Luke chapter 9 seem pretty horrifying to most. Many sky pilots use them to scare the livin' dickens out of their passengers. Some chap comes up to Jesus and tells Him he's goin' to follow Jesus wherever He goes. Jesus told the guy "foxes have holes and birds have nests, but the Son of man hasn't even got a pillow to lay His head on, so, good luck."

Jesus told another fellow to follow Him. The guy says, "Sure, no problem. Oops, maybe there is one slight problem. Dad's dyin' and I've got to go home and make arrangements for the going away party. I'll be back after the bucket gets kicked." Jesus isn't too impressed. "Hey, you're dad will die when he dies. This is now."

Ouch!

Another fellow agrees to follow Jesus too although he wants some time out to go home and say goodbye to his family. This time Jesus tells the guy a person who starts work only to take a java break isn't fit for the kingdom of God.

Whoooaaa!

I know the purpose of this chapter is to discuss the parable of the Good Samaritan, however, I want to just throw in my take on this preceding portion because I believe it's relevant to what's coming down the printing press.

I think Jesus was simply letting us in on a significant truth concerning our ability to accomplish enough on our own to get into the kingdom of God.

Self-righteousness would never be an answer. There's no hope for anyone because the standard is just way over our heads. The bar is set way too high. The hoop is totally out of reach.

Live like a nomad with nowhere to call home. There isn't any room for a person to take care of their parents in their old age. What's up with that? You can't even go home to say good-bye to your wife and kids? Don't you dare take your hands off the plow! Push the pedal to the metal. Don't you dare look back.

Sounds like a pretty impossible standard to me. And yet religious leaders of Jesus' day continued to expect strict adherence to the laws, rules, and regulations they established.

Luke 10 begins with the appointment of another 70 folks, sent out two by two, to beat the pavement with appropriate instructions.

Oh, I've got to stop here for a second.

The number 70 is pretty significant for Jewish folk. That's the number of elders chosen to help Moses lead and direct the hippies of another generation out in the wilderness. The supreme council of the Jews, the Sanhedrin, was comprised of 70 members. It was a common Jewish view of the day that there were 70 Gentile nations in the world. Now isn't it interesting the universalistic Luke would pick on this number to identify the mission of Jesus to the whole world.

Here was the commission given to the 70:

- Travel light.
- Bless folks with peace.
- Stay where you're welcome, don't where you're not.
- Eat what's put in front of you (a test I'd flunk for sure!).
- Heal the sick.
- Tell folks the kingdom of God is almost here. If a city doesn't respond then just dust off and tell them again the kingdom of God is at hand, warning them of dire consequences for not paying attention.

It may be of some interest for you to be informed of a piece of work called "The Teaching of the Twelve Apostles," written around 100 A.D., giving a variety of instructions for itinerant prophets. If a prophet wanted to stay in any given town for more than 3 days without working he was considered a false prophet. If a prophet asked for money or even a meal he was considered a "false" prophet.

Anyway, the 70 came back from their mission and told Jesus even devils were subject to them with the mere mention of His name. Then Jesus says something phenomenal that is often glazed over.

"I saw Satan as lightning fall from heaven" (Luke 10:18).

Whoops! That Satan character is on a bit of a downer.

He continued to explain to them how much power they now had with Satan out of the way. The real secret wasn't the power. The real cause for rejoicing was the fact their names are written in the good book! Then Jesus offered up a prayer.

"I thank you, O Father, Lord of heaven and earth, that you've hidden these things from the wise and the prudent. You've chosen to reveal these things to babes. Yes, you did Dad, 'cause it seemed like a good idea to you. All things are delivered to me from my Father, and nobody knows who the Son is with the exception of the Father. Furthermore, nobody knows who the Father is except the Son, and yes, even all those to whom the Son will reveal the Father to" (10:21,22).

Then Jesus turned to His disciples and told them how lucky they were to get to see what they were getting to see. Hey, prophets and kings would have given the toga off their backs to have the same view the disciples were enjoying. They'd have given their eyeteeth to hear what the twelve of them had been privileged to hear.

D'ya get it?

Let there be no doubt the Son knows who the Father is. Equally, let there be no doubt that everyone the Son chooses to reveal the Father to will also know who the Father is!

Now, who'd that be?

I'm convinced Jesus revealed the Father to the whole world. Look, the wise and the prudent couldn't figure the message out. Go figure. It took a babe to let the babes in on the heart of God.

Just as luck would have it a smarty pants lawyer piped up to catch Jesus, what he hoped would be, off guard. Here's what the exchange sounded like.

Barrister Bob: "Teacher, what must I do to inherit eternal life?"

Jesus: "Hey, you're a lawyer, what does the law say about it? Read it from the cheat notes on your wristband. Enlighten me."

Barrister Bob: "Love God with all you heart, soul, strength, and mind. Oh yes, love your neighbor as yourself."

Jesus: "Well chump, that's exactly what the law tells you to do. Live like that and, according to the law, you'd inherit eternal life. Does that answer your question?"

Barrister Bob: "Not quite so fast there big guy. Who's my neighbor?"

This lawyer was a real piece of work. He thought he had Jesus on the ropes. He presumed the law was the be-all and end-all of everything. I wish he would have asked Jesus what He thought was the way to inherit eternal life rather than what the "law" thought. The pompous lawyer probably figured he had the loving God with his whole heart, soul, strength, and mind portion taken care of. Loving his neighbor as himself, if he could figure out who his neighbor was, would be the only thing left to do before he could claim his eternal inheritance.

And now, finally, we get to the parable of the Good Samaritan, or so it's been called. I'm going to presume the real message went right over his head just like it has over the heads of all the wise and prudent since his time until the present.

Once again, in the version according to Roger...

"A man was traveling down from Jerusalem to Jericho. Unfortunately, as he was walking along the highway, a nasty pack of thugs accosted him, stripped him naked, beat the crap out of him, and then fled the scene leaving the poor guy for dead. Just by chance, a certain priest happened to be taking a trip on the highway too. When he came upon the scene of the robbery and assault the priest simply kept his distance so as not to get involved."

"And just as fate would have it, a Levite showed up on the scene some time later. This person at least came a little closer to get a better look, and yet, he too wanted to keep his nose clean. He figured expediency was preferential to helping the poor fellow out of a right tight jam."

"Next, along comes a Samaritan. When he saw the virtually naked, half-dead fellow lying there he couldn't but have compassion on the victim of a most vicious attack. Like a paramedic he ran over to him and immediately started administering CPR. He bandaged up the wounds as

best he could, soothing them with oil and alcohol he had in his "Samson-ite" bag. He lifted his patient onto his bestial ambulance and headed off to find a place he could get some proper medical help."

"Arriving at the nearest city the Samaritan checked into the local Hebrew Holiday Hut Express and continued to tend to the poor guy through the night. The next morning he knew he had to get back to work, and yet, he knew he couldn't just leave his patient to die on his own. What to do?"

"As he checked out of his room good Sam pulled out a few hundred bucks, gave it to the hotel purser and said, 'Look, there's a chap up in room 777 who's been beaten up pretty bad. I've to go now, but I'd like you to arrange for him to get all the help he needs to get back on his feet, literally. I hope this covers the cost, but if it doesn't, spare no expense. Simply put any overage on my tab and I'll settle the account when I return.'"

"There you have it buckwheat: a priest, a Levite, and a good Sam. Which one of these three do you think was a neighbor to this robbery victim?"

It didn't take long for the lawyer to admit he figured it was the chap who had showered the victim with grace and mercy. Jesus told him to go out and treat others with mercy too.

Jerusalem sits at 2,300 feet above sea level. Jericho, near the Dead Sea, sits at 1,300 feet below sea level. Do you understand why Jesus said this fellow went "down" from Jerusalem to Jericho? I'd say a drop of 3,600 feet over a mere 17 miles or so is quite a drop!

The highway was more like a narrow, windy, rocky, happy hunting ground for dirt bound pirates. Jerome, in the 5th century, tells us the highway was still called "The Red Way," or "The Bloody Way." If you wanted to travel in relative safety as late as the 19th century you were advised to pay a "safety fee" to local sheiks.

The traveler who got beaten up must have been either very brave, stupid, reckless, plain naive, or perhaps, all of the above. Anybody traveling outside a caravan or convoy was doing so at an incredible risk of encountering peril to life or limb.

Don't be too hard on the priest. He'd be out of commission for 7 days if he touched a dead person (Numbers 19:11). When he saw this poor chap lying helplessly in the ditch he decided he couldn't miss a week of work, losing as well his turn of duty in the Temple. Charity gave way to ceremony and obligation.

Criminals weren't all that stupid either. They had enough ambition to match any level of commitment to their cause, as heinous as the cause was. Decoys were often used to lure in unsuspecting do-gooders. "Safety first" was more than likely the Levite's motto. Why do good unto others when bad things could happen to you in the doing?

Samaritans seemingly were nobodies to many, a people without a race to call their own. The capital of Samaria fell to the Assyrians in 720 B.C. and foreigners were brought in to repopulate the land. Jews and foreigners began to intermingle, and I mean intermingle! The resulting children were called Samaritans. Jews and Samaritans have antagonistic feelings toward one another since the exile. When Cyris released the southern nation of Judah from the Babylonian captivity it was the Samaritans who generously offered to help rebuild the Temple. The Jews said "thanks but no thanks." Consequently, the Samaritans built a rival place of worship on Mt. Gerizim.

We've all been taught Jews and Samaritans don't mix. Sure, it's been a no-brainer for interpreters to play the race card. Somehow it makes the whole story more dramatic doesn't it?

Bad guy does good guy. Bad guy helps good guy.

Good conquers evil.

Well, I can't figure out why it is we always seem to paint "good" Sam as being a guy who has at least a portion of compassion in his heart where it's not expected to be.

Did you know the title "Samaritan" was sometimes used by Jews to describe a heretic or someone who broke their ceremonial laws? And did you know the Jews on occasion called Jesus a "Samaritan" (John 8:48)?

Boy, this is all coming together better than I could have imagined. Read on.

Strict orthodox Jews would wear a little leather box (phylactery) on their wrist. In it was contained a number of passages of scripture: Exodus 13:1-10, 11-16; Deuteronomy 6:4-9,11:13-20. Barrister Bob was sharp enough to add even another scripture in his response to Jesus just for good measure (Leviticus 19:18).

PUT IT ON MY TAB !   PARABLE OF GOOD SAM

Now, to a Jew a "neighbor" could be just about anybody as long as it was a fellow Jew, or then again, just about nobody. It was even illegal to help a Gentile woman in a desperate time of childbirth 'cause that would help bring another Gentile into the world.

Oh my. The parable of the "Good" Samaritan is a winner. You know it well, but humor me as I highlight some of the traditional interpretations you've heard before.

Central Truth:

We should be a neighbor to anyone who needs our help, regardless of race, religion, or entitlement. The question isn't "Who's my neighbor?" It's "Who proves himself neighborly?"

Traditional Interpretations:
- The lawyer is given a lesson by Jesus that the Samaritan achieves the will of God where the priest and the Levite fall short of it. Jesus isn't merely stating an issue of simple compassion, but rather, He's raising the issue of obeying the will of God.
- The standard of judgment is not our respectability but our willingness to help.

Practical Applications:
- Anyone who needs your help is your neighbor.
- Pity that issues in help is my duty to a trouble neighbor.
- Regardless of the reasons for the troubles, even those that are self- inflicted, we have a duty to respond to help alleviate the trouble.
- We must help even if it places ourselves at risk.
- Our obedience to God is best displayed when we're responding to opportunities around us to do good things.

Once upon a time, when I was in the throws of learning how to be an eloquent spokesman for the traditionalist cause, I prepared a sermon which I was convinced should have been an award winner. The title was "Yours, mine, and ours!" Sounds good, eh?

And every great sermon has three basic points.

This is beautiful.

79

Read it and weep.
1. The robbers-what's yours is mine.
2. The priest and Levite-what's mine is mine.
3. The "good" Samaritan-what's mine is yours.

What talent I had. The sermon couldn't have been written any better to exhort and invoke my attentive, listening audience to get off their duffs and practice what they preach not only on Sunday, but throughout every other day of the week as well.

Well, that was then, and this is now. I now know there's way more to this wonderful little story we've been hearing since our earliest days in Sunday school. Instead of putting myself in the role of the good Sam character I feel compelled to identify with the poor dufus who was rudely interrupted on his journey.

You can accuse me of being stupid for choosing the path. You can berate me of poor planning. You could even pity me for having a terrible streak of bad luck. And most surely some of you would conclude my unfortunate situation is a direct result of sin in my life. Well, try as they might, religion and the self-righteousness behavior of works were unable to help me out of my helpless state. Apathy, lack of time, too many things on the plate, money, laws, rules, regulations, and many other things simply blocked the way of meaningful assistance and good intentions.

Folks, the factory of religion has spawned an industry all on its own. Denominations and creeds have arisen around the world to fight the good fight against the depravity of man. Designed to give hope it has instead fostered hopelessness. Fashioned to inspire faith it has instead cultivated doubt. Born to engender worship it has instead developed ritual. With every good intention, religion, of any stripe, has set its agenda to turn man to seek God for help.

The result? What we've got is a religious world full of laws, rules, and regulations. Religion maintains its absolute grasp on the hearts of its adherents by establishing boundaries of performance. It tells you what you can and can't do. It's developed various standards of what God considers the acceptable way to get into His good book.

Isn't it interesting the Samaritan didn't take the victim to a hospital, or at the very least, an emergency care facility. If there had to be any taking care of to be done he'd see to it personally. Isn't it funny how we're taught to bring folks with spiritual problems to the church, our religious hospital?

80

Preachers, pastors, and teachers are all trying very nobly to cure the ills of society. The symptoms usually get taken care of, and yet ultimately, most people end up dying in a hospital. Unfortunately, the way I see it, most people end up dying in church too as the abundant life gets sucked right out of them!

Well, my life took an abrupt change the moment the "good" Sam of all good Sams laid His hands on me. He soothed and bandaged my wounds. He took the load off my feet and transported me to a place where healing and restoration were just what any doctor would order. He checked me into the "all-inclusive" inn of abundant life and liberty. Furthermore He told the big innkeeper of all to spare no expense to make me whole. Then, He took care of the bill.

"Whatever it takes, put it on my tab" (Jesus, the "good" Samaritan)!

Jesus paid it all!

That's right. Someone even wrote a song about it. "The crimson stain, which sin had left, has been washed white as snow." Hallelujah!

Yes, the great taker of care did just that! I didn't have to pay a thing. I didn't have to believe. I didn't need faith. I didn't have to give 10% tithe. I didn't have to get up at 5 a.m. to pray. I didn't have a target for church attendance or for saving a certain number of souls each year. As noble and worthy as any of these things are, they are not the key to access the resort.

I was beaten down and He made me whole. I didn't have to beg him to do it. I didn't have to confess I'd been a bad boy. Nor did I have to plead with Him over and over again that I'd dedicate the rest of my life to His cause if He'd only rescue me.

No, the "good" Samaritan saw my need. With compassion, grace, and mercy He saved me!

While the traditional interpretation of this parable has some merit of instilling in us the spirit of compassion and generosity, it has focused once again on "our" responsibility and obligation to serve our fellow man. It's all about "us" doing something to gain acceptance in the "will of God" contest.

While Jesus told Barrister Bob to "go and do likewise" the instruction was in accordance with the lawyers' understanding of the rule of law. Remember the context of this parable? Go back and read the entire chapter again if you must.

Time and time again Jesus laid out the difficulty, no, the impossibility of doing what it would take to follow him. When folks got all excited about having the power to manipulate devils at their command, in Jesus' name of course, Jesus reminded them Satan was no longer a problem. Then He told them they'd be better off if they understood their names were recorded in heaven.

What?

Be content with being saved? What a novel concept!

Did Jesus not continue to give a revelation as He prayed? The wise may not understand, however, babes would get the message. Jesus knew who the Father was, and it was His intention to reveal God to the whole world. Indeed, that's why He came.

I prefer to see this parable as a great illustration Jesus used to help us understand the heart of God towards all mankind. The lawyer thought Jesus was trying to tell him who his neighbor was but he missed the whole point.

Jesus responded to his question with a question. What does the "law" say is the way to eternal life?

Of course Barrister Bob could only speak from his understanding as he responded, adding even an extra dose of self-righteous behavior of loving others as oneself.

Jesus introduced legal minds around the world to a new and living way as He saw it. God did through Jesus what nobody or nothing could do to resolve our eternal problem.

He sent someone to save us, without merit, without cost.

"Put it on my tab!" said the "good" Sam?

Now that's a cure for what ailed me, and I'm all over it!

12. **COMIN' and GOIN'!**

THE PARABLE OF THE GOOD SHEPHERD
John 10: 1-21

"Martha, Martha, Martha. Stop pouting. There are different ways of serving. Just 'cause you know how to throw a fantastic hoop-dee-do doesn't mean that Mary's obliged to minister to me the same way you do. Don't get your nose out of joint" (Luke 10:38-42)!

Jesus is taking perhaps his last break from the mayhem in a tiny village near Jerusalem. He was on His way to an appointment of eternal consequence and what He wanted most was a cool wobbly pop and Martha wanted to throw a huge bar-b with all the fixins'. Mary, suspecting as much, offered probably a good foot rub and a soft pillow for Him to take a few doze dives.

The point of this inclusion into the record books on our behalf is interesting. Jesus wasn't demeaning servitude. He wasn't condoning an apparent lack of consideration, (at least as far as Martha was concerned), nor was he bashing the apparent good intention of Martha to minister to Jesus. There are many ways to serve and just because you to choose a certain way to share your heart that is no reason to expect others must express their servitude in the same fashion.

In John chapter 9 we've got some more jewels. Jesus, when confronted by the disciples about whether sin caused a man to be blind from birth, told them that He was the light of the world. Then He promptly put some spit onto a chunk of clay, placed the mud wrap on the guys face, then told him to go take a bath down at the local Siloam spa.

Oops. Here's what the disciples and a whole lot of other folk were thinking beneath the cobwebs.

"Give us all a break. Why do You always have to heal the sick and give eyesight to the blind on a Sunday? Couldn't You just pick a Monday once in a while."

Well, news traveled fast on the outer-net (remember they didn't have the inter-net yet) 'cause the Pharisees didn't take long to get wind of what Jesus had done. Their reaction?

"How in the world could this dufus be of God if He doesn't even know what you can and can't do on Sunday" (9:16). Ah shucks, he probably wasn't blind. Perhaps we shouldn't have got our dander up so quick. Go find his parents."

"Yep, he was blind."

"Oh shoot."

"Hey, you bucktooth buckaroos, he's old enough, ask him yourselves if he can see now when he couldn't a few hours ago."

"Look fellas, I could care less if He was a sinner or not. I was blind as a bat my whole life, and now I got 20/20. Got a problem with that? Too bad, I don't."

"So how'd he do it, huh?"

"Are you brain dead? I already told you what happened. Are you as deaf as you are dumb? O.K. I'll play along. If I tell you again will you become a follower of His too?"

"Are you freakin' nuts man? You can follow him but we're stickin' it out as disciples of Moses. We know and appreciate what Mo said, but we don't have a clue where this dude's from."

"Whatever. I just know you have to be pretty connected with the big guy upstairs to do what He did. I can see now and that's good enough for me."

"Listen up chump. You were born sinning and you think you have something to teach us. Get lost!"

Well Jesus found out about the incident and went looking for this fellow with a new insight into life.

"Hey, do you believe in the son of God?"

"And who'd that be? I'm quite sure if I knew who he was I could get into it."

"Well, son, you're lookin' at 'im, and you're talkin' to 'im!"

"Alrighty then. I'm good with that. Good on ya! In fact, I'm all over it."

And then Jesus laid out a mitt full of information we'd be well informed to pay attention to.

"I came to this world to discern who can see and who can't. I've come so those who are blind will have their eyes opened wide, and unfortunately, those who think they can see clearly, will become blind to the realities around them!"

Ouch!

"Are we blind too?" questioned the Pharisees.

"If you were blind you wouldn't be sinners. Just the fact you think you see condemns you in your sin!"

OUCH! OUCH!

A dose of double-hurt.

And now we come to the marvelous chapter 10 recorded for us by John. It is perhaps one of the most admired passages in the scripture by those charmed by the adorable nature of sheep. The picture of the shepherd with his sheep is woven into the Biblical tapestry and imagery like no other image. Well, we actually didn't study this as one of the parables in our class in Bible school. Not sure why.

It's a dilly.

The traditional understanding is quite perceptible.

Central Truth:

Jesus is the door and the good shepherd of the flock. Jesus is the master example of those who lead and shepherd the flock under them.

Traditional Interpretations:

- Jesus is the door in relation to the fold.
- Reference to thieves and robbers most likely relates to seditious characters like Barabbas who attempted to seduce Jews to follow their lead into paths of power and prestige.
- Jesus is the shepherd in relation to the fold.
- Jesus was establishing an understanding between Him and His disciples concerning the unity of Himself and His Father.
- The unity Jesus spoke of was not an ecclesiastical unity, rather, a unity of loyalty to Jesus.
- Jesus was laying out His intention of bringing into the fold of Judaism those not yet included through His vicarious, voluntary submission to the will of God.
- The parable is an obvious attempt by Jesus to reveal His obedience to a task set out for Him by God.

Practical Applications:

- Tune in to hear the voice of the good Shepherd.
- Beware of wolves, the false prophets whose intentions are control and destruction.
- Be a part of the missionary endeavor to assist in the effort of bringing into the fold those who don't recognize the voice of God in their lives.

- Folks won't hear if there isn't a pastor there to call
them and guide them. The fulfillment of the dream of
Jesus depends on us. It is we who can help make the
world into one flock with Him as its shepherd.

A central plateau covered the main part of Judaea from Bethel
to Hebron for a distance of about 35 miles, varying from 14 to 17
miles across. The prime pastoral, agricultural land was rough and stony,
fertile ground for herding sheep.

Sheep rarely roamed without a shepherd to protect them.
Sheep were not immune from the folly of thinking the grass is always
greener on the other side. Many of us who have a few miles of tracks
under our walkin' shoes will know this ain't necessarily so. It was the
shepherd's never ending task to guard the sheep from straying to close
to the natural walls that surrounded them. The perilous opportunity to
drop off some ledge into unknown craggy desert loomed large. Wolves,
hyenas and other predators were a constant threat knowing full well
where they could find the butter for their bread.

The Jews gave the name of "shepherd" to their King. They
gave the shepherd the symbol of providence. Constant vigilance to
protect, fearless courage to defend, and patient love to comfort. That's
what a shepherd was all about to the people of Israel.

The Old Testament abounds with testimony to this resolve.
Psalm 23 is perhaps the world's favorite example of God's character as
a Shepherd. But there are many others. Psalm 77:20; Psalm 79:13;
Psalm 80:1; Psalm 95:7; Psalm 100:3; Isaiah 40:11; Song of Solomon
17:45; Jeremiah 23:1-4 and Ezekiel 34 are renowned as expressions of
God's undertaking for His sheep.

Not to be undone, the New Testament is laced with references
to a new good Shepherd, namely, Jesus Christ. Matthew 9:36, 18:12;
26:36; Mark 6:34, 14:27; Luke 15:4, 12:32; I Peter 2:25; and Hebrews
13:20 join with John's account of this parable in chapter 10 in revealing
the role of Jesus as a good shepherd.

A common name used to for someone who leads a
congregation or parish is "pastor." The name is actually the Latin word
for "shepherd." Neat eh? Peter (I Peter 5:2,3) Paul (Acts 20:28;
Ephesians 4:11), and indeed, Jesus Himself (John 21:15-19) used the
reference to encourage and guide those who are charged with the care
and keeping the sheep of God.

Here's a bit of legend used by the Jewish people to explain the reason God chose Moses to become the leader he was destined to become. When Mo was out in the wilderness feeding his father-in-law's sheep one day a young sheepie took off on him. Mo searched and searched until he found it tucked away into a ravine lapping it up from a tiny brook. Mo said, "Hey, you little muffin, why didn't you tell me you were so thirsty. Now I know you must be worn out from having to go to this much trouble on your own." He packed up the soft bundle of woolite onto his shoulder and carried it all the way back to the rest of the flock. God, duly impressed with such character, praised Mo by saying, "Because you've shown such pity and tenderness in caring for the animal of a human caretaker, I want you to lead my flock Israel."

Quite a story, eh?

How did a shepherd operate? His equipment was very simple. No shepherd would be without his purse. Just kidding, it was more like an over the shoulder duffle bag. His "scrip," made of animal skin was used to carry his lunch of bread, cheese, olives, and dried fruit. Trail mix perhaps.

You didn't dare leave the barn with a "sling." Judges 20:16 tells us that a shepherd could "sling a stone at a hair and not miss." Pretty impressive! It was an offensive weapon as well as a defensive one, the precursor to the sheep dog. The shepherd would sling a rock just out if front to keep any stray little wool factory in line. Let there be no mistake it was a nifty weapon to ward off impending doom.

Let's not forget the "staff." This short wooden club had a lump of wood at the end, often studded with primitive nails. There was a slit in the handle near the top through which a thong passed. When defending himself or his flock the shepherd would attach his belt to the thong and swing it like a giant hammer throw like in the Olympic games.

The "rod" was similar to the shepherd's crook. You're perhaps most familiar with the pictures of Jesus with the crook of His rod wrapped around the neck of the "one who got away" from the other 99 little member of His flock. As the sheep were being tucked in at the end of the day the shepherd would hold the rod quite low to the ground at the entrance of the fold. As each little gentle creature passed under the rod the shepherd had the opportunity to examine it for any injury it may have suffered during the day (Ezekiel 20:37; Leviticus 27:32). What a lesson just in that little picture!

The relationship between shepherd and sheep is unique in different parts of the world based upon the purpose for which the sheep are raised. In Palestine the reason was wool. Thus, the relationship became very close over an extended period of time. The term "family pet" aptly works as the shepherd called his sheep by name. The sheep, not to be undone, recognized the voice of their caregiver, fleeing in dramatic fashion when an unfamiliar voice tried to offer a command. What a lesson just in that little picture too!

Well, if I keep going with this stuff we're never going to get through this parable. So let's get started. In my lingo of course:

"Listen up. Anybody who tries to get into the barn other than through the door is like a thief or robber trying to sneak in through some alternative method."

Sorry, I have to stop. This is so important. Folks, this is revolutionary. Don't let this thought get away. The parable is dramatic as it is absolutely incredible.

In the day there were two kinds of sheepfolds. Within any town or village there were communal sheepfolds (barns) that housed the animals at night. A porter was posted at a lockable, strong door. He held the key. Remember that thought. A shepherd would indeed be recognized by the security guard, however, the sheep would also recognize the shepherd, expecting his guidance for day trips and thankful for a safe return for a good night of kickin' back for some shut eye.

The other kind of sheepfold was out in the countryside, far away from the safety of the village. Hillside folds were open spaces enclosed by a wall with an opening through which the sheep could come and go during the day. At night, the shepherd would lay his body across the opening, and the only way a sheep could exit would be over the shepherd's body. In the most literal sense the shepherd was "the" door." Just think on that concept a moment.

"Coming and going" was a very popular Hebrew phrase. The ability to come and go as one pleased described a life absolutely secure and safe. Read passages in Numbers 27:17; Deuteronomy 28:6, I Kings 3:7 and Psalm 121:8 to discover the bliss of one covered off in the security of a doorkeeper/shepherd. These are powerful pictures. Enjoy.

"Only the shepherd of the flock could go in and out of the door unabated. Let there be no doubt the shepherd is the top dog, so to speak. The sheep recognize his voice 'cause he calls them by name. (Heard this idea before?) As they head out for a day on the slopes to catch some rays and to do some down-hillin' the shepherd walks before them to scope out and prepare the way, he walks beside them as their friend, and watches from behind, covering their back. And they obediently follow in his covering, accepting unquestionably his provision. Should a stranger attempt to distract them they simply run away from them 'cause they don't recognize the voice of strangers."

Now, Jesus spoke this parable to them but they didn't have a clue as to what He was talking about. So He had to clarify His thoughts so they'd clue in.

"People. People."

"Don't you get it?"

"I am the door!"

"Everyone who has tried to be a shepherd before me has been an abject failure, unsuccessful as thieves or robbers. The sheep didn't pay any attention to them whatsoever. Let me say it again."

"I'm the door."

"If any body wants in to be safe and sound, they have to go through me. If any body wants to head out into open pasture for a day of wining and dining they have to go through me. There are those who expect nothing less than to plunder, kill, and destroy. I, on the other hand, am all about life, abundant life at that!"

"I'm the good shepherd. Any good shepherd would give his very life for his sheep.

Once again, let me take you back to some neat Old Testament passages to broaden the scope of your understanding. Amos (3:12) refers to a shepherd who rescues a couple legs or a piece of an ear of one poor little sheep out of the mouth of a lion. "If it is torn by beasts, let him bring it as evidence." That was a law (Exodus 22:13)! Any shepherd who lost a treasure better have some pretty strong evidence that the prevention of harm was unavoidable.

We also have the heroic tale Dave told Saul how he had to battle with a lion and bear to protect his father's sheep (I Samuel 17:34-36). Isaiah also spoke of a crowd of shepherds who had to be called into duty to deal with a lion (Isaiah 31:4).

"Then you've got the hired hands. They're not really shepherds at all. Man, they see a wolf and they're gonzo. The wolf simply scoops in and ravages and plunders to their hearts' content. Look, the hireling takes off because he's just someone hired to do a job. He don't care. He has no vested interest in the safe keeping of the sheep other than some wages at the end of the day. He wouldn't have any interest in putting his life on the line for even one of the sheep in his care.

"Let me say it again if you didn't get it the first time."

"I am the good shepherd."

"I am intimately familiar with my sheep and they are intimately familiar with me. Just as my father knows me, even so I know my father. It my honor and privilege to lay down my life for my sheep."

Etymology lesson. "Agathos" simply describes the moral quality of a thing. "Kalos" is used of goodness, a winsomeness that makes the characteristic lovely and peaceable. The latter is the expression of "good" that Jesus used on this occasion. More than efficiency, skill, strength, and power there is a tone of sympathy, empathy, kindness, and graciousness that Jesus uses to describe his efforts as a "good" shepherd.

"Look folks, I've also got other sheep to look after. They might not be sheep you might recognize but I do. I intend to bring them into this fold too 'cause they will hear and recognize my voice. There is actually one sheepfold, and there is but one shepherd."

"That's why my Father loves me. He just digs it that I'd be willing to put my life on the line for those in my care. Giving up my life is the very way I'll get it back. Look, nobody's going to take my life without my blessing. I'll give

my life of my own volition. I have the power to lay down my
life and I have the power to take it back."
   "Who says? Well, my Father did!"

   Whooooa! Perhaps I should have said, Baaaaaaaaaaaaaaaa! Can
you just imagine the hoopla this little lesson frothed up?

      "This fellow's a little touched!"
      "This dufus is a bit deceived if you ask me!"
      "Me thinks he's lost his marbles!"
      "Loonie tunes!" "Cukoo!"
      "Why in the world are you folks paying any attention
to this wacko-J character?"
      Someone else piped in, perhaps playing shepherds'
advocate. "Hey, maybe this guy's got it together. Maybe he
is telling the truth. Have you ever seen somebody with his
nerve and vibrato ever give some blind dude his sight
back?"

   Golly gee, this is good stuff.
   In context we've got the interesting story of Martha and Mary
where servitude and the importance of doing what you feel in your
heart is pointed out. Jesus sure did.
   Next we had the rambunctious intercourse with the blind dude.
Jesus gives the guy his sight simply because He could, and to prove a
point that He'd be the one to open the eyes of all to see. The sad truth
is that those who should be seeing remain blind while those who
thought they'd never get a glimpse have their eyes opened to see a
world of possibilities.
   Following the parable of the good shepherd is a wild exchange
that John recorded for us in the remainder of chapter 10. The religious
industry simply refused to believe Jesus' claim that He was who He
said He was, namely, the Son of God. He claimed His sheep know
whom He is and nobody will be able to pluck the eternal life out of
them.
   They responded by wanted to throw a rock'n'roll party. Jesus
wanted to know why they'd stone Him for doing nothing but good.
The issue of equating Himself with God didn't sit too well with the
religious community. Apparently this was blasphemous. You see, it was
the "law."

"He who blasphemes the name of the Lord shall be put to death; all the congregation shall stone him" (Leviticus 24:16).

Folks this is priceless. Read it for yourselves in verse 34 through 38. Here's my take:

Jesus: "First of all chumps, read your own rule book. Check out Psalm 82:6. 'I say, you are gods, sons of the most High, all of you!' You can claim "god-dom" for yourselves, why can't I?"

Now this particular Psalm is a warning to unjust judges to cease from being unjust and to defend the poor and innocent. The Hebrew word translated judges is actually "elohim" which means "god" in Exodus 21:1-6 and 22:9,28. Other scriptures support the identification of men specially commissioned to some task by God that they indeed were gods. So the rationale employed by Jesus was: if their very own law could identify men as gods, why couldn't He speak about Himself as being one. Sounds reasonable.

Jesus: "Furthermore, God sanctified me for a particular job, namely, to come down here and make things right. You in fact are the blasphemers 'cause you're denying my right to claim I'm the Son of God. Hey, if I can't get done what I'm supposed to get done then, well, don't believe me. But, if I do get it done, well, if you don't believe what I said, you'd better believe what I did! My work will give you the knowledge and understanding you require to verify that the Father and I are indeed one!"

Outstanding!!!

Context.

Hang in there.

Sandwiched between all this extra-ordinary events was the parable. Remember. It was the parable of "the" "good" "shepherd." Is this not good or what?

God's the porter. Folks, He holds the keys to the kingdom! As an aside may I mention the keys of what was we've called "hell" are also in His care and keeping. No need to exercise that lock any longer! Satan is not only fallen, he's toast. Gonzo!

Anyway, when the sheep come home for some r & r and protection it is He who lets Jesus lead them in for safekeeping. When time comes for the sheep to hit the path for some liberty and abundance of blessing it's the porter of porters who opens the door for Jesus to lead their flock to pastures green, valleys low, and to streams of plenty.

I'm not bound to perpetuate a doctrine that there are sheep, and then there are "other" sheep that don't belong any longer. I find nothing in the lingo of Jesus that precludes any from being sheep that He cared for on the cross. In fact, I gain great comfort and solace to support the doctrine of "all-inclusiveness" that I've adopted. This passage has lent credence to my position, theologically speaking, of being somewhat on the other side of "universalism," a somewhat frowned upon position that holds that someday up the totem pole we'll all meet up in heaven.

Well, so much for my status in the religious world since I've taken up a position many would claim to be even worse than that of an unbalanced universalist. I can live with that. I've come to the wonderful, liberating discovery that the cross and the resurrection is where liberty and abundance got their legs! Folks, contrary to popular belief, there is only one sheepfold.

Sheep are we "all."

Likewise, there is only one good shepherd, Jesus!

The place Jesus came to do the work of God was on the cross. The mission He was sent to earth to do found its fulfillment at the cross. Jesus had the power to lay down His life because He was sanctified by God to do it. The devil didn't make Him do it, no, on the contrary, God made Him do it. The Son obeyed!

Not only that, Jesus told folks point blank that if He had the power to give up His life, He also the power to take His life back again. How do you spell "resurrection?"

Folks, contrary to all sage advice, the grass is not greener on the other side. I'm content to track with the good shepherd into His good pleasure day in and day out. Wherever He leads me I'm content to follow.

I'm a comin' and a goin'!

13. **KNOCK ! KNOCK !**

<u>THE PARABLE OF THE FRIEND AT MIDNIGHT</u>
Luke 11:1-13

Somewhere, someday, Jesus was spending some time in prayer. When He finished one of His disciples approached Him.

"Master, teach us to pray like John taught his disciples."

"No problem grasshopper. When you pray, say something like this:"

"Our Father in heaven, may the day come when Your heart and character will be revealed and acknowledged throughout the earth. May Your kingdom come and Your will be done on earth just as it is in heaven. Day by day provide our needs. And forgive us our sins, for indeed, we also forgive each one indebted to us. Furthermore, don't lead us into situations which challenge our fidelity and integrity, but deliver us from wickedness."

And Jesus continued, "Which one of you would go over to your friend's house at midnight, bang on the door and start yelling out your demands before he even gets to the door."

"Hey George, sorry to disturb you so late but a friend of mine was just passing through town and decided to pop in for the night. I don't have anything in the fridge. I've fired up my Bar-b and was wonderin' if you could spare a pound of burger, maybe a few buns, hey some garlic rings wouldn't be too bad either, so I can feed the starvin' fellow and his family? What do ya say buddy?"

"Not surprisingly George is a little ticked at being awakened in the middle of the night. "Have you lost your marble bag Bill? D'ya know what time it is? Folks told me you were one sandwich short of a picnic and now I'm inclined to believe them. Get lost! The door's locked. I don't want to wake the wife and kids, and I have no intention of getting out of bed to go to the kitchen either."

"Look," Jesus continued, "George might not get up to give Bill what he wants simply because he's a friend, however, George would get up and give his friend whatever he had in his fridge and pantry if Bill stood outside the door, persistently pounded the door knocker and caused enough of a general ruckus to get the collective tongues of the neighborhood wagging for weeks to come."

"Seek, ask, and it'll be given to you. Seek and you'll find what you're looking for. Knock on doors and they'll be opened up for you. You see, everyone who asks get, those who seek find, and those who knock have doors opened for them."

"If a son would ask his dad for some bread would any father in his right mind give him a stone? Of if the kid asked for a fish would a father give him a snake? Or if the son asked his dad for an egg do you think he'd be given a scorpion or two?"

"Dah!"

"Well, if you, normal human beings, know how to give good gifts to your children, how much more so is your Heavenly Father prepared to dish out of Himself to those earnestly seek to recognize Him for who He is."

That's my version of Luke's account and I'm sure you can already imagine the traditional scoop of the instructional prayer and this little parable that followed. Let's do a short review.

Central Truth:

In contrast to the reluctant neighbor who eventually would give his friend some leftovers because he was causing such a persistent ruckus, our heavenly Father is more than anxious to bestow His blessings upon those who persist in the petitioning prayer of faith.

Traditional Interpretations:

- The parable contrasts earthly reluctance with heavenly willingness. It doesn't mean to imply God is disobliging.
- It's not merely the place, manner, or frequency of bugging which is important, but, it's the loving willingness of God to give to His people that which they request.

- The parable is to encourage prayer of faith and persistence among God's people.
- Principles of prayer:
    a. Pray with humility (Our Father...).
    b. Pray with reverence (hallowed...).
    c. Pray with submission (Your will be done...).
    d. Pray with trust and dependence (give us...).
    e. Pray with penitence (forgive us...).
    f. Pray with holy aspirations (lead us not...).
- Prayer is:
    a. Based on a friendly relationship with God (have friend).
    b. Intercession for others (with need...).
    c. Definite and specific (three loaves...).
    d. Done with earnest desperation (nothing for him...).
    e. Done with importunity (bugged him at 12...).
    f. Gloriously rewarded (as much as he needed...).

Practical Applications:

- Persistent, energized effort is required to reach any goal in every other sphere of life. Why should the same not apply to the greatest of all strivings-prayer?
- There are certain laws to successful praying:
    a. God knows better than we do what's good for us.
    b. God alone sees all time.
    c. Prayer must be absolutely sincere.
    d. Effective prayer must be definite.
    e. Our cooperation is absolutely essential.
- The best prayer doesn't attempt to extract from God what we want rather, it expresses the willingness of our heart to accept what God wants to give.
- If a neighbor could be counted on to supply a need, if a father could be counted on to give his kid what he asked for, how much more can God be counted on to respond with equal immediacy, understanding, and without the possibility of deception when our sense of need removes our hesitancy or childlikeness and

replaces it with confidence to ask, seek, and knock with
persistence.
- If we are to learn how to pray we must become like Bill
in the story.
- If we're serious, then so is God.
- If you don't mean what you pray, don't.
- Jesus was teaching the disciples, and us by extension, of
our helpless condition and our need of help beyond our
own capacity.

Verses 1 to 4 are Luke's version of the teaching of Jesus to His
disciples concerning prayer. Matthew has a version too, although
Matt's version is somewhat longer. It was a familiar custom for a Rabbi
to teach his disciples a form of a simple prayer that they might use
habitually. John the baptizing chap certainly did.

Houses are definitely a far cry from what most of us are
familiar with today. Apartment buildings, condominiums or houses
with 4500 square feet weren't the norm by any stretch of the
imagination. Homes were designed to be multipurpose in nature. Two
level homes were built to provide housing for both the family as well as
for their livestock. Since animals aren't all that proficient at climbing
stairs the main floor became the animal habitat while their human
caretakers took to the second floor.

Most folks in Palestine were modestly poor. Often their homes
were no more than one room with a small window. No hardwood or
carpeted floors here. Dried reeds and rushes covered the hard packed
earth. Did they have three bedrooms, a kitchen, a family and living
room? Nope. Rooms were divided all right, into two parts, not by walls
mind you, but partitioned by a low platform. One area occupied about
2/3 of the space on the level ground. The other 1/3 was slightly raised
on a low platform of wood.

The upper floor (if you could call it that!) was where the
charcoal stove was used for cooking as well as for heat through the
cool nights. The family would gather to sleep around the stove like a
camp stove, not on comfort cushion, posturepedic beds but on
sleeping mats right on the wooden floor. Animals were relegated to
sleeping on the grassy floor. Leaving one's door open during the
daytime was a hint of open hospitality. A closed door was akin to
putting up a "do not disturb" sign.

While traveling late into the evening wasn't all that uncommon 'cause it was the coolest time of the day, even by our own standards midnight was a little late to drop by on someone so unexpectedly. The obligation to be hospitable with a bare cupboard was no doubt an embarrassing situation.

And what's with the bread/stone; fish/snake; and egg/scorpion thing?

Well, a loaf of bread wasn't the beautifully sliced loaf of bread wrapped in a colorful plastic bag you're probably accustomed to. Pita bread or thin crust pizza is more likely what it was like. A loaf of bread was round, flat and rather dark in color. They were made of crushed whole wheat or barley, baked beside an open fire in a brick oven, often covered with ash and cinders.

Yummy!

D'ya get it? Covered in ash and cinders. Yep, the bread actually had very much the same appearance as ordinary stones out on the ash heap. If a loaf were placed next to a stone of similar size a person would quite possibly be unable to tell at a casual glance what was which.

Similarly, there were certain kinds of slender, edible fish that closely resembled deadly water snakes. An innocent child probably wouldn't know the difference between the two if confronted with the various species, encountering potentially unfortunate consequences in their enthusiastic, explorative nature.

What about the egg and scorpion thing? Now that's a vivid comparison. Many scorpions are actually dark in color, however, in the mid East there's also a light colored variety sometimes called the "white scorpion." When curled up into its relaxed state this creature could easily be mistaken for an egg. Fatal consequence to an unsuspecting child was indeed a serious possibility.

Context.

Context.

Context.

Unfortunately, we've taken out of context an extraordinary teaching of Jesus concerning the heart of God and replaced it with an instruction manual of "our" role in prayer. The mantra of self-righteousness is:

- Bug the tar out of God.
- God will cave if we don't.
- Hitch your success on the post of persistence.

KNOCK ! KNOCK !   PARABLE OF MIDNIGHT FRIEND

The contrarian form of prayer Jesus taught His disciples was instead a wonderful example of His insight into the heart of God.

It included an awesome understanding of the scope of God's ultimate power. Jesus full well knew the "name" of the Father would be recognized throughout the world. You see, in the Semitic language the usage of the "name" is closely intertwined with the "person" or the "being," thus, acknowledging the "name" of God is the same as acknowledging the very "person" or very "being" of God.

Why in the world would Jesus include this petition as part of the learning curve for the disciples other than to illuminate for His disciples the heart of God? Why would we have to pray in any other fashion than with a heart of awe and gratitude when we have a God as illustrated in the little parable?

I tell you, Jesus had a sense of humor. This story is laced with situation comedy, reality stand up comedy with a punch line. The situation described by Jesus certainly wasn't out of the realm of possibility and, in addition, sure makes for good clean fun.

We've got a chap here who got some unexpected company. He's caught with his pants down, perhaps literally (it was midnight after all), with nothing left in the bowl. The cookie jar was empty. The cupboard was as bare as the woman with the staple in her belly button.

What to do?

Wake up the neighbor! What a plan.

His crib, however, is a marvelous monument to silence. The door's shut, the animals are just bagged from a hard day at the office, the kids are tucked away, the temperature's just right with a gentle breeze flowing through the window, and the little woman is spooned in snug as a bug.

What could be better? Hey, what could be worse?

Probably a pesky, out of munchies neighbor, that's what.

Bang! Bang! Whine! Whine!

According to the story Jesus does admit that persistence does have it's perks. Just keep it up and eventually you'll overcome the obstacles of closed doors. Many of you with children know the reality of keeping your head above water down 'til you finally throw in the towel.

Jesus said if you want to get something you most likely won't unless you ask for it. If you look long and hard enough you will get what you ask for. Nobody in their right mind will get doors opened for them if they don't knock first.

99

Why is this Jesus?

Well, if you ask you, you'll get, if you look, you'll find, and if you knock, doors will open.

But here comes the context with the kicker packed with the message of the parable.

What father in his right mind would trick his kids just to get a rise out of them? What kind of father would knowingly and intentionally deceive his kids to teach them a lesson? Would you hand your little children a small stone and tell them it was actually a candy.

"Here you go sweetie, some candy. Rock candy. Ha! Ha! Fooled ya!"

NOT!

Would you give your beautiful offspring some celery and to their horror and shock they found out it was actually broccoli? Yuch!

NOT!

What's the point?

If you, being a mere mortal, wouldn't do that to your kids, what makes you think your Heavenly Father would withhold His very best from you? Jesus wasn't telling the tale to inspire a sense of hospitality in us. He wasn't challenging us to become vigilant whiners, nor was He trying to extol the virtuous qualities of one who'd interrupt his sleep to keep the peace with his neighbor. After all, what kind of friend could he be if he had to be nagged and cajoled into doing his little act of kindness?

It may just be that Jesus told the story to discourage the kind of prayers that bask in an abundance of urgent, strident demands. Such drastic measures may be necessary when dealing with folks under the next cabana however God isn't inclined to act like humans. You see, I think we've got it all wrong. We've always understood these verses to be an inspiration to a successful prayer life. To me, it's a beautiful story of God's love towards His children.

My grandkids will never have to ask for my love. I've become a whole lot more aware of the kind of love God has for the whole world since I've become a grandparent. I never thought I'd say this but it's true. I just look at Ryan and Keira and am filled with so much love it's incredible. They know I love them. They never question me about it, never doubt it, and accept all of me without a care.

Why? They're kids! I sometime think it's too bad we grow up. When we mature we somehow lose the childishness that blindly accepts love for what it is.

KNOCK ! KNOCK !   PARABLE OF MIDNIGHT FRIEND

My wife on occasion has questioned my love. Hey come on. Thirty-seven years is what I'd call a pretty successful marriage, but don't kid yourself, we have our minutes. My grown up children probably wonder whether I'm missing a few drawers in my toolbox once in a while. But my grandkids, hey, they just love me 'cause I'm me!

Why is it we just can't seem to accept God for who He is without questioning His love or His motivation? This is the bottom line of this parable as far as I am concerned. God is a Father who loves us more than we could possibly imagine.

What could be more loving than simply being a Father? What could be better than knowing God's name is recognized throughout the world as the one and only Father, worthy of all honor and praise? What could be better than living in a kingdom of His creating? What could be better than living in a world where the will of God is done exactly the same as it is in Heaven?

That one just blows me away!

What could be better than knowing the daily necessities of life have a source beyond compare? Yes, in whatever circumstance we find ourselves in. You could be living in Detroit driving a Chevrolet taking the kids to school. You could be living in Muana Lani and driving a VW Passat CC. to the magnificent north or south golf course. While that wouldn't be too hard to take I'm convinced God's blessings aren't extended or withheld based or dependant upon where you live or what sled you drive. Well, perhaps He might be withholding some if you don't drive a VW. Oh, give me a break I'm just teasing. After 33 some years of the blue in my blood vessels I just had to throw that in for the fun of it.

What could be better than having our sins forgiven? Can you imagine? No more sin? WOW! What could be better than the liberty from temptations and the deliverance from evil?

"How much more? How much more has your heavenly Father given?"

Indeed!

Folks, the prayer isn't a prayer of petition, it's a prayer of praise. This parable isn't an exhortation about the virtue of beating the drum 'til the sticks break (persistence), it's a revelation of the nature of God's love and care of His children!

Knock. Knock. Wakie, wakie.

Hey, where's the beef?

14. **DUFUS !**

THE PARABLE OF THE RICH FOOL
Luke 12:13-21

Let's mix things up a bit. Before I give you my translation of the text, as well as what I think of this parable, I'll brief you with a summary of the information you'll discover if you read a few commentaries.

Central Truth:

> Distrust God's providential care and you're bound to make covetousness a lifestyle.

Traditional Interpretations:

- It seems to teach the need for constant vigilance and preparedness of being engaged in the interests of God.
- Jesus is warning of the danger of ignoring the signs of the kingdom and of refusing its call.
- The rich man forgot God, forgot his neighbors, and he forgot a man is what he is, not what he has.

Practical Applications:

- Our task is to choose between the riches of this life and the riches of the life to come.
- Materialism is still a present menace of our era, sapping us of a relationship with God and others.
- All we have belongs to God and should be used to serve Him.
- Your heart is where your treasure is.
- Jesus doesn't oppose providing for the future. Bend all your life to obeying God's will and rest content with that.
- Work for things that last forever, things that you need not leave behind when you leave this earth, but which you can take with you.
- A fool is a man whose decisions about the present don't take into consideration the possibilities of the future.

Alrighty then. Let's get to the passage.

Oops, can't do it yet. I have to set it up for you first. Context, context.

If you've been paying attention chapter 11:13 is where the parable of the midnight-door-knocker ended. Verse 14 of chapter 11 begins with Jesus casting out some dumb devil dude. Confusion reigned supreme and the throngs wondered aloud how the heck Jesus was doing what He did and, almost more importantly, who gave Him this kind of authority to do it.

I love the answer Jesus gave to them.

"A house divided against itself will fall."

Sounds simple enough. Folks had accused Jesus of casting out devils through Beelzebub, apparently the top dog in the devil hood. Now why would a bad guy kick out another bad guy out of someone? How could the kingdom of darkness stand if it's fighting against itself (11:15-17)?

Don't be fooled, Jesus was no pushover. He didn't just come out of a hole in the wall or something. He was tapped in.

You might be inclined to think the practice of kicking the devil out of someone started in 1973 when the movie "the Exorcist" hit the screen. Not! Josephus the great Jewish historian traces the practice back to the days of Solomon who employed herbs and incantations to scare the devil out of folks. Josephus tells us he'd seen Solomon's methods with his very own eyes (Antiquities of the Jews; 8:5:2).

Jesus confronts His detractors in a way they could have hardly expected with good old-fashioned logic. In the Aramaic language the name Beelzebub is open to the derogatory interpretation: "lord of dung."

Now that's priceless!!!

I wonder if Paul knew this when he called the witchcraft-like doctrine of works a "pile of ____. Oops, I think he did say "dung" in the King James Version didn't he?

Now, if Jesus could cast out devils with the authority of Beelzebub, wouldn't this make everyone else among them who cast out devils in the same league with the prince of devils?

Listen up folks! Jesus didn't get His marching papers from the devil. If He, with the finger of God, could cast out devils then you'd better believe the kingdom of God is here to stay (11: 18-20)!

Furthermore, greater strength will overcome lesser strength! It doesn't matter what kind of army you protect your things with, if someone comes along with a stronger army, you're toast.

Whoever isn't on God's side simply won't be winning any consolation prize. Satan and his kingdom have been not only neutralized, they're as good as impotent (11:21-23).

Some woman piped up from the crowd and shouted out at Jesus. "Good golly Miss Molly, the woman who bore you and let you suck her boobs sure must be a happy camper" (11:27).

Trying not to blush too much Jesus responded. "Well, she probably is, but the ones who have more to be happy about are the ones who hear the word of God and understand it" (11:28).

Priceless comeback!

Well, the crowd grew to massive proportions as Jesus laid on some more of His teaching. Here are a few of the highlights.

The Son of man would be to His generation what Jonah the prophet was to the Ninevites way back when. Jesus said folks took notice when Jonah spoke, and behold, one greater than Jonah "is" here (11:29-32).

Your candle's been lit, so hide it under a bushel? NOT! The eye is the portal for allowing light into your body. Don't let darkness overtake the light already in you (11:33-36).

Oh. Oh. Here we go again. Another recipe for disaster.

A Pharisee gets up the nerve to ask Jesus out for lunch. What is it about food that it never loses its appeal? Anyway, Jesus accepts the invitation. Oops. Guess what? Jesus didn't wash His hands before sitting down to eat His clubhouse on manna. Apparently, this slip up didn't sit too well with the host 'cause he must have let into his guest with some disdain.

For those of you parents who get disgusted when your kids show up at the supper table with dirty hands this particular incident has nothing to do with the sanctity of cleanliness. Oh no, what we have here was a matter of ceremonial law.

It was the law!

Before you eat you better wash your hands. No ifs, ands, or buts allowed. In fact, you had to wash them between courses. Talk about details. Since ordinary water could be unclean it was necessary to keep "bottled" water in large stone vessels for this specific observance. Evian would have been a big hit back then too I'll bet.

You wouldn't just slosh the water carelessly like my grandkids do. Oh no. You'd only use enough water to fill one and a half eggshells. Someone would have to pour the water over your hands beginning at the tips of the fingers and rinsing right up to the wrist.

Then the palm of each hand would be cleansed by rubbing the fist of the other into it. Once again a rinse, this time in the opposite direction, wrist to fingers. Skip a detail and you broke the law!

Jesus wasn't going to take this particular accusation of breaking the law sittin' down, and you're about to read Jesus lay on a lickin' like you've never read before. I doubt you've heard too many sermons on this passage. If you don't want to accept my summary of it read it for yourselves from verse 37 to 54 of Luke 11.

What a treat!

"You guys might clean your cups and saucers but you're filthy on the inside, full of conniving and wickedness. You fools, didn't God make everything around you, as well as what's inside of you? Bless others with some of what you've got 'cause everything has been made clean for you" (11:39-41)!

Honestly now, you don't hear this preached very often, do you? Oh, here comes a bunch of "WOE" verses. Look out! This is wicked good stuff.

"Woe to you, Pharisees! You wrap yourselves in a knot over what and how you tithe and sacrifice instead of getting in awe of the justice and love of God towards you. Get your priorities straight" (11:42)!

Pharisees were meticulous at paying their dues. First, there was the offering in the Temple of the first fruits of seven different harvests-wheat, barley, vines, fig trees, pomegranates, olives and honey. Second, the "Terumah," a tithe of 1/50th of the total yield was a contribution to the upkeep of the priests. Third, there was a tithe paid directly to the Levites who, in turn, had to give the priests a tithe of what they received! Hey, they did it whether they wanted to or not, and yes, whether they felt like it or not. Tax upon tax. Sound familiar? You must like in Canada to appreciate that kind of humor.

The best seats in the house were the ones that had the greatest visibility. Cheap seats were found in the back, the great seats were in the front rows. The best seats were on a semicircular bench in front of the ark on the platform facing the rest of the synagogue crowd. Guess who got the best seats? They were reserved for the folks who "gave" the most. I guess Jesus had a bone to pick with those who gave for all the wrong reasons.

"Woe to you, Pharisees! You just love your high falutin' lifestyle don't you" (11:43).

"Woe to you scribes and Pharisees, you bunch of hypocrites! Dead-men walking. (Sounds like a good movie title.) You're like graves that nobody even recognizes as such. Your corrupted influence serves only to contaminate those whom you come in contact with (11:44).

Ouch!

Boy, this guy knows how to wing it.

You see, for the dufus who happens to touch a grave out in an open field Numbers 19:16 lays down the prohibition from all religious ceremony for seven days. They were declared to be unclean whether they knew they had come in contact with the grave or not. What an indictment on the Pharisees. No wonder they didn't like what Jesus was telling them.

Wouldn't you know it!

A lawyer was in the crowd. Food and lawyers. Can't escape them.

"Would you be talkin' 'bout us too?"

I suggest this chap would have been better to keep his mouth shut (11:45). Jesus proceeds to accuse the scribes (legal profession) of three different crimes against humanity.

Charge #

"Woe to you too, you pompous, arrogant lawyers! You do nothing more than place folks under extreme bondage, and yet, you won't even lift a finger to ease their burden" (11:46).

What were the burdens folks often had to carry? Well, the burden was the application of individual precepts of the law that had been developed, accumulated and interpreted over the centuries. Lawyers were very good at burdening others with a thousand and one ceremonial laws. However, because they were lawyers, they were also expert in the practice of law evasion.

What do I mean?

You weren't supposed to travel more than 1000 yards from your house on Sunday (Sabbath). But, if you attached a rope to the end of the street, the end of the street became your residence and you could go another 1000 yards. Another thing you couldn't do on Sunday was to tie knots. A woman was, however, allowed to tie a knot in her girdle, so, if water had to be drawn from a well, a girdle could be used to raise the bucket and not the knot. Go figure.

Lawyers also codified a law to get around the prohibition of carrying a burden. Get a load of this: "...He who carries anything, whether it be in his right hand, or in his left hand, or in his bosom, or on his shoulder is guilty; but, he who carries anything on the back of his hand, with his foot, or with his mouth, or with his elbow, or with his ear, or with his hair, or with his money bag turned upside down, or between his money bag and his shirt, or in the fold of his shirt or in his shoe, or in his sandal is guiltless, because he doesn't carry it in the usual way of carrying it out."

Oh for stupid.

Charge # 2

"And woe to all of you! You've built monuments to prophets your very own fathers killed. You not only condone their actions, you exalt them. The blood for the sins of every generation from the beginning of time 'til now is on your hands. Look, God's no dummy (11:47-51)!

D'ya get that? Perhaps it bears repeating. Jesus said the wisdom of God was at play throughout the entire history of mankind. How? Well, He sent prophets and apostles to instruct people about God. What did they do? Folks simply killed the messengers of God.

Now what?

The wrath of God has been brought to bear full force on the generation Jesus was talking to. Could this be the reason Jesus showed up when He did?

Stop for a moment. Re-read the last charge. Read it again. Read it again. Let the impact of this statement whack your brain around for a few moments. Have you ever heard this before? Jesus has just said God took His history sweeping, pent up wrath out on the generation Jesus was born into!

Amazing! Do you realize the implications of the cross and the resurrection for all of us? I don't know about you, but I'm inclined to believe what Jesus said. This concept is mind boggling to me.

Charge # 3

"Woe to you lawyers! You've taken the key of knowledge from the people. You've not entered into the door of wisdom yourselves, in addition, you've also prevented everyone else from understanding the truth as well" (11:52)!

What a stinging indictment upon those who'd been entrusted with knowledge and responsibility! What a rebuke upon the religious leaders and guardians of the repository of truth and tradition! In their hands the scriptures became a book of riddles, impossible for common folk to make any sense of.

Is it any wonder they were ticked off when they heard Jesus call them out? The line was drawn in the sand.

O.K. it was more like a ditch. The waiting game began. The strategy to trap Jesus into making even the slightest slip of the tongue was initiated.

Game on (11:53-54)!

Don't worry folks we're getting closer to the parable. We're into chapter 12 now.

While the Pharisees and scribes are off plotting little war games countless multitudes are trampling all over each other to check out this Jesus character. Before addressing the throngs Jesus took the disciples off to the side to give them a little heads-up.

"Watch out for the yeast (leaven) of the Pharisees. The only character trait they're good at spreading is hypocrisy. Trust me, there's nothing covered up which won't be revealed, nothing hidden which won't be understood. Whatever you speak in the dark will be heard in the light. Say something in a closet and it will be broadcast from the rooftops" (12:1-3).

Hypocrisy is an interesting word. A hypocrite originally meant "someone who answers," while hypocrisy means "answering." Hence, if you were engaged in any ordinary conversation involving a question and answer session you'd be a hypocrite. Eventually the word became associated with this type of dialogue in a theatrical play. Acting out a part was, by its nature hypocritical thus hypocrisy became the basis of insincerity and play-acting.

Jesus certainly didn't mince words! Pharisees were quite the characters, literally.

"I'm telling you my friends, don't be afraid of those who kill someone 'cause all they're doing is killing a body. What else can they do? If you want to be scared of someone, be scared of one who has the power to do something to the person after they're dead. Be scared of the guy who'll throw your body into Gehenna. Look, God is awesomely acquainted with every sparrow, indeed, He even knows how many hairs you've got on your head" (12:4-7)!

"Hell, my Bible says 'Gehenna!'

Why did you use the word "Gehenna?"

Well, the word refers to the valley of Hinnom, a ravine to the south west of Jerusalem where in the Old Testament certain Israelites during the monarchy worshiped Molech by making their children pass through the fire in the valley. Josiah polluted the valley with the bones of men to put a stop to this pagan cult (II Kings 23:10-14), but the cult was revived under Jehoiachin. Jeremiah prophesied one day it would be known as the "valley of slaughter." (Jeremiah 7:30-32) Kimchi, a Jewish commentator (around A.D. 1200) on the Psalms says Gehenna was used as a garbage dump for the city of Jerusalem and that a fire burned there constantly.

Puts a different spin on things, eh? Hell, overkill or what?

Sparrows? Sparrow steak was among the cheapest chunks of meat sold down at the public market. The maximum price for ten sparrows was set at the equivalent of seven cents by an edict of the late third century (A.D) emperor, Diocletian.

It's been calculated blondes have about 145,000 hairs on their head, brunettes have 120,000, and red heads have around 90,000. Who got the government grant for this study? The last time I checked there are quite a few blondes walking around, not to mention brunettes, red heads. I wonder if someone's calculated the number for gray heads 'cause I'm getting my fair share of those. And God knows the accurate number of every one of us?

Wow!

"Be careful, those who publicly acknowledge who I am will be acknowledged before the angels of God, but those who don't, won't. Say what you want against me. That's forgivable, but, speak against the very Spirit of God and there's nothing that can help you. Listen, when you get dragged before the powers that be for hangin' out with me don't worry about what you'll say to defend yourselves. The Spirit of God will help you out" (12:8-12).

I know. I know. Why don't I use the words "Holy Spirit?"

Context. Context. Never forget Jesus was talking about the Spirit of God as the Jews understood it. The audience of Jesus had no such conception of the Holy Spirit as we seem to have developed over the centuries. God's Spirit to the Jew had basically two functions. First, God used His Spirit to tell His truth to men. Second, it was the activity of God's Spirit in a person's mind and heart that helped them recognize and understand His truth.

Look, Jesus wasn't talking about losing an eternity of the Holy Spirit as many would like us to believe He was. The Pharisees had become so deaf, blind, and dumb to the Spirit of God they actually called Jesus the devil! He accused them of losing their understanding of God's truth, and was warning the Pharisees of the difficulty of falling into a state of complete isolation by neglecting their responsibility of hearing God's Spirit relate His truth and, what's probably worse, of the dangers of missing out on living in the wealth and warmth of the wisdom and understanding of God's loving grace, mercy, and peace.

God doesn't shut folks out!

Did you get that? God hasn't closed the book on anyone! Folks do it to themselves! Ignorance isn't just bliss, it's stupidity. Apathy isn't a symptom, it's a disease, and it's a plague, a plague worse than the swine flu, aids, SARS, or mad cow.

In the writing of John a favorite title of the Spirit of God (Holy Spirit) is "paraclete." "Parakletos" means "someone who stands by to help." Is that good or what? In the Spirit of God we have an advocate to plead our cause.

My. My. What a beautiful picture.

And now, in the middle of some outstanding teaching by a most incredible advocate standing out there somewhere in the midst of folks who couldn't believe their ears, comes "the parable of the Rich Fool."

Finally. Someone in the massive crowd of folks called out to Jesus.

"Hey Master, can you talk to my brother? Tell him he's supposed to share our father's inheritance with me."

"Hey player, who made me a judge or estate attorney for you? Watch out. Don't let greed overrun your life. Life isn't about what you possess or wish to possess."

"Let me tell you a little story. There was this rich dude who harvested an incredible crop. He thought to himself saying, 'Self, what am I gonna do 'cause I've got no more barns to store the grain? I know, I'll tear down these small barns and just build bigger ones.'"

"And after he did just that he thought to himself some more, 'Self, you've got enough to last you for quite a few years, take a break, eat, drink, and party on!'"

"But God said to this rich dude, 'You dufus. If you died tonight who'd get everything you've acquired?'"

"What's the moral of the story? There's no security in things. You're a fool if you think what you acquire will help you out get when you get to heaven. You're a fool if you're not rich in your understanding of what God has done for you" (12:12-31)!

Let's tie a few things together.
- Satan doesn't stand a chance 'cause his kingdom is divided up against itself (11:17).
- If I can cast out devils then, no doubt, the kingdom of God is come upon you (Jesus) (11:20).
- Those who understand God's words are happier than mother Mary herself (11:28).
- Jesus was a greater sign or prophet than Jonah (11:32).
- Be careful the light in you doesn't come off like darkness (11:35).
- You dummies! Didn't God, who made you so perfect on the outside, also purify your inside (11:40)?
- Get your priorities straight (11:42).
- Don't be a hypocrite (11:44).
- The blood of sin for all humankind is upon the generation of Jesus (11:51).
- The key to understanding God's mercy and grace is a powerful tool. Use it wisely (11:52).
- Hypocrisy is a plague like leaven (12:1).
- Nothing's covered which won't be revealed, nothing hid which won't be known (12:2).
- Be more in awe of the one who controls the "after" life than the one who controls the life (12:5).
- God knows how many hairs you have on your head (12:7).
- You're a fool if you think what you do or store up will accomplish anything as far as your eternal destiny is concerned (12:13-21).

Wanting more out of this life, or more in this life, is hardly a result of distrusting the providence of God. Vigilance and preparedness are no longer concepts I can accept in the light of what God did back in Jesus' day.

Yes indeed, the story illustrates a rich fool who amassed the luxury of things. Was he a fool for amassing things? No. Was he a fool because he lacked a perspective of what God had done for him? Well, that's the conclusion Jesus offered.

Anyone who tells you money is the root of "all" evil doesn't have a clue about life from the perspective of one tapped into the blessing of God. The problem Jesus describes in His teaching concerns those who can't wrap their imaginations around a God who's blessed them more abundantly than they could possibly imagine.

We have so much in God we don't even know it. We squander our lives trying, trying to "be" good, trying to "do" good, trying to impress, and trying to make sure our heart is firmly planted next to the right treasure.

I'm convinced the message of this parable, in the mix of an entire body of teaching, is that God's provision in Jesus is adequate to cover us all. God knew what we'd need and was equally aware we were totally incapable of meeting the need. Hence, the cross and the resurrection.

What's the secret to life? Get on with it!

You will have no trouble sitting next to your treasure when you know where your heart is.

Dufus me?

Not!

I'm so blessed I can really stand it.

15. **DIG IN !**

<u>THE PARABLE OF THE WATCHFUL SERVANTS</u>
Luke 12:22-59

Hang on. Jesus ain't done yet!

While we may have just wrapped up the parable of the rich fool I don't think the teaching of Jesus to the disciples and the assorted folks surrounding Him ended at the conclusion of verse 21. That particularly brief parable might have hit the outside marker on the target set up by the one bold enough to request the intervention of Jesus into their inheritance problems, but, the teaching sure wasn't over as far as Jesus was concerned. Hey, Peter was also a tad confused 'cause he had to ask Jesus whom His parable was meant for. He wasn't about to give up until He hit the bull's eye.

Once again I'd like to draw your attention to the context of this entire group of verses then return to the parable of the watchful servant to see what sense we can make of it. In my words of abbreviation...

"Food, clothing and shelter? Hey, life's more than meat we eat, the body's more than clothes we wear. Check out the ravens! If you can't add an extra year, month, day, hour, minute, or second to your life by just contemplating about it, why would you take too much time thinking about other things you can't control" (12:22-26)?

"Check out those wild flower lilies. Solomon didn't even come out looking as beautiful as they do. God will take care of you. Seek an understanding of the kingdom of God and you'll figure out what really counts in life" (12:27-31).

"Little sheepies, don't worry. Be happy! It's your heavenly Father's good pleasure to give you the kingdom" (12:32)!

"Your heart can be found right next to your treasure" (12:34).

"Get dressed! Let your light shine" (12:35)!

And now the parable...

"And you yourselves should be like the caretakers who wait for their master to come back from a wedding. When the master knocks they'll be ready to open the door the moment they hear the knock on the door announcing his return. Those expectant caretakers the master will meet at the door will be tickled pink at his return."

113

"Listen, I'm not exaggerating. I'm telling you the master will be so happy to see his caretakers he'll get all dolled up in his cookin' duds, get out the bar-b, and cook up some huge eyes of rib and cobs of corn for the whole crew. I don't care if he comes sometime between 10 pm and 2 am or between 2 am to 6 am. If he finds his caretakers can't get on without him it'll bless his heart and they'll reap the rewards of his joy."

"Don't kid yourselves, if a home owner would know what time a thief planned to come and break into his house he'd have kept his eyes on his watch and prepared to defend himself against the burglary. Well, get on doin' what you ought to be doin'. Why? Because the Son of man will show up when you least expect it" (12:36-40).

Peter pipes up...

"Master, are you telling this parable to us, or are you talking to all these other folks" (12:41)?

And now here comes the explanation from Jesus. This is really interesting folks so pay attention. Notice how Jesus didn't even answer Peter, instead, He continued to expand on the theme.

"Who is the faithful, wise caretaker? Who's the character that will become the top dog in charge of the entire estate on behalf of the master? Who'll get to share in the big pig out? Well, let me tell you the one doing what they're doing properly will be a happy camper" (12:42-44).

Here comes the "but" and the "if."

"But, and if, the caretaker starts goofin' off figuring his master isn't coming back when he said he would and starts whaling on his co-workers, he's in for a rude awakening when the master does show up unexpectedly. He'll get his portion all right" (12:45-46).

"The plain old workers who don't do their jobs properly won't get whipped as bad as their boss 'cause those who have more responsibility and understanding are expected to perform on a different level" (12:47-48).

"I've come to rain down fire of this earth. My goodness, the match is almost set to ignite the kindling, but I've still got some work to do so I'll just have to sit tight 'til my job's been accomplished" (12:49-50).

"Do you think I've come to bring peace to the earth? NOT! On the contrary, what you're going to see is nothing but controversy and divisiveness. You're going to see three members of a family gang up on the two other members. Dads and sons will fight with one another. Moms and daughters will scrape their nails. What about the in-laws? Now there's another story" (12:51-53).

"Look folks, when you see dark clouds in the western sky you just know it'll be rainin' pretty soon. And when you feel the south scirocco wind blowing you just know a heat wave is comin' on. You're actually a bunch of hypocrites. You're capable of predicting the weather, and yet, you can't seem to discern what's happening right before your very eyes. You can't even figure out the difference between the right and wrong way to conduct yourselves" (12:54-57).

"When you take someone to court thinking you've got all the rights, think again, you might just want to settle your differences out of court 'cause the tables might get turned around. Here's what your card might say when you pick one from the pile. 'Go directly to jail. Do not pass go. Do not receive 500 dollars.' In fact, you may just sit there 'til you've paid every last penny you owe to cover your debt" (12:58-59).

My goodness, the fellow who asked Jesus to intervene in his personal estate problems back in Luke 12:13 finally got his answer to his question!

We've come full circle, haven't we?

Jesus gets in the parable of the rich fool and now this parable of the watchful servant, in addition to a whack of other stuff, and the guy's told to settle out of court.

If we had gone over this passage in Bible school I'm sure this is what we would have come up with.

Central Theme:

Knowledge and privilege always bring responsibility. For those who know better, better is expected. For those who have the opportunity to do better, nothing short of better will suffice.

Traditional Interpretations:

- Waiting servants=church; absent master=risen Jesus; master's return=second coming of Jesus; marriage feast=heavenly banquet.
- It's a warning against the priestly aristocracy.
- A day of reckoning is coming, be ready!
- Sin is twice as sinful for the one who knew better. Failure is twice as blameworthy for the one who had every chance to succeed.

Practical Applications:

- Get your ducks in a row.
- Live at peace with yourself and your fellow man.
- Don't be a slouch. You don't have as much time as you may think.
- If you're in charge, you'd better be aware of the consequences of your responsibility.

Once again it must be the context that ought to drive our understanding of this parable. Surely we must understand the teaching of Jesus in light of when He spoke it. The warning indeed was as severe a warning as Jesus could deliver. He knew the arrival of the long awaited kingdom of God was at hand. Indeed, folks were acutely unaware of just how fortunate they were to be seeing the manifestation of the kingdom of God being realized at that very moment.

Jesus wasn't pussy footing around. His mission wasn't to soft peddle or mince words. His visitation to earth would result in the rain of fire all right, and He'd bear the brunt of it. Furthermore, I can't conceive of any possibility Jesus didn't know how much His coming would upset the apple cart. He must have been acutely shocked by the complacency and downright hypocrisy displayed by folks who truly should have known better.

In the parable Jesus exhorted folks to be like caretakers with the responsibility of running the estate while the boss was off tending to some other business.

They had a job to do and were expected to carry out their tasks with a sense of pride and professionalism. Those with more responsibility were expected to exercise their authority with honor and dignity. The fact some who rule over others don't know how to exercise their power should come as no surprise. The fact some abuse authority is a no-brainer. The reality that some workers are void of commitment and accountability is surely evident to even a casual observer in any work force.

The one thing Jesus could guarantee was His accountability to exercise the will of God. Consistent with all of His other teaching is the fact accountability is the very reason why He came. His coming was to accept the accountability for the inabilities and depravities of the whole world.

Why?

He came to satisfy the righteous justice of God.

We live in a world with an ever-increasing storm of criminal activity invading the very places we tend to think are sanctuaries protecting our families and possessions, our homes. There's no time table posted by vandals in my neighborhood's postal kiosk. The random appearance of criminals is often unscheduled and vicious in nature. The rape of dignity and personality is a crime of vengeance we should never tolerate. I wonder how many would be victims without weapons if the time of the travesty of injustice were known beforehand. Gun control? People would be lining up to buy their weapon of choice like they do for house or car insurance on the appointed date of renewal.

Being prepared isn't to be thought of in negative terms. It's an exercise in smarts. Most of us have some form of insurance, whether medical, dental, car, liability, or house insurance. I haven't had a claim against my car or house insurance in decades, and yet, the potential threat of an accident provokes me to protect my family. Only makes sense.

Likewise, living life in the kingdom of God in a prudent and responsible way is surely consistent with the teaching of Jesus. The parable was definitely about the future. I just don't happen to think it was as far into the future as we've adopted it to be. I'm convinced the coming of the kingdom has already occurred. Jesus can come a second time if He wants to, however, the work God sent Him here to do was accomplished when He came the first time.

The banquet some of you are anxiously awaiting in the future is already happening, and you don't even realize it. Most of our religious communities are just like those folks in Jesus' day. They can predict the weather but can't see the kingdom of God right in front of them!

Doing good things, or not doing bad things, is not a requirement for reward. It should be a natural way of living. Treating others with respect and dignity is not a prescription for future reward. It ought to be joyful response to the respect and dignity we were shown by the head honcho of the kingdom. Doing our job with diligence and professionalism isn't merely a means to an end. It a way of life born out of gratitude to One who did the real work on your behalf.

Watchful caretaker?

Start enjoying the trip!

The kingdom has been laid out for you to enjoy. The banquet hall is a smorgasbord of sights, sounds, smells, touches, and tastes.

Dig in!

16. NOW, THAT'S THE PITS !

<u>THE PARABLE OF THE BARREN FIG TREE</u>
Luke 13:6-9

"Suffering is the consequence of sin."

Even today this dogma is as popular as tape on a hockey stick, as peanut butter chocolate ice cream on a waffle cone, or as skimpy bikinis on a Brazilian beach. Isn't it interesting Jesus tried to debunk this goofy theology when He told this parable?.

I'm afraid folks didn't get it back then, and we don't seem to have understood it to this very day.

Let me set it up for you.

Pilate, (remember him?), couldn't avoid trouble for the life of him, even when he had one of those "greeeaat idea" moments which assault all of us every once in a while. Hey, what could possibly be so problematic for a politician who proposes a major government project? Certainly it would be good for the economy. Think about the jobs it would create.

Well, let me tell you, I'd love to have been a fly on the wall of the assembly room where an astute collection of bureaucrats convened to discuss the merits of the top dog's bright new plan.

"Say fellas, let's build a new and improved water supply system. The old aqueduct has run its course and it's high time we do an update."

"And tell us, dear Pilate, where can we come up with the money to pay for this kind of monumental project?"

"Let me think...thinking...thinking. Hey! I've got a greeaaat idea! Let's expropriate some funds from the Hebrew Bank of Jerusalem to pay for it!"

While it may have been a laudable project requiring a justifiable expenditure, the notion of using the Jewish Temple treasury to fund the endeavor no doubt went over like a sack of rotten figs to the Jews. If Pilate wanted to get a reaction out of the Jewish folk all he had to do was think about touching their well-endowed kitty.

The religious leadership made no effort to conceal their disgust for Pilate's intention, inciting the crowds into a frizzy. Pilate, not to be undone, developed contingency plans of his own. Orders were given for a clandestine, covert infiltration of a Sabbath gathering.

Soldiers were given the not so ingenious command to wear cloaks over their battle garb as a disguise, and given short stubby clubs called "cudgels" instead of swords. At an appropriate signal they were to appear out of nowhere and break up the crowd.

Sounds like a good plan, eh?

NOT!

Those bad boys laid a lickin' on the poor Jewish worshippers like they'd never seen in their lifetime. I doubt very much Pilate intended, or expected, his troops to carry out such a massive, deadly attack.

Now Pilate found himself in a pickled herring jar all right, dropped unwittingly into a no win situation. It was impossible for him to take back the destruction he initiated, and indeed, it was completely out of the question to start all over again with a different approach.

Not only was he in deep doo-doo with the Jews, he brought himself into some serious trouble with Herod, who, needless to say, wasn't ever exactly enamored with the antics of Pilate. It seems they didn't patch things up until after Pilate sent Jesus to appear in a trial before Herod (Luke 23:6-12).

That being said, the question posed to Jesus by some Galilean folk who had recounted this tale to Jesus was intended to garner a status quo response from Jesus.

Nice try.

"Do you really think the folks slaughtered in the Temple died 'cause they were better sinners than those who didn't die (13:2)?

Don't you just love that question?

"NOT!"

Don't you just love the answer?

"Look, let me lay this on you. You're all going to die too if you don't alter the program you're on" (13:3)!

Ouch!

The tower of Siloam, both an aqueduct and a pool belonged to a system of canals and reservoirs in communication with the spring of Gihon that had been radically altered through the history of the area. A tunnel drained water into the reservoir pool between two walls in the tower of Siloam. More than likely it was by this pool of Siloam where Jesus gave a man his sight back. (John 9:7) Aqueduct means "the sender" of water therefore the aqueduct of Siloam is sometimes symbolically referred to as "the one who was sent" by John.

Tragic, unfortunate accidents sometimes occur on construction projects to unsuspecting workers. A serious incident must have occurred during the construction of the water system improvement project. Eighteen workers lost their lives when a portion of the tower toppled around the pool of Siloam. Tell me, how in the world could it be possible for a group of dead workers to be more in debt to God than anyone else living in Jerusalem?

Well, money earned by bricklayers working on the hated aqueducts was stolen money. Stolen money? From whom did they steal it? Remember the fly on the wall moment? From the Temple treasury, the bank of God! If it was God's money, they should have worked for nothing, or, at the very least, given it back to God. Popular consensus probably assumed the tower toppled over causing the death of 18 poor chaps 'cause they consented to work on the project, placing themselves in an over abundance of debt to God.

That brings us to the second question posed by the crowd to Jesus.

"Do you really think those poor 18 workers who lost their lives when the tower of Siloam toppled on top of them were more indebted to God than everyone else who lived in Jerusalem (13:4)?

Another great question, another great response.

"NOT!"

"Hey, you're all going to die too if you don't alter the program you're on!" (13:5)

Ouch. Twice in 4 verses.

"NOT!" "NOT!"

The concept of connecting sin with suffering was well entrenched in Jewish tradition. One only has to read the account of the conversation between Elaphaz and Job (Job 4:7) to appreciate this popular doctrine. But Jesus wasn't about to leave the occasion pass by without offering up another little parable to instruct the folks.

Here's the parable in a scoop of my own understanding...

"There was this chap who had a fig tree planted in his vineyard. One day he came to check to see if there was any fruit on the tree. Nada! So he said to the keeper of the vineyard, 'Look, I've been coming here for the last three years to check on this fig tree and haven't even come close to seeing a single fig on it. You might as well cut it down 'cause all it's doing is taking up valuable ground space.'"

"The head botanist replied, 'Boss, let's give it another year. I'm going to work the soil around it and fertilize it. If it bears some fruit great, if not, you can cut it down next year.'"

Alrighty then. As is our habit, let's take a brief look at the traditional approach to the interpretation of this particular parable.

Central Truth:

Judgment will surely come to those who don't measure up. Of those to whom much has been given, much will be required.

Traditional Interpretations:

- There's strong support for the idea this parable is aimed at a national audience rather than a personal one. The intense privilege given to the Jewish nation to exhibit fruitfulness among a patchwork garden was an indication of what occupied the apple of God's eye. The destruction of the Temple in 70 A.D. may have been the limit of God's patience toward the Israelite nation.
- Each individual, society, or nation has a specific role God's expects fulfilled. Failure to perform will result in judgment.
- The parable exposes the tolerance of the owner (God) and the spirit of graciousness of the keeper of the vines. (Jesus).
- The failure to bear the fruit you're supposed to is akin to sinning.

Practical Applications:

- Responsibility is proportional to privilege.
- In the calamities that assail others are the loud calls for us to repent.
- Uselessness invites disaster.
- The greatest failure is the failure to recognize our own possibilities.
- There's a limit to the patience of God.
- Sucking the life out of others without giving back is a no-no.

- Second chances happen once in a while, but don't count on them.

Folks didn't get slaughtered in the Temple fiasco because they sinned anymore than folks who didn't sin. Neither were they wiped out because they were more proficient at sinning than those who were spared. I refuse to believe the amount of sin has any consequence to the amount of punishment God has in store for any of us.

Folks, the "wages of sin" was always the same-death. Sin was sin. God's view of sin never altered. The wrath of God never abated towards sin. He couldn't stand it, was keenly aware of our inability to overcome it, and consequently, He decided to do something about on our behalf. Hallelujah!

I've arrived at the understanding the consequence of sin was indeed death, and the punishment has been enforced. I'm utterly convinced sin "was" dealt with and the empty tomb is the culmination of the incredible revelation of God's provision for sin. The cross was a one-time event. Sorry to disappoint many of you, but, the cross isn't something which will ever be required again. One time is all it took. And it happened once for all. Sin, as well, as the wages of it, were paid for once and for all.

The folks who were slaughtered weren't better at sinning than others. They didn't die because they sinned and others didn't die because they sinned not. They happened to be in the wrong place at the wrong time. Something bad didn't happen to them because they were bad. And furthermore, something good didn't happen to some folks because they were good.

I can assure you Jesus gave a good answer to them. Why? Because there isn't one of those folks in the crowd who survived the stupidity of Pilate who is alive today! Trust me, they all died. Even in the "spiritual" sense Jesus correctly told them they'd all end up in the same death boat if they carried on up the same creek without a paddle like the ones who did die. And what creek was that? The creek is called "self-righteousness!" Furthermore, by now it's a full-blown river!

The very same message applies to the 18 construction workers who were tragically killed on the job. They weren't any more indebted to anyone else than any other citizen who worked on the aqueduct system. To imply their death was because of some lack in their spiritual life is the height of arrogance and ignorance.

How did Jesus conclude this question?

He told folks their arrogance and ignorance would lead them down the garden path to a death as sure as those who died in the tower collapse.

Did it? You bet. Sure, even in the "spiritual" sense.

Just keep thinking what you do to win the favor of God will make an eternal difference to you, and you'll die too, sadly, without knowing what bearing fruit is all about.

The parable isn't about us being "fruitful" or "unfruitful." Please, this isn't just some kind of glib statement. There ought to be no question in our minds concerning our "unfruitfulness." Ever hear of the little phrase? "No, not one!" Let there be no doubt "unfruitful" is an apt description of the entire human race.

Jesus tried to make a strategic point by bringing up His favorite snack. He told a story of a fig tree that hadn't figged out yet in its entire life. Fig trees usually took about three years before they exhibited any sign of fruit and it wasn't uncommon to see a fig tree sprout up anywhere, right in the middle of an orchard or vineyard for that matter.

Please understand I don't usually get the shivers when the science of numerology is applied without merit. However, I'd like to simply remind you of the number of years it is commonly agreed Jesus spent in ministry before that cataclysmic date He had with a crossed piece of beam furniture. Let's just say it was "3" and move on.

Anyhow, the owner had his eye on the fig tree. In the economy of farming an unproductive fig tree had little value. The tree could have been the best looking tree on the farm. It may have had the most beautiful color of leaves. It may have had the knarliest (I'm not sure that's a word but I like it) bark. It may have provided a wonderful amount of shade on one of those hot and humid days of summer. No matter. Fig production was the bottom line. Fig trees are supposed to do figs.

The owner calls in the vineyard prunist to chat about the problem fig tree. Tender love and care is the agreed upon prescription. If this won't fix it nothing will! Precisely!!! I'm going to tell you right now there was absolutely nothing the fig tree could do on its own to get where it needed to get! Talk about an "unfruitful" situation.

The point of the parable?

The chap who owned the farm showed how much he cared for his vineyard. His patience was exemplary. His heart desire to see wholeness, maturity, and productivity is unquestionable. Furthermore, He trusted His prunist.

Perhaps this trust was His greatest gift to the vineyard. In addition, the prunist cared for the farm as much as the owner did.

On top of it, he had faith in his own ability to breathe life back into the fig tree.

I wouldn't be surprised if the bee on the flower next to the hapless looking fig tree could tell a side of the conversation many of us would like to have bugged. Perhaps it sounded something like this...

"What d'you think J.C.? Sure doesn't seem like it's going to make it on its own, does it? We planted it and gave it everything it should have needed to become a big time fig producer. Think we should just cut it off at the knees and get it over with? Perhaps we should just cut our losses and get on with it."

"Ah, shucks pops, it wouldn't be right. I'm seriously convinced it won't make it on its own. How 'bout I get in there and get my hands a tad dirty. I'm convinced I can get this thing turned around in short order, with your permission, of course."

"Alrighty then, go for it. Stir things up a bit. Do what ya gotta do. I'll back you up on this one."

"Thanks Dad. I won't let you down. If we can't resurrect this thing, no one can!"

And you thought the parable was about you. Give your head a shake. Without the compassionate heart and committed activity of the orchard caretaker in consort with the orchard owner, fig tree no longer would we be.

All of us were destined to share the same fate as those slaughtered in the Temple, and with those killed in the tower collapse. And yes, all of us were destined to share the same fate as those who weren't murdered or killed too. Why? Because we were all on the inescapable path of "unfruitfulness." Self-righteousness and unfruitfulness are synonymous.

Now, that was the pits!

But, here's the good news. Three years after the seed was hatched we got some production. No foolin.' The fig tree bore fruit! What fruit it was!

Folks, righteousness and fruitfulness are also synonymous. And the only way we could attain to fruitfulness and righteousness was through the graciousness of the owner, and through the intervention of the prunist.

Now there's a parable worth it's weight in figs.

17. **BRASSICA NIGRA !**

<u>THE PARABLE OF THE MUSTARD SEED</u>
Matthew 13:31,32; Mark 4:30-32; Luke 13:18,19

There are three accounts of this parable and I've packaged them together into one synopsis. Here's my version.

"How can I possibly illustrate for you what the kingdom of God is like? With what could I compare it to?"
"I know."
"The kingdom of God's like a grain of mustard seed. When the farmer plants the seed into the earth it's smaller than any other seed, and yet, when it's full grown, it's like this gigantic tree. Man, the branches become so large birds build tree forts in them."

"Brassica nigra."

Who'd have thunk it?

The kingdom of heaven is like brassica nigra, a tiny, black kernel commonly known as "mustard seed."

I know. I know.

The orchid seed is smaller. But it's not in the herb family, so the mustard seed still claims the tiny title for herbologists. Stay tiny forever? Not! It literally grew to become a tree, reaching the towering heights of seven or eight feet. Birds were so delighted to see the branches stretching out their arms in glorious praise they gladly accepted the open invitation to set up shop in the shadow of shade they provided from the scorching heat.

Field. (Matthew) Earth. (Mark) Garden. (Luke)

It's curious to note the different locations for the seed planting in the three different accounts. Planting mustard seed in a garden was actually forbidden in rabbinical circles 'cause they regarded it to be a "field" crop (Kilaim 3:2). I doubt if I'd want herb trees growing in my garden either. Size and location may seem like petty differences, however, size and location are actually more a part of this parable than you might think.

Hold this thought. We'll come back to it after I review the traditional approach to the parable of the mustard seed.

BRASSICA NIGRA !   PARABLE OF MUSTARD SEED

Central Thought:

The kingdom of God may have originated out of the most insignificant beginnings, and yet, in the end, many nations will eventually be gathered together into it.

Traditional Interpretations:

- For the listeners of the day Jesus was attempting to compare the current insignificance of the seed and the future extent of the kingdom of God.
- For the disciples Jesus was attempting to instill confidence in His immediate followers to hang in there. Perhaps Jesus was becoming all too aware that the disciples were frustrated by the lack of progress in attaining results. He was letting them know the end result would be way beyond their wildest imagination.
- For the listeners of today we're taught the kingdom of God and the church are synonymous. The church, once a speck, has become home to nations.

Practical Applications:

- Great things start from small beginnings.
- Some bright folks, with perhaps little else to do, have calculated the Holy City (Revelation 21:16) encompasses some 2,250,000 square miles. Certainly this must mean the kingdom of God could accommodate a whole whack of folks!

Oh my, we've got to talk.

It took two whole verses (for those of you who think Matt, Mark, and Luke wrote in verse format) for Jesus to profoundly describe what the kingdom of God is like. Read the verses again. Is this what you read?

"O.K. Be prepared to start small. It may take a little time so hang in there. Plant the seed. Sooner or later you'll see results you can hardly imagine. Trust me. The kingdom of God won't reach its pinnacle until I come again way off in the future. What object lesson could I give to illustrate how you'd better get out there and spread the gospel message to the enormous mission field until everybody wants to take refuge in the shadow of my branches."

NOT!

Jesus did give us a revelation of the kingdom of God all right, however, it wasn't a revelation of the future. It was a revelation of the present!

He said "the kingdom of God "IS" like a mustard seed" which produced a home for even the very birds of the air!

To me "is" isn't in the future tense. It's in the present tense. The kingdom of God is already in place because God chose to make it so in Jesus. It's not because you were good enough, because you believe enough, or because you have the faith of a mustard seed.

It's not about you.

How small is the kingdom of God? It's small enough to touch the smallest of the small. How big is the kingdom of God? It's big enough to become an abiding place for all.

I have this funny feeling Jesus was a bookworm. He was no dummy. The influence of a great nation was often depicted as an enormous tree, with subjected nations under its control as birds finding rest and shelter within its branches (Ezekiel 31:6; Daniel 4:11-21).

So Jesus grabs this little analogy out of His bag of object lessons and feeds folks a revelation of the scope of God's heart for all of His creation. Talk about an empire without equal!

You're livin' in it. Here and now!

Ya just gotta love it!

18. **LEAVENHOOD !**

<u>THE PARABLE OF THE LEAVEN</u>
Matthew 13:33; Luke 13:20,21

Moments ago it was mustard seed. Now, the kingdom of God is like leaven. Interesting. Once again I'm laying out for you a compilation, in my lingo of course.

> **"What in the world is the kingdom of God like?**
> **Well, it's like leaven a woman stuck into a batch of dough**
> **until the whole batch was infected by the leaven."**

So, for all you wanna-be-loafers out there, here's a lesson in leavenhood. Get it? Loafers-bread makers? Move on. I know.

Leaven is actually a piece of fermented dough. It's any substance added to dough or liquids to produce fermentation. Usually a piece of fermented dough was reserved from a previous batch to be used for the purpose of infecting a new batch. The element or mixture tempers, moderates, debases and corrupts, or otherwise changes the whole through an internal operation.

Can you see where this is going yet?

Three measures (seahs) of meal were just over a bushel, an enormous amount of dough mixture for a single baking. You'd have to have a fairly large family, or be throwing a pretty good-sized party to think about baking this much bread at one time. Mind you, Sarah used three measures of fine meal to prepare bread for three guests (Genesis 18:6). Must have been mighty hungry folks I'd say. With friends like that who needs a family?

Let's be honest, unleavened bread isn't all that great. It's hard. It's dry. It's as unappetizing as it is uninteresting. Eating bread started from leaven is just the opposite. It's sweet smelling, soft, porous, spongy, tasty, and it goes down oh so good.

Throughout Israelite tradition the use of leaven in any sacrifice to Yahweh was absolutely prohibited (Exodus 23:18; 34:25), including meal offerings (Leviticus 2:11; 6:17). Oh, there was an exception to the rule. Leaven could be used in offerings such as the peace offering, which were to be eaten by the priest or others (Lev. 7:13; wave loaves Lev. 23:17). Sure, let those pious religious leaders have all the good stuff.

Peace offering! Leaven. Peace offering. Hmmm.

The Passover season brought unparalleled scrutiny. The Israelites were forbidden to eat leavened bread during this period. Hey, it was a no-no to even have it in the house or in one's possession. Unleavened bread came to symbolize the haste of flight from the tyranny of Egypt. It served as a reminder of the exodus as well as the manner of life that service to God requires (Exodus 12:39; Deut. 16:3). During the preparations and ceremonies of the Passover feast each family was responsible for scouring their homes for any scrap of leaven. Every bit of the invasive product was to be burned.

Rabbinical literature generally equates leaven with evil desires. The fermentation process was emblematic of the process of corruption. An insignificant amount had a polluting effect upon the whole. Paul even challenged the Corinthian folks about how a little leaven can leaven a whole lump of bread (I Corinthians 5:6-8).

Polluting the whole! Leaven. Polluting the whole. Hmmm.

Alrighty then. Bakery 101. Done. Let's get to the traditional way of looking at what's been called the "parable of the leaven" I studied in Bible school. Here's the approach you'll generally hear from the bakers behind the stove, I mean preachers behind the pulpit.

Central Truth:

Just as leaven alters the character of dough into which it is inserted, so the kingdom changes all things.

Traditional Interpretations:

- The kingdom of heaven starts from the smallest of beginnings.
- Like leaven, the workings of the kingdom of God occur in the realm of the unseen, slowly, and inevitably.
- Contrary to the point above, some interpreters insist the action of leaven is indeed visible, turning the dough into a bubbling, seething mass. Thus, it represents the disturbing power of Christianity upon the heathen world.
- As long as leaven is kept on the outside it is powerless. Thus, like leaven, the kingdom of God works on the inside.
- Dough doesn't have power to change on its own. Thus, the power of the kingdom must come from the outside.

- The "three measures" is symbolic of the vastness of the world that the kingdom must irresistibly transform.
- The leaven of the Pharisees is hypocrisy, the leaven of Herod is secularism and worldliness, while the leaven of the world is Jesus.

Practical Applications:
- The kingdom of God is the leaven which altars men and women at the core, filling them at the very same time with the peace of God as well as with a divine discontent that won't rest until the evils of earth are eradicated by the changing, revolutionary power of God.
- It is also an exhortation to watch the miraculous, apocalyptic character of the growth of the kingdom of God.
- We all should strive to be leaven, to make an impact, and to stir up the pot.

Before I go any further I want you to carefully look at the following notes I just jotted down on a scrap piece of paper as I reread my brief introduction concerning leaven. By no means exhaustive, these few tidbits are fascinating considering the object lesson Jesus chose for His revelation.

Unleavened bread:
- Unfermented, hard, dry, sour, and tasteless.
- Useable in sacrifices and only during Passover.
- It is the religious symbol of the haste from oppression and of required service to God.

Leaven bread, on the other hand,
- Fermented, soft, moist, sweet, yummy good.
- Unusable in sacrifices and never during Passover.
- It is the religious symbol of evil desire, of corruption, and of an invasion to scourge badness into oblivion.

Don't kid yourself folks.

Jesus was abundantly familiar with the self-righteous crap being espoused by the religious community. When He picked out leaven for His homily He knew exactly what He was doing and why.

He was more than aware of the significance of leaven in the Jewish mind than we give Him credit for. He also knew the disciples themselves were having trouble understanding the wealth of His teaching.

So He picked out leaven, and with this choice, He stroked on the whole lot of them a lesson of profound proportions. Jesus was laying out for all to see a new and living way, letting them in on one of the most amazing, astonishing revelations of all time.

Hey, Jesus was the "leaven!"

Jesus, in fact, was making an unadulterated mockery of the self-righteous approach to acceptance with God being propagated by the religious establishment of the day. Leaven, to them, was a most recognizable symbol of evil and its influence in the world. Leaven was a most corruptible agent.

Boy, did Jesus ever corrupt their world! Did He ever become the most evil person and influence they had ever witnessed! Curious. Amusing. Jesus took the most appalling agent the religious leaders could think of to describe what the kingdom of God was like.

Good on 'im!

During the most important time of the year they were bound and determined to rid themselves of this incorrigible infestation, and Jesus made a point of saying leaven is precisely what the world needed, moreover, what it was about to get a good dose of!

No wonder they hated Him so much. They went so far as to try to eliminate the very One they needed to give them abundant, wholesome life!

The world of religion is an unfermented pile of goop. It's hard. It's dry. It leaves a bitter, unappetizing taste in one's mouth. In the moments of most serious gratitude the religious community exhausts itself with pious remembrances of an exasperating flight from the oppression of an evil empire. It revs itself up with a self-righteous, fanciful dedication to a life full of service. The religious community has become convinced one of its primary missions is to scourge the world of an invasive and pervasive evil.

Well, the big baker on high had a better idea. Consider the link between the Passover and leaven. The whole concept of leaven and the Passover are linked in Jesus. The ultimate Passover took place on the cross when Jesus became the leaven of all leaven! In the Jewish system of religious endeavor leaven wasn't to be used during the Passover in a sacrifice to God.

132

Why? I think it's because God wanted leaven to be the symbol of God's intervention. A picture was being painted and folks didn't even understand it, let alone appreciate it. Religions, including the Protestant ones I'm most familiar with, have developed with the notion acceptance of God is attainable through something we must "do" to get the freely given grace. Tell me this isn't a work. As far as I'm concerned the stench of self-righteousness is an unappetizing as an unleavened piece of bread.

Now, when leaven was introduced to the process guess whom benefited from it? Was it not the whole loaf? Track with me now. Think about what Jesus said. He proclaimed the kingdom of God is like leaven that a woman placed into an enormous amount of dough before she baked it into the most fantastic, tasty batch of bread.

Did she put just a snippet in there? Did she separate some out and just put leaven into a small portion? If she had she would have ended up with a whole lot less bread. No, she literally hid the leaven in the dough until the "whole" was leavened.

Did Jesus suggest the leaven would only be effective in the dough that approved of its introduction? Would it only affect the portion of the bread that "believed" leaven had been introduced for its own good? Did He say the leaven would only impact the portion of the loaf that would be willing to give a tenth of its production back to the baker? Did Jesus say the leaven would only impact the faithful, bread-producing component of the dough?

NOT!

So, how have we screwed up His intention so badly?

Let me suggest a few reasons.

Someone came up with the preposterous idea we, the church and those who are members of this establishment, are the leaven. We've been sold a bill of goods. The fallacy of a cooking schedule that places the completion of the baking process way out in the future sometime has been manipulated to control our thoughts and activities.

Apparently, the workings of the kingdom of God occur in the realm of the unseen, slowly, and inevitably. In addition, the kingdom of God is thought to work best internally 'cause leaven is powerless when left out of the dough, implying somehow it's an individual occurrence, a process that must occur in each and every life.

Well, I've come to understand Jesus is the leaven, and His affect upon the whole dump of dough occurred in three days or less.

What He accomplished isn't mysterious at all to me anymore, what He came to do has already been accomplished, and what He did had an affect upon the whole world.

Furthermore, I'd like to suggest Jesus could never have accomplished what He did had God kept Him at home!

Did you get that?

Had He not come to this world His impact on our behalf would have been negligent at best. We'd still be in deep do-dough if God kept the leaven up on the kitchen counter. God did know what He was doing! Jesus didn't come to be a band-aid to cover our wounds. He didn't come to soothe our aches and pains with some silky, soft ointment or magical potions. Nor was He sent to do a tower of terror job of scaring us out of our whits at the mercy of self-righteousness on the roller coast of life.

The symbolism of three measures apparently represents the vastness of the work yet to do. Not. In my understanding, it represents the vastness of the work already done!

The traditional approach would have you believe you've still got a long way to go to become a smell God would appreciate. Well, God did vastly more than I ever thought He did! In our unleavened state the most we had to look backward to was a desperate attempt to escape from the tyranny and oppression of self-righteousness. I find it quite frightening I spent much of my life, like my Old Testament fore-folks, longing in desperation to return to the apparent pleasures and security of slavery to a taskmaster whose only objective was to suck the very life out of me.

No more. I'm quite content to affirm the power of the "leaven." I'm discovering more and more what the kingdom of God is all about. I've a heart of gratitude I'm livin' in the bliss of leavenhood.

When was the last time you went into a bakery and just stood there taking in every scent you could of the sweet fragrance of freshly baked bread, buns, and doughnuts?

Oh my!

Do you ever wonder how God must feel when He gets a whiff of you? Something you've done?

NOT!

Blame it on the leaven!

19. **GOOD EATS !**

<u>THE PARABLE OF THE GREAT SUPPER</u>
Luke 14:1-24

In my reading of the gospels it seems eating out was a particular activity Jesus relished. I guess it shouldn't be a surprise given the fact He didn't really have a permanent resident, nor did he have an incredible wife like I do who can cook the most fabulous meals and create deserts which wow both the eyes and the tongue, and yet, makes me eat virtually nothing I don't like. It's true! Folks who know me accurately say I'm a picky eater. I prefer to say I really love everything I eat, which, of course, is just another way of saying I won't eat anything I don't like.

Back to Jesus and His dining experience associated with this parable. What could be better than having a big time dinner party on the Sabbath? Keep in mind there'd be no breaking of the myriad of procedural laws concerning the preparation of food at this soiree. No rib-eye bar-b special this time around. Since the Sabbath law forbade the cooking of any food everything would have been prepared on Friday before the sun went down. Food to be served hot would have to be kept warm in some fashion overnight.

Get a load of this.

Food could be kept warm for the Sabbath as long as it wasn't put into "oil dregs, manure, salt, chalk or sand, whether moist or dry, nor into straw, grape-skins, flock or vegetables, if these are damp, though it may be if they are dry. It may be, however, put into clothes, amidst fruits, pigeons' feathers and flax tow."

Jesus was to be a guest of no less than a hot dog Pharisee. Jesus was becoming quite an attraction and the paparazzi were out in full force. Let's be gracious to give the host some credit for inviting quite a few of his buddies over for the meal. Let's be generous to dismiss potential ulterior motives he may have had. NOT!

Let there be no doubt Jesus was under intense scrutiny at this point in His ministry. Luke tells us "they" were "watching" Him very closely. It's interesting that the word used for "watching" is the very same word used to describe "sinister espionage." Assembled were a host of lawyers and Pharisees to keep their eyes on this most auspicious fellow who was capturing the hearts and minds of so many Jews.

A set up was in place. Jesus was walking down the sidewalk about to walk through the front door of the private residence when He encounters a chap, who evidently had a touch of dropsy, sittin' on the doorstep. No, he wasn't into dropping things. It was like way more serious than that!

What the heck is dropsy? Well, the condition is actually more of a symptom than a disease, indicative of an advanced organic attack against a particular location of the body. Abdominal dropsy is known as "ascites," "hydrothorax" attacks the pleural cavity, and cardiac dropsy is called "hydropericardium." Dropsy constitutes a disproportionate effusion of watery fluid into the tissues or cavities of the body.

So, here's this poor fellow planted on the front steps suffering from some kind of cardiac, renal, or hepatic problems.

Planted? Oh that's good.

Given the composition of the dinner guests it wouldn't surprise me. Jesus was already considered a lawbreaker, so what could be better than setting up a little trap for Him. The host and his guests had no problem obeying all of the most trivial rules and regulations formulated to foster health and welfare, and yet, they were so hostile to one whose mission it was to ease pain and suffering, even if it was on the Sabbath. The irony in their stunning lack of sensibility isn't only sad, it's tragic.

I'm really starting to appreciate Jesus more than ever before. He's hilarious. I just love this guy. Nobody could accuse Him of being politically correct!

Listen to this. Remember, Jesus is speaking to high fallutin Pharisees, lawyers and scribes.

"Say boys, is it all right with you to heal someone on the Sabbath" (14:3)?

Chuckle. Chuckle. Can't you just see the horror in their eyes? Every single one of them had the answer on the tip of their tongue. Hands attached to arms went up all over the place.

"Teacher! Teacher! I know! I know! Pick me. Pick me!"

NOT!

That's right! Not one hand went up and not one word was spoken. What to do? I guess Jesus figured if nobody was going to object He might as well get on with it. I don't know how Jesus did it. Perhaps He just looked at the dropsyite or laid His hands on him. Maybe He prayed to God and called all the angels of mercy to restore him to health.

Whatever.

Luke tells us Jesus healed the guy and told him to get lost.

Back to address the assembly of googly-eyed congregation of folks with their Jewish noses way out of joint.

"Tell me fellas, which one of you would leave your donkey or ox at the bottom of the well without going out of your way to rescue the animal, even if it was on the Sabbath" (14:5)?

Nada. No comment. Blank faces. What, cat got your tongue?

Take a look at Exodus 21:33 if you are not inclined to believe donkeys or oxen didn't occasionally fall into an open well. Since it was fairly obvious an animal would need to be rescued from such a predicament it would be expected and obligatory for the owner to lend assistance right away, even if it happened on the Sabbath. Jesus, with a stealth blow of searing contempt, wanted to know how it could be wrong to help a man with his infirmity when it was perfectly all right to help an ass out of its predicament!

Alrighty then. Let's eat.

With chins struggling to find their way back to their appropriate place everyone proceeds to get their food from the buffet table, seek out a place to sit down, and stuff themselves. With a keen eye for detail Jesus took notice of the procedure while someone went to throw together a plate for Him.

The parable is coming. Trust me.

Oh, have you ever read Proverbs 25:6,7? Evidently Jesus had. Allow me to refresh your memory.

"Don't claim any honor in the presence of the King; nor stand in the place of great men. Why? Well, it's better to be beckoned to approach the King than to be told to get out of the way of the prince whose spot you took."

Remember Jesus is now going to address everyone as they're chowin' down.

O.K. Wise counsel ahead...

"When you get invited to a wedding reception don't just walk in and make yourself comfortable at the head table. Why? More than likely the bride had other plans for that honor. The father of the bride will tap you on the shoulders and tell you to get lost so the bride and groom can enjoy the close company of the bridesmaids and groomsmen. There'll be nothing left for you to do but squirm away in embarrassment to find a seat at the back of the banquet hall."

"Rather, when you show up to honor the invitation to the wedding reception give respect to your host by finding a nice, inconspicuous table. You'll be filled with honor when the host comes over to you and asks you to come and sit and celebrate with him at his table right next to the head table."

"You see, the one who exalts himself will come to be humbled, and the one who humbles himself will be exalted" (14:8-11).

Then Jesus had a few choice words for his host who'd kindly invited Him over for dinner.

"Look pal, the next-time you're planning to throw a luncheon or supper party don't call your friends, your family, your coworkers, your relatives, or your rich neighbors. Why? Well, the chances are they'll return the favor and you'll simply be repaid for your generosity."

"But, the next time you throw a soiree invite the poor, the lame, the crippled, and the blind. Why? Hey, you'll be a happy camper 'cause there's no way any of them could repay you. Don't worry, you'll get yours at the resurrection of the just" (14:12-14).

Wait. There's more to chew on. Context. Context. Context.

Jews were known for their wonderful spirit of hospitality, rarely extended, unfortunately, beyond their own kind. It's also important to remember the pattern of understanding is akin to blinders on a horse for Jews considering a Messianic banquet. As far as they were concerned guests at that particular feast would be Jews. It was almost inconceivable for an orthodox Jew to even dream Gentiles and other sinners would find a chair to sit on at the table feast of God, let alone get an invite.

Surprise! Surprise!

The thought of this kind of reward Jesus spoke of must have caught the attention of more than a few of the diners. In fact, one of the dinner guests piped up thinking he'd get an extra slab of warmed up goat cheese lasagna for his great wisdom.

Get a load of this...

"Boy, the guy who gets to eat bread in the kingdom of God is sure going to be a happy camper" (14:15)!

I can just see Jesus giving His head a gentle shake. He probably put His hand over His brow covering His eyes to hide His frustration at the lack of understanding this fellow obviously exhibited. Jesus couldn't help but answer with a parable.

Finally, the parable!

"Listen up chumps. A certain man planned to throw a great party and sent out a whole batch of invitations. When everything was prepared he called his butler in and gave him instructions to go out and announce 'Game On!' to all the invitees."

"Lo and behold the butler discovered a whole whack of folks seemed to come up with some very convenient reasons to excuse themselves from the party."

"The first person said to the butler, 'Hey, I'm sorry, but I just bought a chunk of property and I've got to go inspect the land before I seal the deal. Please accept my apologies and give my best regards to your boss.'"

"Another said, 'Sorry bud, I just bought the new ten oxen-power machine and I've got to go yoke 'em up for a test drive. Please accept my apologies and give my best regards to your boss.'"

"And yet another came up with a different excuse. 'Bad timing, dude. I just got married and I'm planning on being tied up this evening. Well, perhaps not literally. Well, maybe. Anyway, please accept my apologies and give my best regards to your boss.'"

"Well, the butler went back home to give his boss the low down on the invite list problems. Needless to say the big guy was a tad ticked off. He had a new set of orders drawn up to give to his butler, who moonlighted as an entertainment coordinator."

"The boss said, 'Listen, I want you to hit the pavement, tuit suite (French I think for pronto, like quick buckwheat). Get out into the city onto the streets and into the back alleys. Wherever. Get the poor, the lame, the crippled, and the blind and bring them to the party.'"

"It wasn't long before the butler was back before his boss. 'O.K. I did what you wanted me to do. There's a whole mess of folks here but there's still some empty seats and space on the dance floor. What do you want me to do?'"

"Overcome with generosity the boss gave out another set of instructions. 'Hit the highways this time, and all those short cut by-pass routes as well. Compel who ever you see to come and join the party. We're having a blast. I

want my house filled to capacity. I'm tellin' ya, those folks who didn't accept my invitation won't get a sniff of the fun we're going to have at this party"' (14:16-24)!

It's time again to examine the traditional approach to the understanding of the parable.

Central Truth:

There's a constant danger of permitting good things to come between God and us. God's banquet table is open to those who'll come and accept it.

Traditional Interpretations:

- The Jews refused the original invitation of God. This great privilege and responsibility is now available to the Gentiles.
- Master=God; Servants=prophets and apostles; invited guests= Jews; poor, lame, crippled, blind=sympathetic to Jews; highway and by-pass folks=Gentiles; banquet=eternal resting place.
- The reasons for refusing the invitation may seem legitimate, however, the priority of relationship was all goofed up.
- The parables must be seen in light of the challenge to commitment Jesus gave.

Practical Applications:

- The motivation for charity ought naught to be self-interest.
- There's a need for humility and concern for others.
- God's house will be filled in spite of the apparent rejection of the invitation of God by multitudes of folks.

Well, convention and political correctness didn't seem to play too much a part in the life of Jesus. In His mind His agenda and mission on this planet certainly wasn't ordered or set by the leaders of organized religion. He was fully cognizant that laws, rules, and regulations established over the centuries by the Jewish establishment were set up for the specific purpose of bringing folks closer to God.

And yet, they were riddled with stumbling blocks fostering nothing less than self-righteousness.

The reason Jesus caused so many problems for the religious leaders was that He was able to answer any concern they might have with such clarity and logic. His understanding of their scriptures was beyond even their comprehension. He healed the chap with dropsy and got away with it. Hey, anyone else would have been put in the slammer. It was the "Sabbath" for Pete's sake and they were hungry. So what if He healed someone!

He even managed to get in some advice to keep the embarrassment quotient under control. The little ditty reminded folks the view is better the higher up the ladder you go. Getting escorted up the food chain is much more pleasant than being asked to slide down it.

Furthermore, Jesus plants on His host the significance of hospitality for the sake of being hospitable. According to Jesus there was more in it for his host if he would give without regard for repayment. In fact, those who followed the dictates of self-righteousness would get theirs.

When?

Well, Jesus said they'd get it at the "resurrection of the just." I'm of the opinion the "just" "has been" resurrected and there's only one person qualified to be called "just." Any reward you thought you could earn on this earth pales in comparison to the reward you've received because God sent Jesus to this earth to exhibit the truth of God's loving kindness, His grace, His mercy, and His peace.

Self-righteousness didn't have a chance to fulfill any hope for reward.

And yet, with amazing consistency folks today continue to be led to understand the parable Jesus spoke is a teaching about "our" responsibility to heed the call of God. The self-righteous "it's all about us" doctrine collides head long into the glowing lights of God's truth concerning heart of God for one and all.

The very reason God sent Jesus to fulfill His will was the appetite of mankind to become self-absorbed. It really doesn't matter if excuses to skip the party have value or not. Some folks actually have no interest whatsoever in attending the party. Many folks have a tendency to procrastinate and think they'll be able to crash the party when it's convenient for them.

141

Well, the party's on whether you know it or not. It's on whether you want to be at it or not. It's on whether you think you'll get there sooner or later. It's on whether or not you think you have to pay for the ticket with belief, faith, tithes, etc., or not.

I'm here to tell you the banquet hall's booked and it's decorated to the hilt. The food's been prepared and the buffet is open for you to enjoy. The band is playing and the dancin' floor is hoppin' with jubilation.

I find it quite interesting there were three sets of instructions given to the butler:

1. Tell those who were invited to come.
2. Tell those who want to come to come.
3. Compel everyone to come. I want the place full.

Fascinating. What a glimpse of the history of reality. If it were left up to us, most of us would miss the party. Excuses and screwed up priorities would negate the possibility of enjoying the party for almost everyone. Even those who did want to show up would go just 'cause something was free.

You can spew the Jews first, Gentiles second scenario as long as you want to. God and His Son got together and figured out a way to make the banquet accessible to all. The kingdom hall of God was to be filled to capacity. There was only one way to get it done.

"You're in!"

"You're in!"

"You're in!"

Done deal.

Jesus concluded the parable with an ominous warning. Many folks are going to miss out on some incredible fun!

No kidding! What a shame. What a waste. Folks just don't know what they're missing. Blessing after blessing are there for the having and many don't even know it. I'm convinced this parable confirms the party's on and you are the big time loser if you're not enjoying it.

I now have the great privilege of telling folks they ought to get to know the party thrower, who just happens to be a party animal. I have the great honor of introducing them to the party thrower rather than trying to scare the living day lights out of them with speculations about an eternal bouncer.

Folks should start enjoying the party they're already at, rather than handing out a set of laws, rules, and regulations on how to get to the party, or what to do when you're finally at it.

Party is on dudes!

Start enjoying the banquet in the kingdom of God instead of wasting your time wondering whether or not you're going to make it to it.

You're in!

The price of admission has been taken care of. You don't have to show some kind of identification to make it through the door. You don't have to supply the food. It's not a BYOB night.

Be here!

Good eats!

20. **BAA, BAA !**

<u>THE PARABLE OF THE LOST SHEEP</u>
Luke 15:1-7

Here we go. A triple-header. We ought to consider ourselves fortunate Luke recorded for us these three parables using three very different things to give us a monumental portrait of one thing, the heart of God towards us. We've got animate. We've got inanimate. We've got human. Sheep. Coin. Son.

Let's start with the baa-baa club. Let me set it up for you.

Jesus has spiced things up with His buffet discourse (Luke 14:1-24). Next up Luke recounts the address of Jesus to the multitudes that tagged along behind Him, befuddling His listeners, not to mention many folks to the present day.

The controversy?

Counting the cost. This, to me, isn't a problem passage. I understand it in the terms of reference Jesus spoke them, namely, before the cross. Clearly it is to me an accurate description of impossibility for anyone to become members in good standing in the kingdom of God on one's own merit or ability.

Salt may be a good thing but if it loses its saltiness it's not fit for seasoning, hey, it's not even good enough to spice up a pile of crap (14:34)!

Dig it (14:35)?

If you've got ears to hear, then listen up!

Oh. Oh.

Now we discover Jesus is hangin' out again with those more than disliked government employee types, namely publican tax collectors, as well as a collection of other loose lip sinners. Together they were eatin', laughin', and carryin' on.

Murmuring. Seems like the Pharisees and scribes had the practice down pat.

"My goodness, there goes Jesus all over again. He's sitting down to eat with trash like it's the natural thing to do. What's up with that" (15:1,2)?

Not to let the opportunity go to waste Jesus lays on them a parable.

"Which one of you having responsibility over 100 sheep, if you lost one of them, wouldn't leave 99 to go after the 1 little rascal who decided to venture off on its own?"

"And when you found it would throw it up on your shoulders and love it to life. I'd bet when you got home you'd call all your friends and neighbors and throw a big party. 'Hey, come on over and celebrate with me. I just found my cute, lost little sheepee.'"

"Look, I'm tellin' you, there's more rejoicing in heaven over 1 whose heart is changed than over 99 who know they have no need to change" (15:3-7).

Matthew relates a similar story in a slightly different context because Jesus is addressing the disciples rather than the uptight religious leaders. In Matthew's account Jesus was referring to the care and keeping of little ones. Jesus summed up the story of the recovery effort with these words:

"Even so, it's not the will of your Father in heaven that even one of the sheep die" (Matthew 18:14).

I'll come back to this thought eventually but, first of all, let's take a quick look at the traditional view of the parable of the lost sheep.

Central Truth:

There's more joy spread around over a small portion that has been endangered than over the continued secure possession of a larger portion. It reflects joy over one who repents than the many who linger in the entryway who refuse to enter the sanctuary of faith.

Traditional Interpretations:
- Jesus was doing what the spiritual leaders should have been doing with respect to seeking lost souls for the kingdom.
- Jesus pictured Himself as the good shepherd seeking lost sheep.
- The parable shows a justification of Jesus in discriminate mission as a policy based on the will of God.

145

- There isn't anyone, no matter how lost they get, who can't be restored to a rightful relationship with God.
- God isn't satisfied with percentages but with totals.
- Repentance is the acceptance of Jesus' fellowship. Forgiveness is the acceptance of the lost by Jesus.

Practical Applications:
- The love of God is always on the lookout for lost ones who need finding and restoration.
- Be good shepherds and get out there looking for lost little sheep that have lost their way. Bring them in to church.

"The People of the Land."

That's the name the orthodox Pharisees and scribes used to identify the group of goofed up sinners who couldn't keep a law even if they tried. The barrier between the religious and the irreligious was higher and thicker than the reality or symbolism of the Berlin wall, or the Great Wall of China.

You might as well expose your daughter bound and helpless to a lion than to give her hand in marriage to a son of one of the "people of the land."

It was forbidden to be a guest of one of them, or similarly, to host one. No business dealings. No sharing a bit of gossip over a few drops of mocha down at the local corner Timmy H. donut shop either.

Get a load of these Pharisaic regulations.

"When a man is one of the 'People of the Land,' entrust no money to him, take no testimony from him, trust him with no secret, do not appoint him guardian of an orphan, do not make him the custodian of charitable funds, do not accompany him on a journey."

No wonder the religious leaders were choked with Jesus when they saw Him sippin' a wobbly pop with the boys in the hood. These chaps weren't just outsiders, they were low down, good-for-nothing losers. Proper religious thought never anticipated there would be joy in heaven over a sinner who turned colors. According to their way of thinking, joy in heaven was achieved when a sinner was obliterated!

And here sits Jesus lapping it up with "People of the Land."
Oh my!
So out comes Jesus with this little sheep story.

Being a shepherd was no easy task. Pasture was scarce, the land rugged. The desert was often a treacherous place, with climate and terrain obstacles to overcome on a daily basis. Shepherds became expert at detective work too, tracking footprints across hill and vale, often risking life and limb protecting and tending the precious livestock entrusted to them.

A flock of 100 sheep would indeed be a large number for almost any poor peasant farmer rather it was more common for a flock of this size to be owned collectively by a whole village. It is also likely more than one shepherd would oversee the entire inventory of animals. At the end of the grazing day the 99 probably were taken back to the corrals and barns by some of the shepherds while one shepherd was sent off to fetch the one which took off on its own to check out the dream of greener pastures elsewhere. Of course, when the shepherd returned with the little rescued sheepie the whole village had something to cheer about.

This parable is such an inspiration to me because I had to do an about face concerning most of what I once believed. I've come to understand the flock numbered 100. It wasn't 52 good and 48 bad sheep. It wasn't 99 good ones and 1 goofed up one. Nor was it 99 bad ones and 1 good one. Each and every one of the 100 sheep belonged to the flock.

The poor lost sheep didn't just magically become disowned because it wasn't with the rest of the pack. The point of the parable has nothing to do with our responsibility to get out there and beat the bushes for folks who've lost their way. It has everything to do with the tender heart of love and care God has for His flock. God, the shepherd of all shepherds, is intimately acquainted with everyone.

The sad reality is many don't even know they're just like all the other sheep on the same big farm. Let me tell you, God is tickled pink when someone discovers they're actually treasured members of the flock, and furthermore, they've always been. Jesus was talking to folks who thought sheep in the fold of their own heritage were the only animals on the farm. These guys were plenty content to understand lost should remain lost. Not so as far as Jesus was concerned.

I'm content to understand God is happy with His flock. He's more than pleased when even one comes to the realization life in the kingdom of God is way more than we could even dream of.

A whole lot of folks actually do get it.

So when one does figure it out there's quite a bit of happiness to go around topside. But there's way more to the meaning of this parable than meets the eye.

I'm confident you'll have a bone to pick with me over my understanding of verse 7 as it relates to us today. I'm about to throw a real monkey wrench into your understanding, or a curve ball into your theological glove.

What does the verse really say about repentance?

Repentance? Do we need to repent from sin?

No, sin was dealt with on the cross! If we need today to repent from anything it's from the lust of self-righteousness. We need a change in our minds to contemplate Jesus as the great shepherd who sought us out and rescued us from ourselves.

Matthew reminded us as well it wasn't the will of the Father any should perish. Far too many folks are perishing all right, perishing in the debilitating struggle of self-righteousness. The spirit of folks is being killed by the inability to "get" good enough on their own. That's just sad.

The religious leaders who Jesus encountered thought they had a patent on understanding the heart of God. Jesus told the parable of the sheep to inform them of a new and living way in the kingdom of God.

We all need to start thinking like everyone's a treasured little sheepie, cared and loved beyond measure by the great Shepherd of all. One of the most exciting things I've come to understand is just how much my Shepherd gave to rescue me from my self. He put His life on the line to make sure I'd never forget I was a member of the barnyard troupe. He picked me up in His tender arms, put me on His shoulders to take the load off my feet, and is loving me to life each moment of every single day.

"BAAAAAAAAAAAAAAAAAA HUMBUG?"

I don't think so!

21. **EUREKA !**

<u>THE PARABLE OF THE LOST COIN</u>
Luke 15:8-10

And now we have the second parable of the triple-header, the object
lesson about an inanimate coin.

A Greek drachma was almost the equivalent to a Roman
denarius. By our standards today it probably wouldn't be worth more
than a quarter. While it may not seem like all that much to us it
represented the standard wage for a full day's worth of work back then.
Loosing a day's pay was no small thing, however, I think there was
something else at play. There had to be some sentimental value
attached to the coin that made the search for it all the more significant.

Indeed. The fondness for jewelry knows no time barriers.
Women are notoriously romantic and have always had an eye for the
bling-bling! It was customary for Jewish women folk to save up to ten
coins so they could string them together into a necklace or a hairpiece.
For married woman the treasured possession was worn with the same
kind of pride a married woman today would display showing off her
wedding ring. It's hard to put a price tag on values of the heart, isn't it?

Have you ever lost a diamond from your wedding ring? Panic
city! Did it go down the drain? Did it fall out onto the carpet during
the weekly vacuum? Sick! You probably didn't even notice the clasp
was coming loose. I'll bet you'd call out the troops to search for that
missing hunk of beveled glass if it happened to you. Every one except
your husband that is, 'cause he ain't supposed to find out just yet.

Hey, at least you've got electricity, windows which let light into
every room, hardwood floors or carpets, not to mention the light on
your vacuum machine. The single window in most homes back in the
day didn't let in all that much light. Most floors were packed dirt
covered with dried reeds and rushes. You might have as much luck
trying to find a pin in a haystack. No wonder the lady pushed the panic
button and lit a candle to do an inch-by-inch search of the premises.

Well, the audience was the same and so was the message. Jesus
went seamlessly from one parable to the next to drive home His point.

**"Here's another one for ya. What woman, having 10
pieces of silver, if she lost one piece, wouldn't light a candle
and scour the house 'til she found it? And when she found**

149

it, she'd call her friends and neighbors together and say, 'Rejoice with me for I've found the coin I'd lost.'"

"In the same way, I'm telling you there's joy in the presence of God over one whose heart is changed."

As we studied it in Bible school, here's a summary of the traditional way of looking at this parable.

Central Truth:

If a woman would act in such a way toward a coin, how much more diligent would God's search be for a lost soul, and furthermore, how real His joy in the rediscovery of it.

Traditional Interpretations:

- This is another form of justifying the mission of Jesus to the outcasts.
- The joy of recovery is contrasted with the critical attitude of the religious leaders.
- The coin was still of value even while it was lost. Even so the soul is valuable though lost.
- The sheep got lost 'cause of its own ignorance. The coin was lost because of the carelessness of its owner.
- The accent is on the loss, the search, and the joy of discovery.

Practical Application:

- People are more valuable to God desiring recovery than the mere possessions of a woman.
- The joy of recovery must be shared with others.

The woman had to go on a search for something that was hers if she was to find something that she lost. The coin was hers. Doesn't matter if she dropped out of her piggy bank or if it became dislodged from necklace. She lost what belonged to her. She wanted it back.

So, she went and found it! Precisely!

This parable illustrates once again Jesus had a wildly different outlook on life than the religious zealots who couldn't even conceive of a God who actually cared for someone outside their little box. The worldview of One from the other side could never be more pronounced.

150

Could we have a better picture painted for us of the heart of God? Something that belonged to Him got separated from the rest of the pack. It bugged the heck out of God. He couldn't take it any more. He set His mind to do whatever it would take to recover the lost. The search was activated.

What happened when the woman found it? Did she throw a party, or what?

And what does Jesus say in verse 10?

ONE is all it would take to get the angels dancin' around the throne. God sent Jesus a lookin'. He not only found one who'd gone astray, He found the whole whack of us.

Of course, because many still believe in the gospel of self-righteousness, the doctrine of sinners yet to repent is still preached around the world. God is still out there looking. At the very least, we're now commissioned to look on His behalf. And don't we get excited when a "lost" sinner is found!

Our arrogance is as strong as those rascal religious fruitcakes surrounding Jesus who couldn't stand the thought of someone being included in the family of God unless they got in according to their laws, rules, and regulations.

The sad truth is many don't object as much to people getting into the kingdom as "how" they get there. Somehow many find great injustice in the fact a dirty rotten scoundrel could get in at the last minute of breath while many a saint has had to live a life of servant-hood to get there. While it might be fair to God it sure isn't very fair to many people.

Good thing the heart of God is what's important! Look, God found what He was looking for all right, and there's been joy overflowing in heaven ever since. It boggles my mind to think it would have only taken the discovery of one, even me, to get things hopping on the heavenly dance floor. To think Jesus would be willing to pay such a heavy price to search for me alone is one thing. To understand He paid the price to recover the entire world is even more awesome.

God's a happy camper folks! So are His angels! So am I!

Eureka! He found me!

The heart of God!

This is what this parable is all about.

22. **PRODIGUS !**

<u>THE PARABLE OF THE PRODIGAL SON</u>
Luke 15:11-32

Needless to say, the triple-header continued because Jesus wasn't finished with the concept of lost and found.

"And Jesus continued..."

"There was this chap who had two sons. One day the youngest approached his father with a proposal. 'Hey Dad, how 'bout giving me my inheritance a little ahead of schedule.' The father consented, divided up his assets, and gave both sons their inheritance."

"It didn't take long for the younger son to pack his bags and hit the road. He traveled to a distant country where he had a riot wasting everything he had in the wildest extravagance you could imagine."

"It just so happened the economy took a nose-dive and a terrible famine struck upon that country not long after he spent his last drachma. Hunger set in so he started begging. He managed to attract the sympathy of a citizen of that fair land who hired him to go out into the fields to feed his pigs. What he wouldn't give to fill his stomach with the pods the pigs were eating 'cause nobody had anything better to offer him."

"The young lad scratched his itchy head and got to thinking. 'Man, how many of my father's hired servants have more than enough food to eat and I'm sittin' here starvin' three quarters to death! I'm gettin' up and goin' home. I'll tell Dad I've done wrong against heaven and against him, that I'm not worthy to be called his son, and beg him to hire me on as one of his hired servants.'"

"The kid did collect his somewhat diminished whits, got up, and set off for home. But when he was still way off in the distance his father saw him shloppin' down the road. The dad was so happy to see his youngest son he almost had a heart attack on the spot. He ran out to greet the boy and almost knocked him over with excitement. Hugs and kisses all around."

152

"The son started to recite the apology he'd been practicing over and over like a habit. 'Dad, I've done some pretty horrible things in the sight of God, not to mention how unpleasant they'd be in your sight. Look, I'm not even worthy to be called your son...'"

"But the father didn't even wait to hear his son finish what he was trying to spit out. He called out to the servants, 'Hey, quickly now, fetch me the best robe you can find and let's get my son cleaned up. Put a ring on his hand and some sandals on his feet. Bring the fattest calf out in the pasture into the barn and slaughter it. I'm throwin' a party. Lets' eat, drink, and be merry!

My goodness, this is my son I'd given up for dead and here he is. He's alive! I thought I'd lost him and now I've found 'im.'"

"Wow! Party-on dudes! But wait, there's more!"

"As the father's eldest son was coming home from tending to the animals out in the pasture he could hear the pipes of bags cranked up and the clogs pounding full tilt on the dance floor. He called one of the hired servants over and asked him what the heck was going on."

"The servant said, 'Your brother's come home and your father's killed the fattest calf 'cause he's so happy his boy has come home safe and sound.'"

"Do I have to tell you the eldest son was a tad ticked off? He refused to go in and party with the rest of the gang. When the father realized his eldest son wasn't celebrating he went out, found him, and begged him to come in to join in the rejoicing."

"The son said, 'Look dad, I've served you faithfully for many years. I've obeyed and carried out every order you've ever given me, and yet, you've never once killed even a baby goat so I could party with my friends. But, as soon this goofed up son of yours has come home, this rascal who's wasted your fortune on prostitutes, well, you go out and kill our best calf in the herd and throw this honkin' huge party. What's up with that?'"

"Somewhat dismayed the father replied, 'Hey, look me in the eye son. You're here with me all the time. Everything I have is yours. Got a problem with this party?

**Well, too bad, so sad 'cause I don't. It's perfectly
appropriate we celebrate. We thought your brother was
dead, but he's alive! Your brother was lost and now he's
been found!'"**

Prodigal: from the Latin "prodigalis" or "prodigus" meaning:
lavish; spending money or resources in a recklessly and freely
wastefully, extravagant way.

Perhaps a few historical/sociological reference points may be
helpful. It might also be interesting for you to know ingredients of this
tale appear elsewhere in Semitic, Greek, and Latin literature. A papyrus
letter written by a fellow named Antonius Longus to his mom in
Fayum in the second century A.D. contains a curiously similar
expression of "hey, I gave my head a shake!"

Jewish law left little room for a father to determine who'd get
his leftovers. The eldest son was entitled to receive 2/3 of the estate,
(Deuteronomy 21:17), however, the practice of distributing the estate
before death was by no means uncommon. Going into retirement and
letting the sons take over the family business provided ample reason to
share the wealth, so to speak. In this scenario the split would more
than likely be a 1/3 split each for the eldest and the youngest. The
father would retain 1/3 until his death then this would pass on to the
eldest. The fact the youngest son in this parable asked for the
distribution is not necessarily out of line as it may simply have been
recognition of inevitability.

Jews don't seem to take too kindly to pigs. A Talmudic parable
announces, "Cursed is he who feeds swine, and the man who teaches
his son Greek wisdom!" Yes, Jews had a way of spinning many
different laws in creative ways. I don't know how much Greek smarts
his father taught him but you can't misunderstand how despicable the
plight of the young man became after he'd squandered away his bank
account.

Rabbinical literature frequently mentions the pods of the carob
tree. The pods were generally recognized as food for domestic animals,
and, as a last resort, considered acceptable for human consumption.

Believe it or not there were folks less privileged than slaves.
They were hired servants. Ordinary slaves were often considered part
of the extended family. Hired slaves were picked up from the temp
pool, usually dispatched at the end of the working day.

Children wore sandals and slaves went barefoot. Our brothers and sisters of African descent sure understood shoes meant liberty! Even I remember the spiritual "all God's chillun got shoes." They lived the experience.

When you wore your robe folks showed you honor. Power and authority followed you around when you wore the family jewels on your fingers.

The Greek word translated "music" in many versions of the Bible may be the name for a very specific wind instrument similar to the infamous noisemaker-the bagpipes! Daniel (3:5) may have been familiar with it.

One of the things I learned from one of my favorite professors in Bible school, Dr. Johnson, was how to construct a sermon that won't put folks to sleep. This classic old school professor believed in using three points. I know he wouldn't say it this way but I'd summarize his plan of attack in sermonology.

1. Tell 'em where you're going. (3 points to chew on)
2. Tell 'em where they've been.
3. Tell 'em where to go!

I particularly like the last point. Some kind brother once came up to me to encourage me as I was shaking hands at the end of the service one Sunday. He said, "Son, I have three points of my own. First, you read your sermon. Second, you read it poorly. And third, it wasn't worth reading!" Ouch! Oh, it's a joke, my favorite church joke.

This particular parable lends itself magnificently to the three-point mantra. Son-son-Father. The focus by and large is on the spoiled little brat. That's why it's known as the parable of the "prodigal" son! It could easily be called the parable of the "spoiled brat." Perhaps both sons could qualify for that title.

To be sure, there are lessons to be learned from each of them, but just because the youngest son recovers from his "backsliding" state he ought not be considered a hero. Nor should the eldest son be vilified for his arrogance and ungratefulness.

I'm convinced a more accurate and appropriate title for this tale Jesus relates ought to be "the parable of the good father." What an amazing portrait of the heart of God! I'm stunned by this brilliant depiction of God's love by Jesus.

But, before we get into it a bit deeper, let's take a look at the traditional approach as I studied it in Bible school.

155

Central Truth:

     The central issue of this parable is the compelling compassion of the Father to receive His repentant children. The holiest, most elevating experience that a soul can know is that which springs from the contemplation of God's mercy.

Traditional Interpretation:

- The parable calls for an opinion. Which attitude toward the prodigal is to be endorsed? The contrast requires the hearer to choose between the father and the elder brother.
- The parable deals with a father, faced with an instant decision to be made that, when made, determines the future. Hope is restored and the possibility of new life begun.
- To reject the attitude of the older brother is to reject the attitude of Jesus' critics. Only by being treated as a son can the penitent again become a son.
- One must guard against making this parable an allegory by identifying the father with God and the elder brother with the Pharisees. The parable may reflect the elements of God's attitude toward the lost, which Jesus Himself must follow.
- One mustn't condone the behavior of the younger son. The prodigal's adventure away from home isn't just to be dismissed because of the restoration to his family. Restoration looks forward to an undetermined future, but at least there was hope.

Practical Applications:

- Christians should endeavor to show to sinners the same spirit that God has shown. The gentleness of God to us should be repeated by us to others.
- Everyone who lives apart from God is living beneath his proper self. He has a spiritual faculty that allies him with God that is truly himself.
- The love of God can defeat the foolishness of man, the seduction of the tempting voices, and even the deliberate rebellion of the heart.

Jesus was a master at illustrating the heart of God. In this set of parables He's used a shepherd, a jewelry aficionado, and now a father to reveal the attitude of God toward those He loves

"Children-ship" was never a question for the father in this story. He had two sons, and both of them were the apples of his eye. Well, his wife probably was the apple, the kids perhaps the oranges. Apples. Oranges. Fruit. As we say in our house, "sames but different." All he had wasn't just his.

Hey, this reminds me of the little chorus we used to sing. I can't remember the exact words but it went something like this. "He owns the cattle on a thousand hills...and I know they're mine as well..." Anyway, everything the father had belonged to his whole family. The distribution of it wasn't even an issue. The fact one went and spent his piggy bank (literally) and one sat on his duff was of no consequence to the father.

When the father saw the kid walking up the path all he could see was a "son." When the father saw the party-pooper all he could see was a "son." You see, it's all perspective.

Jesus didn't mention a thing about how the father required a video to confirm "sonage." Nor did He want a playbook of activity. Amazing! The father didn't even ask for confession. In fact, Jesus tells us the father didn't even let the kid finish the sentence as if it mattered not a whit.

Now don't confuse the loving attitude and unconditional love of this father with consent. Paul wrote extensively on the subject of liberty. In Jesus you have absolute liberty, however, just 'cause you have liberty doesn't mean you should take the responsibility and privilege lightly.

What about the eldest son? Here's a particularly nasty sort who couldn't stand the fact his loyalty and duty seemed so unappreciated. His resorting to name-calling might almost be hilarious if it weren't so terribly sad. I'd really like to know if he was mightily ticked off his younger brother had a particular way with women. Perhaps he wished he could have sown a few wild oats of his own given the father's attitude. "Hey, why didn't I think of going there or doing that? Rats."

The father only saw the oldest boy as a son too! The father didn't back off, nor did he cave in to the pouting of the eldest son. He didn't go into some long speech of gratitude for years of uncompromising service. No, he told him to grab a dose of reality and join the party.

157

Perspective.

There are companies of folks today who think they've a better idea. Many are convinced there's a way to ultimate happiness beyond the warmth and protection of the family.

Well, Jesus has news for y'all. You're a valued member of the family of God and nothing will ever separate you from the love of God. When you come to understand this kind of love you'd never even give a thought to wanting to leave for something better.

Something better doesn't exist!

There are also a whole lot of folks so committed and faithful to serve they can't stand the thought some two bit good for nothin's would get even a sniff from God. The mantra of legalism and self-righteousness are perhaps more detrimental to the family of God than anything else, for this self-serving doctrine and logic communicates nothing less than hatred, bigotry, and intolerance.

Oh, but what a lesson in this parable! I can't help but marvel at the heart of God for His kingdom. His love doesn't diminish one iota when a member of His family determines to seek an alternative route to happiness. His love doesn't depreciate even one degree of centigrade for the one who serves Him faithfully day after day.

Family is family. Always was. Always will be.

Someone once asked Abraham Lincoln how he'd treat those southerners who'd rebelled so vigorously after they'd been defeated and rejoined to the union of the United States. Expecting a sour note of vengeance the questioner was shocked when good ol' Abe said, "I'll treat them as if they'd never been away."

Now, like Jesus, there was someone in high places with a whole heart of special insight!

23. FINGERS IN THE COOKIE JAR !

<u>THE PARABLE OF THE UNJUST STEWARD</u>
Luke 16:1-18

Here's another beauty. Most scholars/commentators consider the parable at hand to include only verses 1 through 9, and some are generous enough to extend it through verse 14. Well, why stop there? Let's allow the context to lead us right through verse 18.

There are a number of interesting individual verses in this little teaching Jesus dished out. For the most part verses 1-9 are glazed over because of the difficulties posed by a rich owner praising his shady manager, the notorious verses inciting the necessity of being faithful in small things so you can be put in charge of bigger things, and of course, we must not forget the killer verses assailing the futility and shame of serving two masters, namely, God and money, all right, the love of money.

Well, as difficult as it may seem to some, I'm overwhelmed by the wealth to be uncovered in this treasure. Why only take a few shovels out when there's simply too much good stuff to dig out the further down you go. Luke tells us Jesus was addressing His disciples, and, although not the intended victims for the teaching, listening in were a group of Pharisees, renowned for their appetite of material possessions.

So, first of all, here's my version of the account...

Then there's this story Jesus told His disciples...
"There was a certain rich man who had an estate manager who oversaw his business affairs. When the rich landowner returned from his summer vacation property someone approached him and ratted on the estate manager, accusing him of mismanagement and of misappropriating the company cookie jar. The top dog decided to call the second level dog into his office to get the scoop, so to speak."
"Not one to beat around the mulberry bush he addresses the alleged cookie thief. 'Hey, what's up? I've been told you're not doing a very good job managing my affairs. I want you to bring in the accounting books so I can

159

figure out for myself if you cooked them. If there's any truth to the reports I've heard I may have to let you go.'"

"The manager was quite taken aback. He thought to himself, 'Self, what the heck am I gonna do now? Man, I'm not about to get my fingernails dirty digging ditches, and I'm certainly not about to be ashamed by having to resort to begging out on the street corners. Hey, I've got a great idea. If I'm gonna be out on my tush I'm going to arrange it so a few people will owe me a favor or two and I'll at least have a place to stay!'"

"So he called every one who was indebted to his boss and arranged for them to meet with him at a specific time and place."

"To the first debtor he said, 'How much do you owe my boss?'"

"'900 gallons of oil.'"

"'Well, hurry up and sit down. Take this blank invoice and write down 450 gallons.'"

"To another he said, 'How much do you owe my boss?'"

"'1000 bushels of wheat.'"

"'Well, take this blank invoice. Write down 800 bushels.'"

"Having taken care of business, so to speak, the manager brought in the books. After looking them over the rich owner was quite impressed with his manager's bookkeeping practices, so much so, he commended the obviously dishonest employee for shrewdly acting with the thoughtful foresight concerning his future employment."

"D'ya know something? The children of this world are, in their generation, wiser than the children of light!"

"Listen, my advice to you is to make good use of the resources you've been entrusted with, tainted as they might be, to do good things for others. Make good with what you've got now 'cause when death comes, as it inevitably will, you'll have nothing to worry about when you're greeted on the other side."

"The truth of the matter is those faithful with a little are also sure to be faithful with lots of stuff. Those who cheat in the small things of life can be counted on to cheat in the bigger things. If you can't be trusted with the things of this world who in their right mind would think you could be trusted with the true treasures of eternity. Furthermore, if you can't look after the possessions of another, who in the world would give you property to look after on your own?"

"It's impossible for any servant to serve two different masters. Either they would hate one and love the other, or they'd cling to one and despise the other. Similarly, there's simply no way you can serve God and material things."

Within earshot of Jesus stood a batch of covetous Pharisees. When they started mocking the teachings of Jesus, He responded to their derision.

"You guys are quite thorough in justifying your activities before your peers, claiming your wealth is proof of your righteousness. Well, give your head a shake. God's intimately acquainted with your hearts. What is highly esteemed among folks is an abomination in the sight of God. The law and everything the prophets have written were in effect until John came along and started preaching a new and living way."

"Ever since then the kingdom of God continues to be preached and everyone's been forced into it, against all the proper decorum of the law. And yet, I'm telling you it would be easier for heaven and earth to pass away than for even one ornamental stroke decorating the alphabetic letters of the law to become null and void. Any man who divorces his wife and marries another woman commits adultery. And any man who marries the woman who was divorced from her husband is also an adulterer."

Whooaaa!
The traditional approach to the parable is quite predictable.

Central Truth:

If a rascal like this unjust steward could act with such decisively shrewd calculation in the face of personal disaster, how much more should we use no less powers of well-calculated foresight in the affairs of the kingdom of God.

Traditional Interpretations:

- The principle applies to Israel's situation in the time of Jesus. It's a stress on the understanding that those who reject their sole calling or appropriate to themselves its benefits have no further hope than to continue in their own chosen way.
- To the disciples the parable is a challenge to remain steadfast in faithful stewardship of the things of God. It's an exhortation to make use of the resources at hand for the beneficial purposes of God.
- The parable is to provoke Christians to outdo the world in qualities while laboring for a nobler end.
- It would seem Jesus is advocating trickery but we must see His intent to draw a contrast between the world and spiritual affairs.

Practical Applications:

- As the children of the world aim steadfastly at their selfish objects, so the children of the light are to keep constantly before their eyes the relation of life to the divine kingdom and to press everything into service.
- The faithful man will be true to his trust, whether it's great or small, for character will always reveal character.
- It's a challenge to a resourceful zeal, to reality, to foresight.
- The use of money and material possessions may be dedicated to the cause of righteousness.
- Be as resourceful and ingenious as you can to get the message of Jesus to the masses.
- Actions for the present should be based on prospects for the future.
- You can't take it with you so send it on ahead.

Right off the bat I'd like to say I'm inclined to think there are enough stinkers in this story to go around.

1. You've got the rat-finks. Boy, I haven't used this poignant insult since I was in grade school. I couldn't stand tattle tales then, and I can't stand them now. I wonder what in the world they had to gain by talking behind the manager's back to his boss?

2.   You've got the rich land baron. What kind of a boss could he be if one of his hand picked employees would rip him off with such incredible, calculated shenanigans?

3.   You've got the business manager. Sneaky rascal to be sure, but dangerously close to getting caught with his fingers in the cookie jar.

4.   You've got the debtors. To what lengths would one go to avoid paying the appropriate amount of fees or taxes to whomever it's due? Don't be so out of touch to think this is some kind of ancient problem. Look around you and you'd probably be able to spot someone who has cheated on their taxes or someone out of something. Hey, maybe all you have to do is look in the mirror.

Let's be careful to spread the shame around if we're going to spread anything around. However, most of the attention of the traditional approach is given to the creative ingenious of the business manager. One translation says, "Turn in the account of your stewardship, for you can no longer be steward." (RSV) The obvious consensus among many scholars is to adopt the understanding the shady manager gets fired in verse 2 based upon this rendering.

Well, I don't buy it. Why?

First of all, even the KJV leaves room open to dispute the notion for there's some doubt in the statement. "Thou mayest be no longer steward" could imply there was a question in the mind of the rich owner as to his capabilities given what he'd heard from a group of gossipers. The more appropriate understanding in this case would suggest he "might be," or he "might not be," fired. A review of his conduct by the rich owner would therefore ultimately determine which of the two options would be taken concerning the manager's future employment.

This brings me to the second reason. In most cases there are two sides to every story, and it's no different in this one for the rich owner had only heard one side. I've been in the business world myself as an owner of a business, as well as a manager of several departments. There's no way I'd fire anybody without hearing both sides of a story.

Look, this rich dude was probably an absentee owner who'd just returned to the ranch from months of drinking lots of froth and bubbly on some white, sandy beach to check down on things.

He heard a rumor. Do you think he'd just up and fire the guy without at least letting him answer the accusations?

I'd also like to disagree with the notion that the rich owner praised the indiscretion of his sneaky manager. What makes us think the owner knew the manager had screwed him over by slashing the two detailed debit accounts that were discussed virtually in half? Why do we presume he could have found out this information on such short notice? He probably never found out.

Here's what I think happened. The owner comes back into town and some schnooks plant the seed of doubt in his mind. He calls up the manager on his cell phone and tells him he's in danger of being fired if he can't come up with a good accounting of his practices. He'd better be in the office asap to turn over the books.

Knowing the possibility of getting his pink slip is too close for comfort the manager is forced into some creative action. Setting himself up with some chips he could cash in if the unthinkable would happen he makes the only rational decision he could come up with on such short notice. He'd have to cook the books, and pronto.

If this weren't enough, he gets unquestioning misfits to become complicit to the point their own handwriting could be used as evidence in any potential litigation. The manager covered his butt. "Hey, that's not my handwriting..."

I've got to hand it to him. He was sharp.

The manager takes the accounting files in to the boss so he could examine the bottom line. The boss hears him out and feasts on the cooked books. (D'ya get it? Cooked books. Feasts on cooked books, ah never mind) "Hey, looks like everything is in order here. Guess you've been doing a pretty good job here after all, and you've obviously done wisely to ensure you're future with my company. So, carry on. Get back to work."

You see, in Luke's recounting of the teaching, Jesus is the one who thought the manager was sneaky. We've come to assume the owner praised the manager for screwing him. Not!

Why? Because of the commentary Jesus gives at the conclusion of the story immediately after this in verse 8. What's the bottom line? There are two kinds of folks out there. First, there are folks who give their attention to the interests of this world. Second, there are folks who give their attention to the interests of the world to come.

Now, this is important. Pay attention. This is what Jesus wanted those around Him to understand.

The folks behind door # 1 are wiser in the attention they give to their endeavors than the folks behind door # 2!

Just think about this for a moment. This is a stinging, nasty rebuke Jesus has just served up like a wicked 110 mph slammin' ace from behind the base line in tennis. Did you get it? He wasn't passing judgment. He wasn't saying bad is better than good. He wasn't implying craftiness out shines towing the party line.

What He did say is that the level of dedication of folks who live in the present is greater than the level of commitment of folks who live in such fear of the future they can't enjoy the present.

Then along comes verse 9.

Material possessions are blessings to cement the real and permanent values of life. The Jews were led to believe the extension of charity would stand to a man's credit in the hereafter. Rabbis had a saying, "The rich help the poor in this world, but the poor help the rich in the world to come."

Jesus took charity to a different level. Be charitable because you can, not because you need to. You're not going to need material things like money after you die so you might as well make as many friends with it as you can in this life. Don't put a whole lot of stock in things, regardless of how they came into your possession. Things are things. Value is found in understanding the permanency and endurance of the blessings of all life.

"Christian" folks have a hard time with the very idea or possibility "worldly" folks have a clue about life and what it's about. According to Jesus, many of them actually have it together better than folks of the "faith." They know whom to trust as well as whom not to trust. They can spot a cheat a mile away. They can spot a schnook from a distance. They can sniff out hypocrites like nobody's business.

Oh. Oh. Here's the verse. The dreaded verse 13.

We've been led to believe there are two masters in the world, namely, God, and, everything else imaginable. We're quick to lump all kinds of things into the concept of "mammon." Money, the love of money, food, sports cars, too much TV, beautiful women, smarts, sex, education, whatever. If you happen to enjoy any of your earthly possessions more than God consider yourself screwed. Well, at the very least, you're screwed up.

Back in the day a servant was the servant of one master. It was an impossibility to be encumbered by more than one. If it were possible to have two masters a servant would literally go nuts.

They wouldn't have a clue which master to obey. One master would give out salted, roasted almonds and another would give out a job to do. One master would say, "Let's go fishing," and the other would tell the servant to "go out and watch the goats cut the grass." Guess which master would tend to attract the most attention, or which master would a servant tend to gravitate to?

Do you get it? Jesus wasn't giving us some kind of trumped out advice about the horror of getting our priorities messed up! He wasn't even warning us about the foolishness of giving an ounce of admiration for the things of this world.

What Jesus did reveal was the impossibility of serving God and things. It's impossible folks! It's not even in the realm of the possible. In the very same way it was impossible for a servant to serve two masters, it's impossible for you to serve two masters. You simply can't do it.

You can't serve things! Things/possessions/money and everything else on the list of "mammons" aren't to be worshipped. They're blessings of God, not something worship-able. God, on the other hand, is God, eminently worthy of worship.

This is what Jesus was saying: God gave you what you've got. Use it. Enjoy it. Bless others with it. Hey, if you can't even do this why in the world would anybody out there want what you've got? You're already living in eternity and you'll be received into your next habitation in due course. Look, you're nothing less than a soul with a body during your stay on this planet. Your time ain't over by a long shot.

Back to the Pharisees 'cause we're at verse 14 where we're informed they were somewhat ticked at the message of Jesus. Why? Because it went against everything they believed in. Jesus picked them apart. He ridiculed them for their self-righteousness, poked holes in their hypocrisy as they continued the tradition of justifying their reputation for stacking the deck of "works." God, in deference to their conceit, was intimately acquainted with the way they thought. What did He say in verse 15?

"What you think is important is actually an abomination in the sight of God!"

Ouch!

That hurts. Don't you just love the way this whole context thing comes together? I'll tell you, I just love it.

There are folks who tend to connect the possession of things with goodness. Wealth surely must be a sign of being on the good side of the big guy upstairs. According to Jesus, just the opposite is true. The bigger the parade to show off the more repugnant God becomes. The more folks exalt themselves the more abominable they become to God. Self-righteousness, in whatever form it's displayed by folks, makes God want to puke.

And the Pharisees serve as a magnificent object lesson of what self-righteousness is all about.

Oops. He's not done. Can you believe it? Get a load of this. According to popular opinion the "final" word of God was embodied in the law and in the prophets.

News flash! News flash! Breaking news!

"The good news of the kingdom of God is being proclaimed ever since the presses stopped on the majority of the Old Testament, the law and the prophets."

Get it? It "is" still being proclaimed! And Jesus didn't even stop with this incredible revelation.

News flash! News flash! More breaking news!

"Everyone is forced into the kingdom of God!"

What?

Who said that? Give your head a shake!

Everyone is pressed into it! We've all come stormin' into the kingdom of God. Jesus just told us we didn't even have a choice in the matter!

Perhaps you need to read this alarming statement again 'cause you may not have seriously contemplated it before.

"Everyone (that's seriously a lot of folks) is forced into the kingdom of God!"

Go figure. No kidding!

What a revelation from the ultimate revelation Himself! Can you imagine the faces of those He was speaking to, the ones with the turned up noses, as they heard Jesus tell them all their self-righteousness didn't amount to a hill of beans as far as accessibility into the kingdom of God was concerned? Good folks and bad folks, self-righteous or not, are "in" the kingdom of God in spite of themselves, because of nothing less than the grace and mercy of a loving Master, the only Master in the whole wide universe. For indeed, there is no other. Not even "mammon" is a master.

Wait there's more.

News flash! News flash! Don't stop the presses just yet.

"Just because the kingdom of God is being proclaimed, and just because the whole world is now included in the membership list of the kingdom of God, doesn't nullify in any way shape or form or validity of the letter of the law."

Oops. How'd this sneak in here? Listen, heaven and earth will be gone before the rule of God is nullified. Guess we'll have to put up with the law for a while yet, eh?

A serif is a little line at the top or bottom of certain Hebrew letters to distinguish words that would otherwise be quite indistinguishable. Jesus lays it on us that not even a serif remains insignificant in the big picture. God's perspective could not be more different from ours.

In verse 18 Jesus throws out a for instance. Fidelity and chastity were hallmarks of the Jewish faith. According to the Rabbis, "God could overlook virtually everything except un-chastity." In fact, "un-chastity causes the glory of God to depart." Idolatry, murder, or adultery is akin to giving up your life. At least in theory, that is.

The tragedy of the day revealed that common practice had a way of working its way all around theory, but never into it. Here's the example Jesus would set out for His listeners.

Jewish law gave little credence to anything female. A woman was no more than a thing. The only way a woman could divorce her husband was if he became a leper, an apostate, or if he ravished a virgin. I wonder how many men took that last requirement up as a way out of a bad marriage. Anyway, other than these three things a woman had no rights whatever and no redress other than that the marriage dowry must be repaid if she was divorced. "A woman may be divorced with or without her will; a man only with his will."

How's this for Jewish law?

Mosaic law: "When a man takes a wife and marries her, if then she finds no favor in his eyes because he has found some indecency in her, and he writes her a bill of divorce and puts it in her hand, he can send her out of his house" (Deuteronomy 24:1).

My version: "Here you go babe. I just can't stand your burnt offerings anymore and I'm sick and tired of not being able to go to the bar after work with my buddies. Here's a writ of divorce, a letter of dismissal and your deed of liberation, now, take a hike."

"I've got two signatures of canvas ball teammates who watched me sign your walking papers. Go check the book of faces and all the dating services. Marry whoever will have you. Now, get lost!"

That's what I call a quickie divorce!

What are the trick words in this particular Mosaic regulation? "Some indecency." Two schools of thought regarding what is and what isn't decent:

1. The school of Shammai: adultery, and adultery alone.
2. The school of Hillel: if she spoiled a dish of food, if she did cartwheels in the street, if she talked to a strange man, if she bad mouthed her husband in his presence, if she talked so loud the neighbors could hear her next door, and according to Rabbi Akiba, if her husband found another woman more beautiful than her.

Guess which school had more students?

No wonder most women weren't all that ecstatic about tying the knot. Is it any wonder Jesus chose to pay honor to the sanctity of the marriage bond? Even for Jesus there are rules that have validity and make for good common sense and practicality.

So there you have it. See what a difference a little context makes. The whole teaching of Jesus is a revelation that what make sense to us in the world of self-righteousness has very little impact upon God's sense of endearment with His children. We'd be wise to realize what we are, and what we have, is sourced in His good pleasure to bless us. It's impossible for us to serve things and God at the same time. God is the only master there is. Everything else is a blessing of abundance served up for our pleasure and enjoyment.

The parable is, in my humble opinion, a stinging rebuke of Jesus to the religious world that many folks who aren't considered by them to be part of the kingdom of God are the ones who actually have it more together. It's an encouragement and exhortation to get on with life, to live it to its fullest, and to share the abundance with others.

Kind of like putting your fingers into a cookie jar!

What a parable!

24. GOD IS MY HELP !

THE PARABLE OF THE RICH MAN AND LAZARUS
Luke 16:19-31

The story you're about to read apparently is what revolutionized the heart of Albert Schweitzer, ultimately provoking him to leave the comforts of home to spread the gospel message to the so called "dark continent" of Africa.

The story, however, wasn't something new from the mouth of Jesus. Stories like this one were not only found in rabbinical sources, they were also available in ancient Egyptian tales, such as one found on a demotic papyrus of the first century A.D. It went something like this:

A very wealthy man, clad in the finest attire, was carried to his grave by a large group of mourners. At the same time, the body of a poor man was removed for burial, unaccompanied by attendants and covered only by a mat. An observer, impressed by the disparity in the honors bestowed on the two, commented on the advantages enjoyed by the rich man, but changed his views when he was permitted to visit the underworld. There he saw the poor man clothed in the linen garments of the rich and given a place of honor, while the rich man suffered torment for his evil deeds. The story concludes with the moral: "He who is good on earth fares well in the realm of the dead, and he who is evil on earth fares ill."

The parable of the rich man and Lazarus is unique in the Gospels for its colorful description of the after life experience. Hades represents the Hebrew word "Sheol," in early thought, a gloomy subterranean pit where spirits of men went after death, in which they suffered some miserable, shady existence. As later Judaism adopted some notion of a resurrection, possibly of a Persian eschatology, Sheol became a temporary abode of spirits departed from the human form. Gradually, as I Enoch 22 bears witness, the belief arose that there would be some separation of the righteous from the evil even before the resurrection "until the great day of judgment."

In this parable a rich guy suffers a fiery torment in a part of Hades resembling Gehenna. The other part, where the afflicted poor fellow ends up residing, is in the dwelling of the righteous, namely, Paradise. While folks may see each other, a great gulf ("chasma" in the Greek) has been permanently fixed between the destinations making it absolutely impossible to travel between the two.

Needless to say, I'm convinced Jesus pulled this charming three scene play out of His duffle bag of insight to shed some light on the Pharisaical perspective on life, and, more importantly, on their perspective of death. He spun it in a whimsical way to illuminate their profoundly blissful ignorance of the perspective of God.

Was Jesus mocking the Pharisees 'cause they had all the apparent associations and parallels with the rich man in the fable? Was Jesus telling them they were toast while those they figured didn't have a chance would get to rest in the bosom of Abraham? If these things were true then it's no wonder Jesus had a target on His back!

Well, let's not get ahead of ourselves. Here's my interpretation of the account Luke recorded for us.

"There was a certain rich dude who dressed in the softest undergarments possible with the most gorgeous, colorful outer threads like he was one of the rich and famous. His table was filled with the most scrumptious buffet spreads virtually every day."

"And then there was this certain homeless beggar, named Lazarus, who was merely able to feed himself on the crumbs he'd find scrounging through the trash after it was brought outside the gates of the palatial estate for garbage pickup. Lazarus wasn't exactly the picture of health either 'cause he was covered in ulcerated sores. They only way he could find comfort to bear the pain and itchiness was to let dogs come by and lick the sores, the ultimate in reducing one's sense of worth to tatters."

"Alas, the beggar died and was carried off by the angels to the bosom of Abraham."

"The rich dude died too, but he was buried. He awoke to discover he was being tormented in what he assumed was one kind of hell or another. When he opened up his eyes he could see Abraham a way off in the distance with none less than Lazarus in his arms."

"He cried out, 'Hey Father Abe! Have mercy on me! If nothing else, at least send Lazarus so he could dip the tip of his finder in some water and cool off my tongue 'cause man, it's hot here in the furnace.'"

"Abe called back, 'Son, remember how you in your lifetime received good things, and how Lazarus received

nothing but bad things? Well, now he's being comforted and you're being tormented! Not only that, between us and you there's fixed a great gulf which would prevent anybody here to get to where you are, and anyone from where you are to get to where we are.'"

"The rich dude wouldn't give up. 'Alrighty then, I'd like to ask a favor of you Father Abe. Send Lazarus to my dad's house 'cause I've got 5 siblings who need to be told about the afterlife so they don't end up like me.'"

"Abraham responded, 'Look, they've got Moses and the prophets. Let them pay attention to hear what they've said.'"

"The rich dude replied, "Ain't gonna happen! Father Abe, nobody will pay attention unless someone comes back from the dead to warn them to repent.'"

"And Abe said, 'If they won't be persuaded by the words of either Moses or the prophets then there isn't a hope in Mesopotamia they'd be convinced by someone who came back from the dead!'"

O.K. Let's do a quick review:

Act I: Life

The first of two characters is the rich dude, often referred to as "Dives" (Latin for "rich") although this name isn't used in the actual writing. The Sahidic version named him "Nineve," while as late as the third century the name "Phinees" had some currency. The second character is the beggar who is named "Lazarus" in the Greek, and "Eleazar" in the Hebrew context. Eleazar is of course a beautiful descriptive and appropriate name 'cause it means "God is my help."

Two diabolically opposed lifestyles are described. One lives at the height of wealth, the other at the depth of poverty. One lives in abundance, the other in abject need. Health against sickness, opposites beyond compare.

Act II: Death.

Death knows no distinction. It recognizes no labels or status. It receives rich and poor, healthy and not so healthy alike.

A Jewish rabbi in the second century A.D. describes how "angels of service" and "angels of destruction" were sent to fetch the souls of the righteous and of the wicked after death. No doubt this idea is based on more ancient tradition.

Act III: After Life and Death.

The figurative expression, the "bosom of Abraham," suggests the deep fellowship of Abraham with all his descendants, receiving them like a father would bear hug his kids. Lazarus ended up in the arms of bliss.

Not so the rich dude.

What he wouldn't give to be where Lazarus ended up. He craved the drop of water like Lazarus once craved a breadcrumb. The ideas of a Paradise and of a Gehenna have practically coalesced with the earlier idea of Sheol, a flame in one part of Hades, and a spring of water in the other.

Then comes the magnificent dialogue between the rich dude and "Father Abraham."

"Hey, Abe! Get me out of here!"

"No."

"O.K. How 'bout a little dap of water on my tongue. It's hot in here!"

"No. You've had your taste of heaven on earth and now Lazarus is getting his taste of earth in heaven. Besides, we can't come there and you can't come here."

"O.K. Can you at least send Lazarus to warn my five brothers and sisters about what's going to happen to them."

"No. They should pay attention to what Moses and the prophets told them."

"Hey, come on. They want to hear it from someone who's been dead."

"No. If they won't believe good ol' Abe, they won't believe any dead guy!"

OOPS!

Let's take a boo at the traditional approach of understanding.

173

Central Truth:

Death is as conclusive as taxes. It's futile to expect any result beyond what's earned in this life, so, heed the important teaching and warnings concerning repentance and service we find in God's word (Moses and the prophets).

Traditional Interpretations:

- The purpose of the parable isn't to present a literal description of the existence beyond the grave, however, it's purpose is to show the finality of individual responsibility in this life which results in the determination of one's future destination.
- The condemnation of the rich dude wasn't because he was wealthy, but rather, because of the neglect to heed the revelation of God, the fearful consequences of unbelief, the failure to use his possessions in the service of God, and his unconcern for those in need.
- The plea of ignorance is unwarranted because God gives to everyone enough light for the performance of duties that He requires. Responsibility is for each and every person proportioned according to opportunity.
- Although we can't predict the future, this parable seems to indicate the anguish of the unrighteous, an eternity of punishment, and that God is aware of the plight and heart attitude of each individual.
- Death can't destroy consciousness, identity, memory, or destiny.
- This is an allegorical appendix which presupposes the conflict between early Christianity and orthodox Judaism. The rich guy and his five siblings represent unbelieving Jews. They didn't believe what Moses told them and Jesus was predicting they wouldn't be impressed by His resurrection (actually, I find this one quite interesting).
- This is an attack on the wealth and worldliness of the sect of the Sadducees, priests and members of the Jewish aristocracy, a highly privileged and wealthy people. They steadfastly refused to believe in an afterlife or admit the Scriptures afforded any warrant for such a belief.

Practical Applications:

- We'll usually get what we want but we must always pay the cost.
- If we understand God's compassion towards us we'll see the responsibility we have towards others.
- One's eternal goal has a bearing upon one's attitude direction for living in the now.
- Duty is fulfilled by meeting the needs of others out of purer motives rather than out of superficial motives.

Now, I want you to stop for a moment and ask yourselves some very elementary questions about this passage.

Who was Jesus talking to? Do you think Jesus was confirming their suspicions concerning the afterlife? Do you think Jesus was actually telling them His perspective on life and the life hereafter? Was He underscoring their lofty acknowledgment of the role of Abraham? Was He extolling the virtue of being poor verses the consequences of being rich?

It's obvious the target of Jesus' attention was the Pharisees grouped around Him. He had just finished rebuking them for their ignorance. I think Jesus was convinced they were even more stupid than they gave considerable evidence of.

Don't think for a moment Jesus was unaware of traditional Jewish thinking. Good gets good. Bad gets bad. Jesus didn't tell them what He knew, He reminded them of the fallacy and desperation of their theology.

Let's see if I can lead you to consider a few things you may not have given much thought about. In this story is there some particular point of condemnation for the rich dude? What was his "sin" which resulted in his eternal banishment from Abe's bosom? What "law" or "laws" was he guilty of breaking? Are we merely to assume he ended up on the black keys 'cause he didn't care about the unfortunate chap outside his gate? Ouch. If this is the case we're all headed for the fireplace.

And what of the folks whom Lazarus is called upon to represent? Are folks getting the heavenly hug 'cause they couldn't rub two shekels together properly or because they weren't endowed with the best of health? I certainly hope not.

Let's talk about the stopover destinations elucidated by some of the traditional theological understandings. Could it be there is truly an intermediary destination? Is there a torment before a final torment? Is there a bosom of rest before some eternal resort is reached? And what about this chasm thing? How in the world could the rich guy see Lazarus wrapped in the arms of Father Abraham? Furthermore, how could they carry on a conversation? The whole thing seems preposterous at best.

I'm inclined to understand this passage as no more than a comedy routine Jesus used to poke holes in the abhorrent claims the Pharisees were perpetrating upon the folks under their control. We've become witness, not to an awesome revelation of the understanding of Jesus regarding life and its consequences, but rather, to an understanding of why He thought the Pharisees were so out to lunch.

The traditional approach to the understanding of this parable spends most of its time on the story. It gathers its theology from the dramatics of the story. Why not? The comical dialogue between the rich dude and Abraham is a great commentary on the sickness that exists in the hearts of those bent on self-righteousness. There's surely enough in there to make you want to land on the pearly whites.

While good-gets-good and bad-gets-bad seems to make sense in the world of human understanding, it sure doesn't have any relevance in the understanding of Jesus.

What mattered to Him?

Let me draw your attention to the moral of the story. Let me focus your attention on the summation Jesus lent to the account. Here's the bottom line from the wisdom of Abraham's in this tale.

Moses and the prophets revealed the heart and will of Father God. What makes you think you'd believe someone who'd come back from the dead?

What an astute observation! In addition, is this an ominous prediction or what? If ever there were someone with insight concerning not only this life, but also the one to come, I'd put my money on Jesus.

Don't use this parable to keep some kind of spiritual score. Don't use it to perpetuate a theology that isn't supported by the substantive remainder of recorded scriptures. Nor should this passage be used as support for a teaching that implies rich folks don't have a prayer and being poor is actually a blessing in disguise.

God isn't in the business of saying "no!" Quite the contrary, for through Abraham and the prophets we have nothing less than a revelation of a God of compassion, forgiveness, and reconciliation. Unfortunately, humankind didn't have a hope on the planet to achieve the righteous standard He set. So the ambassadors of God prophesied a day in which the whole would see a salvation only God could bring to fruition.

We have the message of Abraham. We have the message of the prophets. As if that weren't enough, we also have the revelation of the One who died, and of the One who has come back to life in a victory few of us can truly comprehend.

God put His foot down. His name was Jesus. And yes, He did come back from the dead. His legacy is our wake-up call to get our collective hands out of the sand and to smell the roses.

As far as I am concerned, I know without a shadow of doubt that "God is my help." I have no fear for life, the eternity of it.

Hey, I'm blessed beyond compare!

25. **TIT FOR TAT !**

THE PARABLE OF THE BOND SERVANTS
Luke 17:1-10

The perversions and exaggerations of this doctrine of reciprocal justice were bountiful in the time of Jesus and they're not only present today, they're flourishing, espoused and measured in the dogma of self-righteousness.

      If I do this, I'll get that.

      Tit-for-tat.

      If I don't do this, I won't get that.

      Untit-for-untat.

      This notion is at the complete opposite end of the spectrum of the grace and mercy of God. God's grace provides us with everything we never deserved and His mercy withheld from us everything we did deserve.

      Just prior to the passage at hand we come across scripture used by control masters to guilt and shame the flock into the terror of continuously questioning attitudes and motives for living in a world that, according to many, has gone amuck. Following those words of wisdom comes this beautiful passage containing even more gems from the perspective of the One who'd seen most everything you could ever imagine, and then some.

      If these words were truly preached the way Jesus intended it we'd have a different insight on the benefits of the pursuit of self-righteousness. From my perspective there is no benefit to self-righteousness, just tragedy. Unfortunately, many still think the lessons contained herein give direction on what our responsibility is in order for us to receive the blessing of God.

      Take a look in many commentaries and you'll discover scholars suggest as many as four different divisions to the first ten verses of Luke 17, each division representing a different thought of Jesus. The suggestion seems to indicate Luke has merely strung them all together at this juncture of his writing, not intending them to be a continuous thought. Verses 1 and 2 apparently deal with the peril of becoming a stumbling block; verses 3 and 4 yield an exhortation concerning forgiveness; verses 5 and 6 impress us with the significance of faith; and of course, verses 7 through 10 are considered to be parable material.

Traditional approaches seem to loathe the concept that verses 1 through 10 might actually came out of Luke's bottle of ink in one pattern of thought. Well, I'm not inclined to believe Luke had some kind of brain freeze the day he put quill to papyrus. I'm convinced the entire passage from verse 1 through 10 of chapter 17 include an uninterrupted pattern of thought which can survive the merits of a singular treatment if we wouldn't be afraid to let context rule the attempt to understand the teaching of Jesus.

By the way, if I haven't mentioned already, I hate chapters and verses. As far as I'm concerned chapters and verses screw with context and we're the worse for it. I'll grant they assist as a point of reference, however, the folks who originally came up with this bright idea clearly didn't think the whole concept through very well. Which brings me back to what must be a common theme to you by now, context!

Remember where we just came from?

Jesus has been going back and forth from the disciples to the Pharisees giving both groups incredible revelations of the heart of God. Jesus just finished updating the Pharisees on the extremely high degree of probability they wouldn't accept the truth of God's activity towards humankind if they had it exposed in front of their very eyes, or more specifically, if they heard it with their very own ears from One who'd seen things from a different perspective.

What a scoop!

Forget what was going to happen to Jesus just around the corner but didn't He already have a different outlook on life given the fact He was God in the flesh? If the congregation of the day only knew "who" was talking to them. Well, obviously they weren't in tune 'cause they simply didn't wrap their collective heads around the teachings of Jesus. Luke continues to record the dialogue and this go around it's the disciples who get a talking to.

Once again, here's my rendition of the account. See, even the first word sets up the context like something else just came out of Jesus' mouth moments before.

Then, Jesus said to the disciples:
"It's impossible to think stumbling blocks won't be put in front of folks by other folks attempting to trip them up. The people who instigate problems for others better watch out. Actually, it would be better for them if someone would simply tie a mill stone around their neck and heave-

ho them into the deep blue for causing such an unnecessary aggravation in the paths of those with little understanding."

"Be careful! If someone offends you, let the person know it. If they say they're sorry, accept their apology. In fact, if you're wronged seven times in one day, and each and every time they apologize, accept their apology each and every time."

And the disciples said to Jesus, "Increase our faith."

And Jesus said, "If you had faith the size of a mustard seed you'd be able to say to this sycamore tree here, 'Pick yourself up by your roots and go jump in the lake,' and it would obey you."

"But, I want you to imagine you've got a servant who's just returned to the ranch from a long, arduous day plowing out in the fields, or, from feeding the cattle out by the barn. Which one of you would graciously say to the servant, 'Hey, come on in here. Sit down and let's have a few wobbly pops and a stuffed baked potato with all the fixins.'"

"NOT!"

"I'll bet you'd say, 'Hurry up, I've had a tough day at the office and I'm starvin'. Hit in the kitchen and get my supper ready. Get cleaned up, put on some decent butler threads, then come and serve me 'til I'm fed up. After I'm done you can munch on the leftovers.'"

"Now, after it was all said and done would you thank your servant 'cause he did everything you told him to do?"

"NOT!"

"Hey, don't think you're any different. When you finish jobs you're given to do here's what you'll have the honor of saying, 'Look, we're no greater, nor lesser, than any other workers, 'cause we've only done what we're supposed to do.'"

The traditional approach, as I alluded to before, considers the parable of the bondservant to include only verses 7 through 10. This following brief summary of the traditional approach to the parable of the bondservant then is a reflection of this premise.

Central Truth:

Whatever good a man does there's no way he can do more than he owes to God. What we receive from God is grace and goodness, not reward.

Traditional Interpretations:

- This parable may not only have been directed at the disciples, but, Jesus may also have been giving a spiritual lesson to the orthodox Jews whose doctrine of works involved a moral balance sheet. Jesus says it's impossible to pay our debt to God so piling up a credit account of good works with God is futile.
- Jesus was warning His disciples against presuming they could press any claim to God's favor or reward for God isn't engendered by service, nor aroused by merit. (Someone actually got it right!)
- One must guard against assigning the attitude and apparent inconsiderateness of the master in the parable as a picture of God.

Practical Application:

- We are servants of God with responsibilities and roles however we have no right or claim to any kind of reward.
- It's a privilege to be of service to God whose grace is ever extended towards us.
- Be a patient person. We are not exempt from the daily toil of life. We must take the example of the servant whose roll in life is to please his master.
- We are warned of the dangers of impatience that arises from an overestimation of our work.
- The parable teaches the insufficiency of mere duty. We ought not expect thanks for doing things which are our obligation to do.
- There are no set hours in the working day of any Christian life. Following our master and serving our God is our obligation day in and day out.
- This parable is a challenge to endurance.

- Service isn't based on feelings, and we must serve with patience and without murmuring or grumbling.
- Don't be content with mediocrity. Do the best you can all the time.

Let me start sharing my understanding by returning to the beginning of the chapter then follow it through to the end of verse 10.

The probability of running up against a variety of screwed up doctrines of theology is pretty close to 100%, at least according to Jesus. The disciples were told it would be an impossibility to be immune to the reality some folks would lead others into a misunderstanding of the revelation of God. I've come to the disturbing realization I've spent the vast majority of my life living in an illusion, and what's even worse, I've been part of an industry that propagates the myth of self-righteousness.

To folks who hold the unchallengeable opinion they have the one and only inspired and infallible truth concerning God I'd suggest they best take their blinders off. That's what Jesus had to tell the Pharisees and disciples alike.

I'll bet Jesus was getting pretty disheartened and dejected by the level of downright stupidity that seemed to confront Him at every turn. People who make it their goal in life to put stumbling blocks in front of others are about as useless as screen doors on submarines. In fact, Jesus expressed an almost unbelievable suggestion that they tie a cement block around their necks and chuck them into some body of water where they'd be quite unlikely to succeed in the sport of treading water!

Did He mean that literally? I'm inclined to think not 'cause the punishment for sin would have to be a whole lot more serious than that. Why do I think Jesus was just messing with His audience? Look at what He said next (vs. 3,4).

"When folks mess with you, let it go!"

Seven times seven. Seventy times seventy. Whatever. The number doesn't matter. The number of times in one day doesn't even matter.

Why?

It's because Jesus was infinitely acquainted with the heart of God. You see, forgiveness is in the heart of God. There's no limit to the intent and extent of His forgiveness. It knows no bounds.

182

Forgiving others when they do nothing but intentionally set up roadblocks for you is the last thing you may want to do, even though it's actually what makes the most sense to do.

Obviously the disciples were having a hard time buying into some of these concepts too. Why would they want to forgive someone who's messing with their hearts and minds? Tit for tat was a concept they were more than familiar with and they seemed to be getting along with the philosophy just fine. Unlimited forgiveness and acceptance seemed like an unattainable proposition so they blurted out a request that has been repeated over and over in rededication and recommitment ceremonies down front at church altars wherever they're found.

"If this is what you expect from us then you'd better increase our faith."

"Pretty Please" (17:5)!

"Well, to tell you the truth," replied Jesus, "you'll never have enough faith."

OUCH!

Is Jesus off his rocker?

Say that again Jesus just 'cause it's more than possible our ears didn't pick up that last sentence quite right.

"Okay, you'll never have enough faith!"

OUCH!

It still stings the second time 'round.

What's up with that?

Why won't more faith cut it?"

"Don't you get it grasshoppers? Look, if you had as much faith as a mustard seed has you could tell a black mulberry bush (sycamine tree) to get itself out of the rut it's in and go play in the ocean instead. Now, if you had the same amount of faith as a mustard seed does, the bush would obey you!"

If this is the case, I have yet to meet someone with even the faith of a mustard seed. Is it any wonder we don't know a world in which forgiveness and acceptance reign supreme?

"But... "But..."

Jesus said knowing full well they didn't have a clue what He was talking about. He decided to lay on them yet another little "parable" which hopefully would assist them in understanding the perspective of God.

The disciples are called upon to imagine themselves as rich land barons who have servants to serve them in a variety of capacities. One of their servants has been out sweatin' in the fields all day and, at the end of it all, he merely wants to get some grub in his belly and hit the hay for some shut-eye.

Jesus offers the disciples (land barons) two choices.

1. Tell the servant to come in and have a seat at the table and enjoy supper with him and his family.
2. Tell him to get cleaned up, put a slick cooking apron and hat on, hit the kitchen, and serve up some fine tasting grits. After that, the servant can clean up the mess before eating and drinking the leftovers.

While option # 1 may be an example of the heart and gracious spirit in the economy of God, option # 2 is an example of the reality in the heart and selfish spirit in the economy of humanoids. Jesus didn't expect anyone to pick door # 1. Hey, it wasn't going to happen.

Jesus, however, wasn't going to let the disciples off the hook just yet. In the story the servant fulfilled the obligations of his position, so Jesus posed the question, "Would you pat the servant on the back for doing the job he was expected to do?"

"NOT!"

The parable isn't complicated folks. It's a story told to let the disciples in on a truism of life. They wouldn't give special thanks to someone in their employ for doing something they were expected to do. The disciples were given the stunning revelation that their dedication to doing a job at hand is no less, nor more significant than it was for the servant in the parable.

Let's do a brief review of verses 1 through 10 so you get a snap shot of what's just happened.

- People are going to mess with you.
- God help those screwballs (fortunately, He did on the cross).
- What should your response be to these jerks?
- Tell them to smarten up, then, forgive 'm.
- "We're going to need more faith to do that!"
- You ain't ever going to have enough faith to do what only God can do.
- "How are we supposed to get on with life?"
- Do what you gotta do 'cause it's what you ought to do.

Sometimes life sucks. Deal with it!

Faith, or an increase of it, is irrelevant. You see, you can never have enough faith. Faith isn't what it takes 'cause the amount of faith you have is so inconsequential in the big picture it isn't even funny.

Doing what you ought to do is what it takes.

This story isn't about what we owe to God. It's not even about how much we're indebted to Him. There is no moral balance sheet here.

It's true.

God's favor isn't engendered by service nor is it aroused by merit. Get on doing what you know you gotta do. I'm convinced most folks actually know the difference between what they know they should and what they shouldn't, they'd just rather not do it.

In life, as you go about your daily routines, don't let tit-for-tat rule your conduct.

26. **A BLACK EYE !**

THE PARABLE OF THE UNJUST JUDGE
Luke 18:1-8

150 feet.

According to one authority a leper, if he were upwind from a healthy person, would have to maintain a distance of at least fifty yards as a safety precaution. And yet, 10 lepers managed to call out to Jesus as He was doin' a walk-a-bout through their village somewhere in Samaria or Galilee on His way to Jerusalem. After gaining His attention can you just imagine their curious expressions as Jesus simply responded to their beckoning by telling them to go see their priests instead of hangin' out with Him?

Novel idea!

Well, on their snail's paced way to the local synagogue the 10 lepers discovered they weren't lepers any more. Nine of them scattered like crabs gone wild. Only one of them did a 180 to find Jesus, desiring to give Him a big thumbs-up.

By the way, Luke tells us, with an element of surprise, the thankful one just happened to be a Samaritan. Even Jesus was bemused only one out of ten recognized the gifting of God (Luke 17:11-19).

The lepers weren't the only ones baffled by their good fortune. Take a peak at another group of confused gawkers, the Pharisees. My goodness! All they had to do was hang around Jesus enough so they could sift through pile after pile of stuff to taunt Him with. Perplexed and perturbed, the best they could come up with after seeing this leper incident was to ask Jesus when the kingdom of God would come.

I love the answer Jesus gave.

"Hey, we're not talking about something you're going to be able to observe. You're not going to hear someone say, 'Here it is!' or 'There it is!' Why? 'Cause the kingdom of God is in you" (Luke 17:21-21)!

Both the lepers and the Pharisees had plenty of company in the "what the world?" contingent. Equally baffled were the disciples. The perspective of self-righteousness the disciples hung on to is at the opposite spectrum of the perspective of the Son of man. Let me do just a brief review of the verses leading up to the parable we're going to discuss.

Issuing lessons concerning the days of the Son of man this is a brief synopsis of what Jesus told the disciples (Luke 18:22-37):

- Even though you may want to see one of the days of the Son of man you won't. You won't recognize it for what it will be!
- The Son of man will have the same affect upon the world as lightning. It's force will stretch from one part under heaven to every other part under heaven.
- When will these things happen? When the Son of man has to suffer many things. When the Son of man will be rejected.
- When will that be? When the Son of man is rejected by this generation!
- Which generation? This one. (The one in which they were living!)
- The days of the Son of Man will be like the days of Noah when folks ate, drank, got married and then, the flood came and God passed His judgment upon "all;" like the days of Lot when folks ate, drank, started businesses, planted crops and built buildings and then, the judgment of God had an effect upon "all;" the days of helplessness when folks can't go back to retrieve what's been left behind
- Try to save your life and you'll lose it. Lose your life and you'll discover it!
- Some will get it. Some won't!
- Where will this occur? If there's a body to be had, vultures would gather above it!

And then, according to Luke, Jesus tells a parable to give them all some clarity. Why? Luke says Jesus told this parable so folks wouldn't wimp out without hope (Luke 18:1). Here's my version of Luke's account of the teaching of Jesus. (Luke 18:2-8)

> **And Jesus said,**
> **"Once upon a time, in a city with no name, there happened to be a judge who had little or no reverence for God, let alone much respect for his fellow man. A widow, who lived in the same city, anxious to have her day in court, came to present her case before the judge."**

"She pleaded, 'Your honor, please protect me from my enemy who's trying to ruin me.'"

"Well, the judge took her plea under advisement and tabled her complaint, preferring to let her wait it out for his decision in the case."

"Some time later the judge was thinking to himself. 'Self, this is pomegranate goofy (plum goofy for some of you). Even though I'm not much of a religious man, and quite frankly, I'm rather put off by the petty problems of my fellow man, there's something about this annoying little widow. I think I've got to deal with her and her situation or else she's going to wear me out by the continuous nuisance she poses to my court.'"

"Now, did you guys hear what the screwed up judge said?"

"Well, why wouldn't God also protect the very precious ones He's chosen to be His own and to see justice prevail for those who've been crying out day and night for His help? Let me tell you God is about to deliver justice in a stealth move the likes of which have never been seen before."

"Unfortunately, I wonder, when the will of God is carried out through the Son of man, whether there will actually be anyone around who'll understand what the heck just happened!"

It really isn't all that incredible a Roman judge didn't have much reverence for the God of Israel. You could probably say the same thing about the Emperor, the senators, the tax collectors, and most every citizen of the Empire. Given bribery was a common way of settling disputes it's no wonder this particular judge didn't see a lot of potential merit or profit in dealing with this widow's particular case.

If you need a traditional figure of misfortune look no further than the nearest widow. If you're looking to find a victim of unscrupulous dealings, grab an Old Testament and look up these passages: (Deut. 24:17; 27:19; Job 24:3,21; Is. 10:2)

Things haven't changed all that much.

Telephone fraud artists specialize in slapping a bull's eye on many an unsuspecting widow.

What tipped the scales of justice in the plaintiffs' favor, at least according to traditional understanding, was the persistent pestering of the plaintiff. The judge didn't act out of compassion. Nor did he act because he had the interests of justice in mind. No, he acted 'cause he wanted to get her out of his hair.

Now, if you insist on calling this judge "unjust" go ahead. "Justice," or "injustice" had nothing to do with it. It was expedience, and little else.

Well, as has been the practice to this point, let me share a summary of the traditional understanding of this parable

Central Thought:

In spite of the seeming delay that sometimes occurs when we bring our petitions before God, we are encouraged to continue to persist in prayer.

Traditional Interpretations:

- Persistence in prayer brings results.
- The parable is used to compare the worst and best of justice, the worst being the unjust judge, and the best being God who desires justice for "His" people.
- The object of prayer is the point of this parable as opposed to the mode of the prayer.
- As far as God is concerned it is both the one who prays, and what they pray, which interests Him.

Practical Applications:

- Believers are encouraged not to allow any influence, however depressing, regardless of any delay however long, to keep them from continuing to pray for the appearing of the Lord.
- Repetitious prayer represents an unworthy view of God, since it implies He will yield to pressure. God know what we need, when we need it, and it's the Spirit who teaches us what to ask for anyway.
- Things asked for that are in harmony with God's "perfect" will is virtually guaranteed to be acknowledged as well as supplied.
- Those who win the reward don't begrudge the toil.

I have little problem with the obvious differences that are discreetly alluded to by Jesus between the ultimate judge and a perverted judge. Don't be surprised by the fact an unjust judge is exposed for what he was. Appointed, no doubt, as a result of some form of kissing butt, the judges of the day were known as "Dayyaneh Gezeroth," meaning judges of prohibitions or punishments. In popular lingo they were called "Dayyaneh Gezeloth," (note the spelling difference) which means "robber judges." The chances you had of ever getting your case settled without the effectiveness of power and influence, or a decent sized bribe, was very limited indeed.

Apparently the judge in this particular case had a couple of things to worry about with this insistent little widow. The terminology suggesting she'd wear him out (exhaust) could also mean she'd give him a black eye. Now whether this meant a literal black eye, or a black eye in the eyes of his immediate supervisor, I'll leave to your imagination. We ought to be careful, however, to assume the widow had a legitimate beef or that her cause was a just one. It's quite possible this widow may have been a whole lot further off her rocker than we've thought.

Well, context is the rack upon which I'll hang my hat. I'm convinced Jesus was continuing His consistent approach in responding to questions inevitably being posed to Him by the Pharisees, as well as the disciples, in regards to the coming of the kingdom of God.

This particular parable was an attempt by Jesus to help them understand the justice of God. Humanoids were familiar with the justice system of mankind, where injustice, more often than we'd like to think, reigned supreme. This wasn't some kind of secret or some unique exposure to a mystical truth. What they weren't exposed to was a deep understanding of the reality of the justice system of God.

The lament of Jesus at the end of this passage was more than warranted. He was no doubt troubled by the reality very few folks were going to be able to grasp the incredible truth of the economy of God's will to wield His justice upon the entire world, "those whom He called to be His own," through the birth, death, and resurrection of the "Son of man!"

The parable isn't about persistence, about an unjust judge, or even about a widow with a mean hook up her left ruffled sleeve. No, the parable is another revelation Jesus laid on us about God and Himself, the "Son of man!"

Context. Go back. Read the verses again about when God was going to make His impact upon the world in a way He never had before. The generation of folks in which Jesus lived on this earth was the generation that rejected the Son of man!

What was the impact likened to? Lightning! It would strike from one end of the universe to the other.

Who did Jesus say would be affected by the justice of God? Well, as in the days of Noah, Lot, and others, justice was leveled against whom?

"ALL!" That'd be everybody.

Who'd figure it out? Virtually nobody would get the revelation.

The disciples wouldn't get it even though the Son of man walked in front of their very faces for three years or so. The Pharisees were surely too blind to see 'cause they were trapped within the paralyzing framework of self-righteousness.

Jesus was right. Folks simply don't get it. We still think it's about begging and persistently bugging the heck out of God in an attempt to get what we think is best for us, when all along we've been given the gift of His love, grace, and mercy the very moment God laid down the verdict and handed out the punishment of the entire world upon the Son of man!

The judgment? Guilty!

The penalty? You die!

You want justice? Well, God dished it out all right. And Jesus took it on the chin!

For me! For you! For all!

Justice was served up for "all" on a rugged old cross and folks for generations haven't even fully understood the scope of it!

Jack Nicholson delivered with great gusto a few lines in a recent movie that cuts to the chase of what Jesus discovered, "You want the truth? Well, you can't handle the truth!"

No kidding!

Jesus slapped on the folks who heard Him, including the self-righteous Pharisees a message that should have revolutionized their lives. It's a preposterously simply message.

The kingdom of God is "in" you!

This is an incredible revelation. Please don't just slip by that last statement. This is so fantastic it should shake your theological boots into bobbling ecstasy like a bowl of jelly.

191

And if you think I now believe or understand this applies "only" to those who "believe" as I once believed, you haven't been paying attention.

You might recall from the very beginning of this chapter that a Samaritan was also included in the healing ministry of Jesus, contrary to all religious rationale. Why should we expect any different from God's world wide ministry in Jesus Christ to heal the "whole" world in one fell swoop, and with a sacrifice of blood to cover the just requirements of His heart for all His children.

"All" whom God loved is a pretty inclusive group in my finite understanding of mathematics. Since I was a little child I was always told God loved the whole world. What happened? How come I stopped believing it for much of my life?

Well, I've started thinking outside my comfortable little sanctimonious sandbox. I took the liberating opportunity to peek out through the window to witness that the skies of possibilities were as far, wide, high, and deep as I could imagine.

Well, I'm on that exciting journey of discovery and I'm having a blast.

My inspirational buddy Tim would say, "Sssswwwweeeeeeeett!" And I know he wouldn't just be talkin' 'bout his phenomenal golf swing, 'cause I've seen him park a few!

27. GOODY TWO SANDALS !

<u>THE PARABLE OF THE PHARISEE AND THE PUBLICAN</u>
Luke 18:9-14

"If there are only two righteous men in the world, I and my son are these two; if there is only one, I am he" (Rabbi Simeon ben Jocai)!

Surely this has to be an example of what a pompous, self-righteous goody two sandals must be like. Jesus spoke this parable to a group of pompous, self-righteous do-gooders inclined to thumb their noses up at others.

"Two guys went up into the temple to pray, one a Pharisee;"

Pharisees, if you don't already know, were religious leaders who went above and beyond the call of duty. The Talmud consisted of the law, as well as the commentary and interpretation of the law by leading rabbinical scholars. The Pharisees adhered to the decrees of the Talmud, following laws and interpretations with unscrupulous devotion and commitment.

For example, while Jewish law prescribed merely one obligatory fast on the Day of Atonement, those who desired to gain special merit (Pharisees) would also commit themselves to fast on Mondays and Thursdays of every week. While everyone else would be helping out the economy, the do-gooders would white wash their faces and walk around the shopping malls in torn togas just to gain the largest possible audience for their self-righteous endeavors.

Folks weren't exempt from death and taxes back then either 'cause they were subjected to poll taxes just for the privilege of existing. Usually ten percent of the produce of a crop was to be paid as part of a land tax while income tax consumed about one percent of one's income. The goods and service tax on imported and exported items was much beloved too.

NOT!

Hey, some places had taxes just for entering their town, for possessing a cart, for crossing bridges, not to mention tollbooths erected at entrances of popular freeways. And who were the most diligent to complete all the tax forms, including all the ever-popular supplement pages?

You guessed it! Pharisees were known to pay tithes for everything even for things there was no obligation to pay. Kind of reminds me of that TV commercial playing lately where a number of folks extol the virtues of paying banking fees. I just love it.

And could they pray. Jews had four specific periods given to the performance of prayer throughout each day (9 am; 12 noon; 3 pm; 6 pm). Pharisees didn't miss any opportunity to be seen and heard.

"...the other, a Publican..."

If Pharisees were loved and appreciated, Publicans were loathed and scorned. Well, show me anyone who does like tax collectors and I'll show you some land for sale at the bottom of the Dead Sea. Yes, Jewish folk who wanted to serve in the field of publicanery (I just made the word up and I like it) were able to bid for the honor of collecting taxes on behalf of the Roman empire, adding to their despised ranking right up there with the scum of the earth. Don't be shocked to learn they used their creative genius to make sure assessments more than covered what Rome expected.

The result? Profit! Not that profit is all that intolerable mind you. What is unpalatable, however, is excessive and unjustifiable profit. It's not hard to get a tad riled when someone else has a hand in your wallet more than you do. Suffice it to say Publicans weren't exactly a good bet to win any popularity contest.

"Get a load of the way the Pharisee stood up and prayed for himself: 'A big high five to You, big guy, that I'm not like other chaps. Most of 'em are just a bunch of losers, extortionists, unjust, and moreover, they're nothing but a pack of adulterers. Man, I'm sure glad I'm not even close to being like that Publican dude over there. Hey, I fast twice during the week, and yes, I tithe a portion of everything I possess.'"

Look who's talkin' about losers!

"On the other hand, and standing somewhat off in the distance, was the Publican. He wouldn't even so much as lift up his eyes towards the heavens. Instead, he beat his chest and cried out, 'God, be merciful to me a sinner!'"

"Let me tell you something. This Publican chap went home justified rather than the Pharisee."
"Why?"
"Look, those who exalt themselves actually behave in a way which belittles or degrades themselves. On the other hand, those who humble themselves will find themselves exalted."

Now, once again, the traditional approach to understanding this parable is quite predictable. Let me share a brief overview of common teaching.

Central Truth:

A person is justified by God not on the basis of religious merit, but, in response with a faith which seeks forgiveness on the basis of an accurate assessment of one's self.

Traditional Interpretations:

- The flaw of the Pharisees' approach stems from his self-justification as opposed to being repentant. He was convinced justification was a reward for going beyond the call of duty.
- The Publican approached God without self-interest, throwing himself on the mercy of God.

Practical Application:

- Prayer springs out of a sense of helplessness and faith.
- The parable teaches all men are sinners in need of repentance.
- True prayer is always offered to God alone.
- No man who is proud, or despises his fellow man, can pray.
- The gate of heaven is so low that no one can enter it except on his knees.
- Humility is of the essence of greatness.

Context, context, context!
Who was Jesus talking to?
Indeed, the parable was directed to those bent on the principle of self-righteousness.

If there ever was a better depiction of the unequivocal failure of "works" I'm not sure where else I'd have to look. The Pharisees were a veritable collage of parable material waiting to be told. Jesus didn't feel any compunction to hold back his feelings towards the self-righteous mentality the Pharisees enshrined.

Equally so, unequivocal acceptance of the will of God is the model expression of one who had no right, in the eyes of most at least, to get even a sniff of the mercy of God. Jesus declared the scumbag publican was justified before he got home while the arrogant Pharisee was left to muck around in the cesspool of self-righteousness.

Go figure!

The whole concept of justification has been bandied about for two thousand years now. What seems to have been forgotten in the traditional approach to the interpretation of this parable is the fact both of the participants in the story just happened to be Jews. Now, if I'm not mistaken, we'd all like to think Jews were included in the family of God by virtue of their heritage, as well as the appropriate adherence to the rules of the Law. The system was set up for them to be justified at least once each year hence Jesus wasn't proclaiming some special inhabitation upon them.

Since I don't believe Jesus was trying to set us up with some kind of revolutionary teaching I want to simplify my understanding of this parable as much as I possibly can for you. I've come around to the remarkable understanding folks who lived before the cross/resurrection were justified in the same way as folks who live after the cross/resurrection. Hey, it's not my understanding that is remarkable. The fact God justified anyone at all is what is so remarkable!

It's amazingly simple. Here's the bottom line:

We're "all" justified by the grace and mercy of God!

This parable is just another noteworthy revelation of Jesus that justification is definitely not a result of religious merit. The realization God's grace and mercy is dependent apart from one's self is a staggering, empowering formula to enjoy an abundant life beyond belief. Those who think they've got in made in the shade as a result of their own accomplishments are the most likely to get sun burnt for they behave in a way so as to belittle or degrade themselves. Look folks, Jesus is telling us self-righteousness is a dead end street. Those who travel it end up disappointed and confused.

On the other hand, those who live in the understanding of their hopelessness apart from the loving grace and mercy of God are truly exalted to live in the luxurious lap of liberty and abundance knowing God is the ultimate dispenser of justification.

Why? Because it's all about the will of God! And what the world did God will?

Nothing less than to love the world, yes, the whole world!

Oh, this particular parable might be over but we're certainly not done. There's more context to confirm what Jesus has just laid on His listeners. It may not be a parable yet it's information Luke fits precisely into place in the scheme of things. It's the story of children, a fellow who thought he had the world by the tail, and of some close associates who didn't have a clue. I'll try to supplement my understanding with a brief synopsis of Luke 18:15-17; 18:18-30; and then 18:31-34.

Luke 18:15-17

Children. The kingdom of heaven, as far a Jesus was concerned, is comprised of children who've been touched. Religious folk of today aren't convinced many folks deserve a touch from God in the very same way the disciples tried to isolate children from the hand of Jesus.

Of course, we've been taught to think Luke 18:17 implies it will take childlike faith for anyone to get into the kingdom. I prefer to understand Jesus is implying that nobody will get in unless Jesus touched their very being. No matter how smart you are, no matter how rich you are, no matter how mature you are, you aren't going to get close to the kingdom unless you receive a blessing of His touch upon your life like He blessed those children with.

Let there be no mistake. You've been touched! It happened some two thousand years ago.

Luke 18:18-30

A man of power and prestige approaches Jesus with a question of ultimate proportions. "Good master, what shall I do to inherit eternal life?"

Great question.

After Jesus listed a whole bunch of commandments the chap says he's kept them all. Jesus tells him to go and sell everything and give it to the poor.

Oops.

Don't want to do that.

Whereupon Jesus says it would be easier for a camel to get through a people door into a city than a rich dude to get into the kingdom of God.

Then the perplexed disciples asked, "Who in the world can be saved then if rich folks can't even get in?"

Here this response of Jesus, and this is great:

"Things impossible for men are possible with God!"

Oops. Peter didn't clue in. "Hey, we've left everything behind to follow you."

"Look," Jesus said to them all, "I'm telling you there's no person who has left their house, their parents, their spouse, or their children for the sake of the kingdom of God who won't get more than they bargained for in this life or in the life to come."

Stunning.

Luke 18:31-34

He gathered His 12 disciples close to Himself and told them they were all going to Jerusalem so prophecy would be fulfilled. He'd be given into the hands of the Gentiles, He'd be mocked, scorned, spit on, scourged, killed, ah yes, and He'd come back to life again.

Did they clue in to His hints? Not! They didn't understand a thing. They couldn't figure out why He would tell them this, nor could they get a handle on any of the things Jesus was laying on them.

The parable reveals the destitute state of self-righteousness. The follow up passages teach us about the necessity of a touch from God, the endless possibilities of God's power, and a revelation of the prophetic scenario that would soon complete the mission of Jesus on this earth to make the whole abundance and liberty thing a reality for everyone.

Folks, it's all about God. It's not about you. It's all about what God has done. It's not in the least about what you've done.

Self-righteousness sucks!

The unilateral, universal intervention of God rocks!

Folks, it's all in the context.

Goody two sandals do you need to be?

NOT!

28. JUST HANGIN' IN THERE !

THE PARABLE OF THE POUNDS
Luke 19:11-27

Luke, as his 19th chapter begins, tells us the wonderful tale of a short, tree climbin' dude. Yep, you probably sang a cute little song about him if you went to Sunday school. Who you talkin' 'bout bro'?

Zacchaeus!

Oh, did I mention he was the chief Publican? And was he rich or what? If he was the top dog of those dirt bag tax collectors there could be no doubt about the size of his bank account. Given his ill gotten gain it's no wonder nobody would let the little rat get a peak at Jesus as He was coming down the main drag of Jericho.

Well, Jesus happened to catch a glimpse of Zach as he dangled from a branch up in the sycamore tree, forever etched into our memory because of this incident. The sycamore is actually a type of wild fig tree, also known as the fig mulberry (Amos 7:14).

I can just imagine the conversation.

"Hey dude, what's up?"

"Not much, just hangin' out."

"Get down here. Let's do lunch."

"You're on..."

Aghast, folks watched in unbelief as the chattering duo strutted off to Zach's estate for some grub and stomped grape juice. I'll bet they were scratching their collective heads around the notion Jesus would even give a nanosecond of consideration to being a guest of such a loser. Zach, on the other hand, was beside himself, amazed at his good fortune not that he didn't already have a sizable one.

Now, I want to stress it's important for you to consider where we've just recently come from-the parable of the Pharisee and the Publican. Here it's Zach's turn to lay out a pile of self-righteousness so deep you'd need a ladder to reach the top of it.

"Look Master, I give 50 % of whatever I get to the poor...(Well, you scammed so much you'd better) and, if I've cheated someone I pay them back fourfold." (Ya right!)

O.K. O.K. I'm being pretty skeptical. Let's give him the benefit of the doubt. Zach's cool 'cause four fold restitution was not only the requirement of Roman law for the crime of stealing it was also the standard of the Jewish law (Exodus 22:1).

Once again, I remind you of the previous passages in which Jesus was less than impressed with incredible expressions of downright self-righteousness. So what was the reaction of Jesus to the gibberish He'd just heard from Zach?

"For so much as you're also a son of Abraham, I want you to know, without a shadow of doubt, you're livin' in the lap of salvation as of today. You got it?"

"Why?"

"Because the Son of man came to seek and save those who've been lost."

I think it would be quite interesting for you to know the name "Zacchaeus" corresponds to the Hebrew name "Zaccai" (Ezra 2:9; Nehemiah 7:14). What does the name mean? It means "pure" or "righteous." I very much doubt Luke was aware of the etymology, and yet, isn't it a wonderful affirmation by Jesus.

What ever became of Zach? Well, according to a questionable testimony in the Clementine Homilies (III.63) our groovy little tree climber ended up becoming a bishop of Caesarea.

And as they heard these things Jesus threw in a parable for good measure. Why? Because He was getting close to Jerusalem and they thought the kingdom of God was going to appear any day now.

"A certain nobleman had the great honor of going on a long trip to a far country to be confirmed as the new leader of his country, after which he'd return home to assume his new commission. Before he left he called ten of his servants in for a little pep rally. He generously gave each of them a whole whack of money, (each was given a "pound," the equivalent of about 100 days of wages for the average daily laborer) **as well as instruction to govern over his affairs until he returned."**

"Unfortunately, the popularity of the nobleman was at an all time low. Soon after he left a delegation of citizens, who couldn't stand the thought of him governing over them, sent a unmistakably uncomplimentary message to the top dog king which read something like this: 'We don't want this goof to rule over us!'"

"Either the king didn't get the message or he completely disregarded it. The nobleman returned home to assume his rule over the country. He summoned the ten

servants to whom he had given the money and the authority to conduct his affairs while he was gone so he could get a handle on how each one of them had done."

"First dude: 'Master, I saw your one pound and raised you ten more.'"

"Master: 'Good on ya mate! Since you've done exceeding well with the little I gave you, I'm placing you in charge of ten cities in the kingdom.'"

"Second dude: 'Master, I saw your one pound and raised you five more.'"

"Master: 'Good on ya mate! Since you've done exceedingly well with the little I gave you, I'm placing you in charge of five cities in the kingdom.'"

"Another dude: 'Master, here's your pound you gave me. I've kept it hidden under my mattress and guarded it carefully. I have to admit I'm kind of scared of you 'cause I've heard you're a very severe man, known for exploiting folks, taking up what you haven't laid down and harvesting what you haven't planted.'"

"Master: 'You numbskull! I'm going to judge you based on the crap coming out of your very own mouth. So, you've heard I'm a tough guy, huh? You understand I have a habit of taking what isn't mine, of profiting without investing? If you knew all of this why didn't you at the very least take what I gave you and put it in the bank to gain some interest on my behalf. Are you nuts man?'"

"Master to others around him: 'Take the pound from this guy and give it to the guy who gained the 10 pounds. I'm telling you all, those who do something with what they've been given will get something out of it, and those who don't, won't. And another thing, go round those folks up who didn't want me to rule over them and kill them right here in front of me.'"

Then Jesus, after He had told this parable, continued on His seventeen-mile journey up to Jerusalem.

I know my versions a tad different than most, but, tell me you've read this one before and understood it.

Most of you, from the most conservative to the most liberal, must be scratching your heads trying to figure out what the heck that was all about, especially the part about wiping all his enemies out right in front of him.

Well, let me keep you in suspense a few moments as I share a few of the traditional perspectives.

Central Truth:

God expects, from His trust, employment that will produce results. To merely safeguard what is entrusted is virtually to ask it be taken away.

Traditional Interpretations:

- Character is revealed by how you handle what you've been entrusted with. Your fitness for positions in the kingdom is revealed by what you do with what God has given you to do on this earth.
- The nobleman's motive was to inspire character, not money making.
- The parable seems to speak to the burning issue of the day concerning the function and future of Israel.
- If an absentee ruler can judge like this, just think how more likely God will so act with reference to His purposes in history.
- The church now stands where Israel once stood, faced by the same demands of performance to grow the kingdom.
- Good and faithful servant = those who make the most of their opportunities.
- Losers and unfaithful servants = those who neglect the whole process of character development.
- The parable's an allegory: the second coming of Jesus will be delayed; He goes to heaven to get new role as king; Jews hate Him and don't want Him to rule them; Christians have specific duties in the meantime; and He'll return to reward and punish accordingly.

Practical Applications:

- Those endowed with gifts above the average have a responsibility to their fellowman and community.

- Do something with what you've been given.
- It tells us of the King's trust, test, and rewards.
- To those who have, more will be given. To those who squander, all will be taken away.
- God doesn't demand the same quantity from everyone but He does demand the same quality from everyone.
- If we want to be in charge of bigger things someday, we'd better start by being competent in the little things.
- The reward of work well done is more work to do.

Irony is a literary technique, originated in Greek tragedy, by which the full significance of a character's words or actions is clear by the audience or reader although unknown to the character. It's the expression of one's meaning by using language that normally signifies the opposite, typically for emphatic effect or humor. In light of the context I'm convinced Jesus is using the technique on His audience.

Jesus has just laid on folks the parable of the Pharisee and the publican, the lesson concerning the kids of the kingdom, and then the story of the rich young ruler. And you think just the disciples were dazed and befuddled. And then there's Zach.

All these wonderful stories are justification for a theological position regarding a doctrine of "works." Let there be no doubt, the revelation of Jesus in each of these accounts concerns the doctrine of "works," except it's not the works of mankind which matter, it's the "works" of God which count!

I can't find it in myself to equate the nobleman of this story with Jesus in any shape or form. If I did I'd be asking questions I find inescapably inconsistent with my understanding of the love, the graciousness, not to mention the mercy of God towards those (the whole world) He loves. The kingdom was already His. Why would He have to go away to a far away place to have His rule established? Why would Jesus leave His estate in the hands of only a few, and then, give each of them exactly the same allotment of funds to carry it on?

What an incredible burden to bear. The staggering effect of trying to achieve the maximum return on investment is mind numbing. It's no wonder so many folks buckle under the pressure of this kind of strategy.

The new king stuck it to the chap who didn't either gain or lose what he'd been given. He ripped the 1 out of his hands and gave to the first guy who'd bumped his stock up to 10.

203

How come he didn't give any of it to the second guy with 5? Wasn't he just as fastidious as the first guy? And perhaps, most confusing of all, how in the world could I anticipate Jesus being satisfied to not just wipe out any who didn't like Him, but want it done it such a degrading and violent way by others who did like Him?

No, I'm inclined to accept this parable in the context Luke recorded for us. Jesus was utilizing a satirical lesson concerning the folly of self-righteousness. In the realm of the kingdom of this world it's all about what you do. If you aren't gaining, you're losing. In fact, you'll be stripped of what you've maintained. You'll be embarrassed into guilt and shame. And what about the fate of those who can't make a sound appraisal of the nature of God? They'll just be wiped out!

Sad. Sad. Sad.

This kind of human justice is just what feeds arrogance, hypocrisy, intolerance and discrimination. Jesus painted the picture for us in this parable of the utter lack of compassion associated with a humanistic approach. He was completely aware of where He was as well as where he was going. He was on His way to Jerusalem where the whole cart of self-righteousness would be upset. He was on the road to fulfill the will of God to secure the eternal destiny of the whole world once and for "all."

There was but one enemy to be wiped out. The enemy was the goofed up notion that what we did could make a difference in the way God would love us. The map on Jesus' GPS tom-tom was set with the specific purpose of establishing the freeway of liberty and abundance for each and every one of us to journey upon. He pioneered a path by cutting a swath through the wilderness of self-righteousness on our way to a haven of love, grace and mercy.

Just like that little guy Zach, yes, the little dude who simply wanted to get a glimpse of Jesus, we've been blessed to get a whole lot more than we bargained for. Like Zach, "pure" and "righteous" are we now in the sight of God.

Not by works of righteousness which we have done,
BUT,
according to "His" righteousness,
"He" saved us!
Just hangin' in there waitin' for a touch of eternal blessing?
Hey, hop down from your perch. Dinner's served!

29. **CHERRY PICKERS !**

<u>THE PARABLE OF THE LABORERS IN THE VINEYARD</u>
Matthew 20:1-16

We have in this parable a fairly typical illustration of life in rural Palestine during the grape harvest season towards the end of September. The significance of getting the crops in on time was paramount since the rainy season followed closely on the heels of harvest.

The vibrant center of most communities was the market place. It served as the place of commerce as well as the hubbub of social interaction. It was perhaps the place where folks came together to sip on a few cups of Jerusalem's Best mocha or some special blend of Galilean Gray herbal tea, accompanied by some melba toast laced with marmalade. Yum!

In the story Jesus tells the market place also served as the employment office. Those needing work for the day showed up early. Early bird gets the worm you know. Those who required employment on a daily basis were usually on the lowest rung of the wage ladder. Common slaves usually had some kind of affiliation with an owner/family so they were taken care of as far as food and lodging were concerned. If you didn't work you often didn't eat, so, being unemployed was quite a serious matter not only for a man but, for his whole family.

The Jewish time clock started ticking at sunrise (6 am) and was counted in three-hour intervals until dusk (6 pm) when the next day officially began. With tools in hand a man would show up at the marketplace at the crack of dawn fully expecting to get hired. The fact some men were still standing in the employment line at 5 pm is an indication of just how desperate some guys were to work. Or, it could be they just decided to sleep in extra late.

Can you imagine working for a penny a day? Actually it was a "denarius" or a "drackma" (Tob. 5:1-4). What ever, it wasn't a whole lot of money. The verbal agreement of the amount and the timing of the dispersal of funds were binding in law. Workers generally were to be paid at the conclusion of the workday (Leviticus 19:13; Deuteronomy 24:15). While this practice wasn't always followed in every case, to demand immediate payment if they so chose.

Some scholars have described this parable as one of the greatest and most glorious of all. I'm not so sure I'd go that far, however, it definitely does add some additional color to the picture Jesus was weaving for us concerning the kingdom of God. Let's take a read in my lingo of course. And let's use cherries as the crop this time just for a change of scenery. We always think it was grapes. Who's to say?

The kingdom of God is like an owner of an estate who went to the marketplace. Here's a synopsis of his schedule:
6:00 am.
- **Hires cherry pickers for a penny a day.**
- **Sends them out to cherry pick.**

9:00 am.
- **Returns to marketplace and notices more workers**
- **Agrees to pay going wage at end of day**
- **Sends them out to cherry pick.**

12:00 noon
- **Ditto.**

3:00 pm.
- **Ditto.**

5:00 pm.
- **What the world? Guys still there who want to work.**
- **Agrees to pay going wage at end of day.**
- **Sends them out to cherry pick.**

6:00 P.M.
- **Tells business manager to pay the cherry pickers.**
- **Pay first those who started at 5:00 pm, then those who started at 3:00 pm, then those who started at 12:00 noon, then those who started at 9:00 am, then those who started at 6:00 am.**
- **5:00 pm cherry pickers got 1¢**
- **3:00 pm cherry pickers got 1¢**
- **12:00 pm cherry pickers got 1 ¢**
- **9:00 am cherry pickers got 1 ¢**
- **6:00 am cherry pickers got 1 ¢**

Jerusalem, we have a problem!!!

6:00 am cherry pickers: "What's up with that? We've worked our fingers off since daybreak and these suckers (pickers actually) who started at 5:00 pm get paid the same amount we did? For stupid! We worked from dawn to dusk, through the bitter cold of the morning through the bitter heat of the day. They worked for an hour. You can't be serious. Where's our union shop steward?"

Estate owner: "Hey, settle down! I didn't do anything wrong by you. You agreed to work for a penny a day, didn't you? Well, I paid you your penny, you earned it, now, get lost. I made an agreement with those who worked for only one hour. I have every right to treat each employee as I wish. Just because I'm generous with each and every one does this give you the right to be jealous? NOT! Those who started last got theirs first, and those who started first got theirs last."

The traditional approach has a field day with this one. Take a read...

Central Truth:

The spirit in which work/service is performed is what makes the difference. While many serve seeking reward, those who serve best serve in the response to loyalty and love.

Traditional Interpretations:

- This was to be in one sense a warning to the disciples. They weren't supposed to get their noses out of joint. Just because they were among the first to be included in the fellowship of believers didn't mean others who followed much later would be any less important in the scheme of things.
- This was meant to be a stinging rebuke to the Jews who resented the concept God would extend His grace to others when they've been the "chosen ones" all along.
- The spirit of grumblers represents the evil principle existing even among Christians.
- We have here the principle of the right of every person to a living wage.

- The parable may illustrate the doctrinal truth of God's grace being extended to each who comes to Him in spite of the time frame of their life.
- God can't be dealt with in terms of service for reward. Service is in response to His love.
- Granting the same wages to those who arrived at the end of the day those who'd worked right through the day is an illustration of the compassion and generosity of God.
- Jesus wasn't so heavenly minded He would forget about the practical needs and problems of this life.

Practical Applications:
- It is the spirit of the worker that is important, not the length of time, nor the magnitude of the service rendered.
- Divine standards are measured according to motives. Divine judgment is measured according to opportunity.
- You may not get as much as you want if you work for reward, while those who work for love will get way more than they expect.

Folks, the teacher was a master teacher. Seldom did He teach in a vacuum. There's always context to consider. Let's look at the wider picture of Matt's record.

Chapter 18: The parable of the king.

Chapter 19: Starts off with the sneaky Pharisees trying to trip up Jesus with devious questions concerning marriage and divorce. Then we have the interesting spectacle of the rich young ruler who came to Jesus to discover what he had to do to get eternal life. Once again, the standard Jesus sets down makes it a virtual impossibility for a rich person to attain it. A camel has a better chance of fitting through the needle of a city gate than a rich man (19:24)!

Not surprisingly, the disciples were floored. Here's the question they then posed.

"Who then can be saved?"

Precisely, if the bar is set so high, who in the world could jump it with any degree of success (19:25)?

What was the response of Jesus?

"With men it's an impossibility!"

But. But. But. But, with God, all things are possible" (19:26)!

Pete pipes up. "Looky here Jesus. We've given up everything to follow you. Will we get to enter the kingdom" (19:27)?

Jesus responds. "Look grasshopper, anyone (all) who follows me in the regeneration when the Son of Man (Jesus) sits in the throne of His glory will also get to sit upon twelve thrones judging the twelve tribes of Israel. Anyone (all) who leaves home, family, or sister, father, mother, wife, children, or land will inherit everlasting life. But many (all) who are first will be last and those who are last will be first" (19:28-30).

Chapter 19 has given some amazing revelations concerning the "all" inclusiveness of the kingdom of God. We've "all" followed in the regeneration. Based upon the accomplishments of mankind? Hardly!

Why do folks have trouble with God's "all" inclusiveness? Paul tells us folks have fallen from grace, having been bewitched into believing what we "do" can change the heart of God. Give it up. What you "do" could never change the heart of God. Your confession and repentance has no effect upon God. In fact, He's the one who did the repenting. He changed His heart from vengeance and justice to salvation, to grace, and mercy for all. Check it out (Exodus 32:7-29, in particular verse 14).

Context has really set up chapter 20.

The parable is a prime example of how folks got their noses out of joint with the justice of God. Folks even today get their wiggles waggled 'cause they've come to think there is injustice in the fact some could join the kingdom of God after serving up a lifetime of badness and misery upon their fellow man. Why should God open wide His arms to receive a last minute confession?

The last minute thing really bugs a lot of folks, just like it did the cherry pickers that put in a full day of work in the parable. They grumbled and complained over the apparent injustice of it all. Oh, to be sure, they didn't begrudge the latecomers their due compensation, they were just annoyed the amount of compensation was skewed. Those who put more blood, sweat, and tears into the basket ought to be rewarded accordingly.

I'd like to know where we get off thinking it's the spirit of our work that will make the difference when the crowns get passed out? Where do we get off perpetuating the idea that it will be those who've served with the most loyalty, love, and dedication who'll receive a reward greater than anyone else?

Why have we drawn the inference from this parable it's the folks who work for profit or reward who are somehow inferior because of their motive? We've developed a "first to the trough" mentality.

Go figure.

One translation refers to the estate owner as "the goodman of the house."

No foolin'!

Why is it so difficult for us to be content to accept the right of God to extend His mercy and grace to include everyone, irrespective of response?

God didn't ask us for our approval before His love sent His only begotten Son to accept His wrath for the ills of the "whole" world. God could have cared less if we were willing to believe it, to work for it, or to beg for it. He simply did it because He had our best interest at heart, because He wanted to.

Isn't this, in fact, the message of this parable? The cherry farm owner went looking for workers and agreed to compensation. His blessing was equitable and just as far as He was concerned. The first got theirs last. The last got theirs first. Hey, they all got theirs! Who should care?

We're back at context. First is the same as last. Last is the same as first (20:16).

This was the message in the last verse (vs. 30) of chapter 19, and it appears again in the last verse of this parable. There's absolutely no difference between first and last in the eyes of God. Why? Because all He sees now is seen through the blood of Jesus!

I'm sure you're wondering why I've excluded the last phrase of the RSV version of verse 16, "for many are called, but few chosen."

First of all, according to most scholars, this phrase isn't actually in the original writing.

Secondly, if it were in Matt's account, I'd offer this explanation. God indeed called many. "Many" is a term Paul used frequently to imply "all." Folks are called on the basis of whom they are-loved of God. "Few," more like none, are chosen on the basis of belief, faith, works, good looks, fame, fortune, etc. Folks are not chosen because of what they've done are called to be the children of God.

This brings me back to context.

Keep reading the rest of the 20th chapter. Read what Jesus says in verse 23.

He says we're "all" going to drink of the same cup as He would. He said we're "all" going to be baptized with the same baptism He would be baptized with. Jesus declared He wasn't the One choosing who'd sit where at the banquet table. It's the role of the heavenly Father to sit at the table with whomever He wants to share His food and beverage with. I'm thrilled to pieces with whom He wanted there.

Me!

Indignation, however, was the response of 10 of the 12 disciples (20:24)

"No Way!"

WAY!

Then look at verse 28.

"The Son of man didn't come to be ministered to, but to minister, and to give His life a ransom for many (ALL)!"

Wow!

The parable estate owner went to the market to cherry pick those he wanted to cherry pick. Furthermore, he rewarded them according to His generosity, not according to work ethic or performance.

Wow! I can dig a kingdom of God like that!

God, the ultimate estate owner cherry picked whom He wanted to cherry pick, furthermore, He rewards cherry pickers according to His generosity, not according to ethics or performance.

Wow! Wow!

(Double wow)

Is God good or what?

30. **NOW, GO DO THE RIGHT THING !**

<u>THE PARABLE OF THE TWO SONS</u>
Matthew 21:23-32

History was definitely in the making.

In setting up the context for several parables to come Matthew records some significant events that had formidable implications for all those who surrounded Jesus. Let's follow along from Matthew's record from verse 17 of chapter 20.

Jesus and His twelve disciples were on their way to Jerusalem when they decided to make a pit stop just before they left the city of Jericho. I'm sure it caught the disciples a little off guard when Jesus gave them a run down of what was to unfold before their very eyes.

Here's a list:
- He'd be betrayed.
- He'd be handed over to the religious authorities.
- He'd be condemned to death.
- He'd be handed over to the Gentiles for mocking, scourging, and crucifying.
- "Oh my Lord!" they cried.
- There was some good news. He'd rise again three days later (20:17-19).

Their jaws were still wondering what to do when Zebedee's wife (mother of Zeb's children, namely James & John) came to Jesus to first of all worship Him, and secondly, to put in a special request (20:20).

Mrs. Z: "Can my two boys sit next to You in Your kingdom, one on the left, and one on the right? Pretty please" (20:21)?

Jesus: "Hey, you don't even know what you're asking, do you? Are you going to drink of the cup I'm going to drink? Will you be baptized like I'm going to be" (20:22)?

Mrs. Z, James, John: "You bet."

Jesus: "Indeed, however, where you sit isn't up to me" (20:23)!

Oops. Jerusalem, we got problems! The 10 other disciples get ticked off with their two compatriots for trying to get a leg up (a chair leg, that is) (20:24).

Jesus: "Power and control, in the Gentile world, is in the hands of those in power. In our little group, whoever is great will be the one who ministers, the greatest-the servant."

"Even as the Son of Man didn't come to be ministered to, but, to minister, and to give His life a ransom for many (ALL)" (20:25-28).

WOW! That's good stuff.

Hordes of folks followed Jesus out of Jericho, including a couple of blind chaps who cried out to Jesus for mercy over the stunning, clambering rebuke of their compatriots. What were they thinking? Alas, they were the ones who got a first hand look at God's gracious gift of mercy (20:29-34).

An interesting band of characters, associated animals and materials are gathered for the processional. Folks bear witness to an ass and baby ass, carpets of robes and branches, super-size me choirs, and a mighty contingent of confused on-lookers. Jesus enters Jerusalem amid pomp & ceremony fit for a king. Those who knew informed those who didn't the dude causing all the fuss was Jesus, a prophet from Nazareth in Galilee (21:1-11).

Oh. Oh. Jesus starts upsetting apple carts. Literally (21:12,13)! If this weren't enough to tick off the religious control freaks Jesus had the nerve to heal some blind and lame folks who approached Him in the Temple, of all places. Before He left Jerusalem for the bedroom community of Bethany where He was to stay, Jesus had to remind the sky pilots of the phrase (Ps. 8:2) which foretold "praise" would be "perfected" out of the mouths of those least likely to be expected to utter it-babes (21:14-17)!

And just prior to our parable we have this big dilly. Jesus curses a fig tree, and tells His disciples they'd be able to do the same thing if they indeed had faith. Furthermore, whatever they'd ask in prayer, believing, they'd get (21:20-22).

Although most consider the parable at hand to start at verse 28 I'm more inclined to consider the context of the above, and then to start off the parable with verse 23. Here's my version of the incident Matthew records for us in chapter 21. Oh, before I continue I've just got to tell you about the audience 'cause it's actually quite crucial to understanding the parable.

Jesus is confronted, more like accosted, by a serious group of headhunters. These guys were no slouches. They really thought they knew their stuff. The target of their contention was to them a serious threat to their industry. Jesus was becoming a pest who, left uncontrolled, could cause dangerous repercussions to the stability of the status quo. Before they left the tarmac these sky pilots questioned Jesus concerning His authority.

This, to me, has got to be one of the funniest scenes in the whole Bible. This is hilarious. I love it.

Chief priests & elders: "What authority do you have and who gave you the authority to talk like this" (21:23)?

Jesus: "I'll tell you what. I'll ask you one question, and if you get it right, I'll answer your question. Was the baptism of John authorized in heaven, or, by men" (21:24,25)?

CP & E among themselves: "Dah, if we say 'heaven' He'll question us about why we didn't believe John. If we say 'men' then folks will get ticked off with us 'cause they revere John. Trick question. We're hooped" (21:25,26).

CP & E to Jesus: "We give up" (21:27).

Jesus: "Oakkey-doughkey. (love my spelling?) I'm not telling you either who gave me the authority to do the things I do" (21:27).

Jesus: "Let me tell you a little story. Tell me what you think of it" (21:28).

What a beauty set up for this little parable.

"A certain chap had two sons. One day He went to son #1 and told him to go out and work in the vineyard. For whatever reason son # 1 said 'NO!' After a while he realized he should have listened to his dad so he went back to him, apologized, and went out to pick some grapes" (21:28,29).

"The father also had gone to son #2 and told him to hit the fields too. 'No problem big guy. I'm on my way.' Unfortunately, he didn't actually do what he said he'd do" (21:30).

"Now, which of the two sons did what the father wanted him to do" (21:31)?

CP & E: "Son # 1" (21:30).

Jesus: "Listen up dudes. The truth of the matter is publicans and harlots will enter the kingdom of God before you guys will. Look, John came to you to declare the way of righteousness and you didn't believe him when publicans and harlots did. My goodness, he drew you a picture of the way of righteousness right before your very eyes for you to understand and believe in, and you didn't turn a crank from the standards of self-righteousness you've set for yourselves" (21:31,32).

Jesus, what are you saying? Are you telling me pimps and prostitutes will get to see the kingdom of God before religious folk? Are you really telling me folks like the dreaded tax collectors, politicians, used car salesmen, lawyers, and whores will be able to understand the beauty of God's gracious and merciful kingdom before religious movers and shakers will?

Absolutely!

Oops, I'm getting ahead of myself. Let's take a quick look at the traditional approach to understanding this parable.

Central Theme:

Promises are never a substitute for performance. Verbal courtesy, surface politeness, nor political correctness can take the place of old fashioned good works. A good person can always spoil a good deed by the way they do it.

Traditional Interpretations:
- Son #2 may well represent religious leaders who profess to do the will of God and yet refuse to recognize their responsibility to do it while son #1 may well represent sinners who initially refuse to have anything to do with God eventually repent and begin doing God's will
- God doesn't condemn making promises with sincerity and performed in earnest. What is condemned is the making of insincere professions and commitments.
- Both sons hurt the heart of their father. The son who would really bring happiness to the father would be the one who would willingly hear the command and then obey it.

Practical Applications:
- This parable strikes at the chaos of modern religion. It shames crude evangelism that imposes its zeal with ignorance and mercenary motives.
- Self-righteousness is a greater obstacle to one's entering into the kingdom of God than sinful indulgence.
- Every Christian is an advertisement for God, whether good or bad.
- Words can't take the place of deeds.

215

* The time to work is now. We're not to procrastinate.

One highly regarded scholar actually suggests there are some folks with little or no professed interest in religion who, when it comes right down to it, actually live more "Christian" lives than many professing ones.

Wow! I think he may be on to something.

Most commentaries, however, seem to agree the first son represents the cast of sinners while the second son represents the Jewish religious leaders. In one camp there are folks who practice what they believe, at least they will eventually, and in the other camp are folks who profess one thing and live out another.

Lest we be directed down another garden path let's return to what should keep us focused on the true intent of this parable of Jesus-context. The whole passage doesn't revolve around our responsibilities and our commitments. The context is all about the authority of Jesus to do what He was doing. Jesus upset the apple cart (literally) in the Temple and the big wigs were miffed. And then He had the nerve to bring up John the Baptist. John was obviously a Baptist long before it became popular.

Whatever denomination he belonged to, John wasn't someone to be messed with as far as the Jews were concerned. There was no greater office of authority other than that of a prophet, an office that had been bestowed on John. His authority, and the authority of all prophets, came directly from heaven itself. Jesus had the audacity to make a direct correlation between the prophetic authority of John and His own. John had indeed baptized lots of folks, Jesus included. Therefore, His authority came from the very same place as did John's, from heaven.

This put the religious junkies in a no-win situation. If they agreed with Jesus' view of John's prophetic ministry they'd be admitting Jesus could do what He wanted to do. If they denied it they'd be in the lurch with the multitudes holding John the Baptist in a pretty high regard.

These fellows weren't altogether stupid you know. They didn't want to get sucked into a trap so they found it quite convenient to duck the question. Seemingly unbeknownst to them, Jesus was no dummy either. The situation was perfectly clear to Him and without actually answering their question, Jesus essentially told them He was speaking and acting out the very will of God.

216

Remember the context. Think back a moment to verse 19. What did Jesus do to the fig tree?

He cursed it! He told it to dry up and wither away. And what did it do? Matt said it withered up presently. When? Immediately!

What's the big deal? Well, when you understand the fig tree in Jewish thought most commonly represented the fruit of repentance you've got to marvel at the incredible significance of Jesus' statements and actions!

He cursed what?

He cursed the fruit of repentance!

D'ya get it? Do not let this truth go by your grey matter too quickly. Repentance is, by the will of God, cursed! I've got to wonder why religion continues to perpetuate the myth of repentance when Jesus wiped out the need for it on the cross.

Onward.

Verse 21 has been used and abused by so many Christians it isn't even funny. It's the supposed charge to summon up faith to move mountains. If something doesn't happen the reason is "lack of faith." If something doesn't go the right way there must be "sin in the camp." Don't doubt.

Folks, Jesus wasn't inspiring us to faith and faithfulness. He employed reverse psychology to expose our "inability." He was poking fun at any mentality that suggests if you have faith miracles will pop out of nowhere or any simplistic, doubled-up belief will result in getting what is requested. De-fruiting trees or creating oceanic mountains are impossible accomplishments!

Why?

It's impossible to have enough faith to curse a fig tree into fruitlessness when it's not even in season to bear fruit! It's impossible for you to have enough belief to uproot a mountain and throw it into the ocean.

That's the whole point. "Our" faith is absolutely incapable of accomplishing anything of eternal purpose or value. I'm here to tell you there's only One who could exhibit the kind of faith to curse fig trees and move mountains, and it ain't you or me!

Religious leaders wanted to make it an issue of control and the issue at hand, in the context of the parable, is indeed one of authority. The story isn't about the sons. Don't ever forget it was the father who had the authority, not the sons.

The question Jesus posed was this: "Who did what the father wanted?"

The contestants put their collective heads together and cried out, "We pick Door # 1!"

Jesus jumped up and down and yelled out, "Hey, you're bang on. Mikey (one of the angels down on the showcase floor), please show our contestants what's behind door # 1!"

NOT!

Go back and read it again. Listen, Jesus didn't answer the first question about authority and He certainly felt no compunction to tell them which pick would win the door prize either. Given two choices, the popular candidate to become a model citizen of the kingdom of God would be the first son. The second son would be the unpopular dufus who lacks sincerity and a sense of obligation, duty and honor to become of fine upstanding citizen.

I don't believe Jesus either agreed or disagreed with the obvious choice His audience would make. How did Jesus respond to their choice? Let me remind you.

"Listen up. Tax collectors and prostitutes understand the kingdom of God more than you do. You see, John (that Baptist chap) came enlightening everyone concerning the way God was going to hand out His righteousness. You blokes didn't even understand the revelation he proclaimed, and yet, tax collectors and prostitutes have no problem accepting the message of God's loving gift of His grace and mercy. And what did you do with the gift when you heard about it? You didn't change one iota away from the path of self-righteousness you plug along on. You just don't get it, do you?"

You know, since I've been on this journey of discovery of a new and living way I've encountered an amazing, consistent pattern to what Jesus was speaking about. I'm finding out folks who have no background in things religious have little problem accepting the love of God. Most of these folks actually don't think they're miserable sinners. They find the spiteful, arrogant disdain of "Christians" to be quite distasteful to say the least. They don't disregard God as much as they disregard those who profess to have the love of God in their hearts at the very same time they display an inordinate amount of hatred and contempt. They'd call that kind of duality "hypocrisy."

On the other hand, those with a background in things religious are the most stuck in the mud.

DO THE RIGHT THING !   PARABLE OF SONS

I'm starting to understand why Jesus must have been so disappointed with religious folks. They had every opportunity to see the light, and yet, they were blinded by a darkness of their own creation. Hey, two of the most frowned upon professions could handle the truth! Why couldn't religious folk?

Jesus quoted the psalmist to remind us all who'd get the drift. Babes! Praise was to be perfected out of the mouth of whom?

Babes!

Now I'm not sure if any of the tax collectors in the IRS in the United States or in Revenue Canada qualify as babes but I wouldn't be surprised if more than a few prostitutes are babes. I'm more than sure these aren't the babes Jesus was referring to. The point is those who seem most unlikely to understand actually do understand. They can relate perfectly to the kingdom of God.

The self-righteous agenda is based on profession, confession, and performance. "Our" profession, "our" confession, and "our" performance are what it's all about. We're invited to the altar for God to change "our" heart, "our" attitude, and "our" servitude. "Get altered at the altar."

Good news folks.

God altered us all right!

Not only that, He even altered the altar.

In fact, He got rid of it!

The parable is about authority-God's authority. Jesus told Mrs. Z, her two boys, and the other 10 disciples that power and control, in the religious world, are in the hands of those in power. The kingdom of God isn't about power. It's about doing what's right.

The sons in the parable didn't lose their children-hood because they weren't the best of kids. The father didn't haul out the spanking strap to reprimand slothfulness or disobedience. The father never told the boys to get lost, permanently or temporarily. He didn't praise one or the other. If there's a lesson to be learned from the boys it's this:

Go do what you know you should be doing. Be who you are. You're children of your heavenly Father. Act like it.

In the uncanny, inspirational words of my favorite internationally syndicated radio talk show host, Dr. Laura Schlessinger,

"Now, go do the right thing!"

31. **MAN, I'M STONED !**

THE PARABLE OF THE WICKED HUSBANDMEN
Matt 21:33-44; Mark 12:1-12; Luke 20:9-18

Matthew, Mark, and Luke all recorded this next parable for the record. It's often been called the "parable of the wicked husbandmen," or the "parable of the wicked tenants." It should come as no surprise to you I like neither one of these titles.

Each of these writers includes certain facts that are common to each other, and each one includes something that the others don't. For example, Luke doesn't include the quote from Psalm 118:23, Matt suggests multiple servants were sent by the owner instead of one at a time, and Mark doesn't include the references to the critical passages from Isaiah 8:13-15, Isaiah 28:16, and Daniel 2:34,44,45. I'm sure we can allow for some creative differences without getting our noses out of joint. With this in mind, please accept my rendering of all three accounts as I've woven them into one expression. Jesus, of course, is the one relating the story, and the chief priests and elders are among the listeners.

"**Listen up, here's another parable for you to sink your teeth into.**"

"**There was a certain estate owner who planted a vineyard and then built a hedge all around it. He dug out a spot for the winepress equipment and had a tower built. After the construction project was completed he rented the estate out to some farmers before leaving for his summer home in some foreign land.**"

"**When the time of harvest approached he sent a servant back to the farmers to collect the rent. The farmers met with the servant, beat the crap out of him, then sent him away empty handed.**"

"**So the owner sent another servant. This time the renting farmers stoned the servant, made a mess of his face, and sent him away as shamefully as the first fellow.**"

"**Once again, the owner sent another servant. This time they simply killed him. The owner continued to send others to collect what was due him, however, the tenants simply beat some of them, killing others.**"

"Finally, the exasperated owner decided to send his one and only son whom he loved very much. He figured, 'Surely they'll honor and respect my son.'"

"But when the farmers saw the son they agreed with one another, 'Hey, this dude's the heir to the estate. Come on, let's kill him and seize everything he would have inherited.' So they caught the son, torpedoed his body off the property, and then had him killed to double their pleasure."

Jesus then posed a poignant question.

"When the owner of the estate comes back, what do you think he'll do to those farmers? Don't know? Well, I'll tell you. He'll miserably destroy those wicked men, and will put others in charge of the vineyard who'll pay the rent when they're supposed to."

The chief priests and Pharisees proclaimed, "Oh no. God forbid!"

Jesus said to them, "Haven't you ever read this scripture? 'The stone which the builders rejected is become the head stone of the corner: this is the Lord's doing, and it's marvelous in our eyes'" (Isaiah 118:22,23).

"So I say to you, the kingdom of God will be taken from you, and given to a nation who'll bring the fruits thereof. 'And whoever will fall on this stone will be broken, but, on whomever it falls it will grind him to powder'" (Isaiah 8:15).

When the chief priests and Pharisees heard His parables they figured He was speaking about them. But all the while they quietly plotted amongst themselves how they could lay their hands on Him they were scared of the multitudes because the people took Jesus to be a prophet. So they just left Jesus and went on their way.

Let's start off with some cultural/historical information.

The story, for the most part, revolves around an estate owner, his property, and the renters who've leased it. The owner decides to develop his property into a vineyard. In order to protect his investment he builds a hedge around the fields of grapes. A thick, thorny hedge was designed to keep out wild, predatory animals such as wild boars, in addition to thieves who had little better to do with their time than create mischief. Over a period of time the property develops into a thriving business.

An essential piece of equipment in any vineyard would naturally be the winepress. Two troughs were usually hollowed out of rocks or constructed of bricks. One on them was a bit higher than the other so as the grapes were pressed in the higher trough the juice would run off through a channel into the lower trough.

The owner also constructed a tower that served a double purpose. It became a watchtower to protect the vineyard from scavengers, animal and human alike, and it also served as a rooming house for those who worked in the vineyard.

Absentee landlords weren't uncommon. A life of luxury seemed to be available in lands beyond the troubled lands of Palestine so many were quite content to lease their property out and reap the profit on the backs of others. Rent could take the form of an amount of cash, an agreed upon percentage of the crop, or it could be a fixed amount of the crop regardless of how good or bad it was.

Keep in mind renters weren't exactly always the most honorable of folks. Economic unrest often led to discontent and rebelliousness. Trying to escape the terms of a lease agreement often led to some pretty unscrupulous behavior much like that displayed in the parable Jesus told.

So here we have an owner who set up his property into a vineyard, gets his business affairs in order (at least that's what he thinks), and hits the road. About five years down the pike he figures it's about time to cash in on some of his grape jam, raisin strudel, and wine.

Five years? Where did that come from? Read Leviticus 19:23-25. It would normally take at least three years just to grow the vines to maturity. The crop of the fourth year was a sacrifice to God. In the fifth year the fruit thereof was yours to enjoy.

The traditional approach to the understanding of this parable is almost as predictable as snow in an Alaskan winter. Let's take a look at the common consensus.

Central Truth:

God, like the estate owner, won't take no for an answer forever. His patience indeed has an expiration date and judgment will eventually be dolled out in spades.

Traditional Interpretations:
- Vineyard=the nation of Israel; owner=God; renters=the religious leaders; servants sent to gather rent=prophets; son=Jesus Christ.
- The story presents a vivid tale of the history and doom of Israel.
- God sent in every age a representative and finally His only Son to receive His tithe.
- It implies the destruction of Jerusalem.

Practical Applications:
- We must recognize the human privilege of being a steward of God's vineyard.
- We have a human responsibility to tend the garden and bring forth fruit. God not only desires, He demands from us spiritual fruit.
- Our judgment depends upon our response to the messengers of God, prophets and Jesus alike.
- The parable is a revelation of the trust God places in men, His patience, and His application of judgment.
- It relates the honor of human privilege, the responsibility of human freedom, the surety of human answerability, and the deliberateness of human sin.
- It tells us of the accuracy of the supremacy of Jesus over the prophets/servants who came before Him, as well as significance of His sacrifice.

After telling the story of the owner and the renters Jesus posed a question concerning the authority of the owner and the fate of the renters. Even though the answer appeared to be obvious to some of the audience, Jesus didn't want the significant question to go unappreciated by them. Following His explanation there was a sudden gasp for air by many of those within earshot of Jesus' voice. Unbelief was supported with righteous horror. A collective "God forbid!" rang out.

Jesus probably wasn't even taken aback by their righteous indignation. However, He seemed to take a few steps down an altogether different path for their illumination. He shifted into high gear and appeared to completely disregard the parable He's just spoken.

Or, does He?

"Have you guys never read the scriptures?"

Now, what kind of question is that? It's akin to asking Mrs. Marcos if she'd ever tried on a pair of shoes, or Wayne Gretzky if he knows anything about a sport called hockey. Didn't Jesus know whom He was speaking with? Weren't many of these guys chief priests and elders?

What scriptures did Jesus have in mind? I don't know about you, but I'm more than a tad curious why He'd start thinking of stones at this point in the conversation. He draws on His recollection of different passages in the scriptures He knew to make a few immensely significant points.

The first is drawn from Psalms 118. Allow me to put this verse in context by giving you a taste of the passage from this chapter. Here's basically what it says from verse 15 through verse 24.

This is great stuff. I hope you pay close attention.

"The voice of rejoicing and salvation is in the tabernacles of the righteous: The right hand of the Lord works valiantly. The right hand of the Lord is exalted. The right hand of the Lord works valiantly. I won't die, but live, and I'll declare the works of the Lord. The Lord has corrected me often, but He hasn't given me over to die. Open to me the gates of righteousness: I will go into them and I'll praise the Lord, this gate of the Lord into which the righteous will enter. I will praise You: for You've heard me, and have become my salvation, the stone which the builders have refused has become the head stone of the corner.

Look, this is the Lord's doing, and it's marvelous in our eyes. This is the day which the Lord has made, and we'll rejoice and be glad in it."

This is the day that the Lord has made and we'll rejoice and be glad in it! We've all heard this verse before, haven't we? In fact, there's a popular song with these very words I'll bet you've even sung before. Did you know it had anything to do with a head stone of the sanctuary corner?

The Psalmist declared the right hand of the Lord had valiantly opened the gates of the tabernacle of righteousness for him to enter. My, oh my. He was bent to praise the Lord for becoming his salvation. What does he call the Lord?

The Psalmist draws a picture for us.

He equates the Lord with a chunk of stone, not just any stone mind you, but a stone which construction crews actually thought was unfit for the job. Indeed, the stone proved to be invaluable, playing a most significant role in the structural stability of the whole building, the head stone of a corner.

It's significant to remember the construction crew had nothing to do with it. It was the Lord's doing, and we can but marvel at His workmanship! If this doesn't give us reason to rejoice and be glad in the day the Lord has made, I don't know what will.

The second reference to "stones" is omitted in the account of Mark for some reason. Since both Matt and Luke do include it let's take a look at the three passages that Jesus drew His reference from.

The first one is taken from Isaiah 8:11-15; 22.

"For the Lord spoke to me with a strong hand, and instructed me that I shouldn't walk in the way of the people. He told me not to get involved with the conspiracies of the people, not to fear what they fear, or be afraid of what they're afraid of. Worship the Lord of hosts Himself, and let Him take care of fear for you, and let Him take care of what you dread.

And He will be for you a sanctuary.

But, He'll be a stone of stumbling, and a rock of offense to both the houses of Israel, a trap and snare to those who live in Jerusalem.

Many among them will stumble, fall, break some bones, get entangled, and be overtaken...and they will look to the earth and behold both trouble and darkness, dimness of anguish, and they'll be driven to darkness."

Isaiah was an amazing piece of work. I think you owe it to yourself to read his words again and again if you have to. Actually, let me sum it up for you with my own words of understanding.

God told Isaiah not to walk in the pathway of deception like most folks who've been sucked into the conspiracy of self-righteousness. He wasn't supposed to fear what they fear. His concentration was to be upon worshiping the Lord of Hosts who'd take care of fear and anything else he had dread of. The Lord of Hosts was the sanctuary.

Moreover, Isaiah sheds some light upon the life of those who just don't get it. For those who persist in the agony of self-righteousness the sanctuary will be anything but a sanctuary.

Folks stunned in their own endeavor will stumble, they'll become entangled, and they'll be overtaken with fear, guilt, and hopelessness.

I'd like to suggest to you the grace of God is a stumbling block to those who believe "they" have something to do in achieving access to the sanctuary. This is Paul's understanding of falling from grace. I've alluded to it before that "un-believers" have an easier time accepting grace than folks who declare their unequivocal belief in God's love.

Go figure.

I'm proud to claim God is my sanctuary. His grace is not a stumbling block to me. He has taken care of any fear I previously had. He has removed the uncertainty of my valiant effort, faith, and belief. I no longer stumble and fall in the darkness of my self-righteousness. I refuse to walk in the footprints of my own achievement.

Jesus also drew from another source in scripture to make His point. The second reference is again found in Isaiah, this time in verse 16 of chapter 28. However, it would be unfair to use only verse 16, so, follow more of the context.

"In that day will the Lord of hosts be for a crown of glory, and for a diadem of beauty to the residue of His people" (28:5).

"And for a spirit of judgment to Him who sits in judgment, and for strength to those who turn the battle to the gate" (28:6).

"For with stammering lips and another tongue will he (a prophet) speak to the people, to whom he said, 'This is the rest who'll cause the weary to rest, and this is the refreshing.'"

"Yet, they refused to hear the word. But, the word of the Lord was applied to them precept upon precept, precept upon precept, line upon line, line upon line. Here a little, and there a little."

"Why? So folks might go and fall backward, be broken, snared, and taken."

"Wherefore, hear the word of the lord you scornful men who rule the people in Jerusalem, because you've said, 'We've made a covenant with death, and with hell are we at agreement. When the overflowing scourge will pass through it won't come upon us, for we've made the lies we've concocted our refuge, and under falsehood have we hid ourselves.'"

"Therefore, this is what the Lord God says, 'Look, I lay in Zion for a foundation a stone, a tried stone, a precious corner stone, a sure foundation. He who rests in the stone isn't anxious or alarmed.

Judgment will I also lay upon the line, and righteousness will be the plum line, and hail will sweep away the refuge of lies..."(28:11-17).

Wow! Heavy duty. Better read that again.

First of all, whenever I read the words "in that day" I think of only one thing. To me "that day" refers to the day God put Jesus on the cross. It's the focal point of all history. It isn't a day somewhere off in the future, near or far off. "That" day has already occurred. When Isaiah spoke the event was yet in the future. When we speak, the event was in the past.

The Lord God, according to Isaiah, wasn't all that amused by the scornful religious leaders who ruled over folks in Jerusalem. In spite of everything He'd done for them, little by little, law upon law, they simply stumbled and crumbled under the weight of their doctrines of self-righteousness.

What had they done? They made a pact with death! They made a covenant with hell! They were convinced that when the flood came it wouldn't affect them. They made lies their refuge. They hid themselves in falsehood.

Is there a better picture of the folly and recklessness of self-righteousness? I think not.

God knew He couldn't leave it up to us. We were a hopeless lot indeed. So what'd He do about it?

He laid out His plan. He built a kingdom based upon a "foundation of a stone, a tried stone, a precious corner stone, a sure foundation." God's judgment would be laid upon the stone. His righteousness would be the plum line. The refuge of lies (self-righteousness) would be swept away!

I'll tell you folks this is good news!

The third reference Jesus used comes from the book of Daniel (2:34, 44, 45). Let's take a look at the context. As chapter 2 begins we find King Nebuchadnezzar starting to dream dreams in the second year of his reign. Unfortunately for him, he can't figure out what the dreams mean.

After a batch of magicians, astrologers, sorcerers, and Chaldeans couldn't interpret a particularly memorable dream, the king ordered all the wise men in Babylon to be killed, among them Daniel and his buddies. Eventually Dan gets brought in to give the 'neezzar his interpretation.

- (27) These goofs can't tell you what your dream meant.
- (28) But, there's a God in heaven who can.

- (29) You dreamed the dream, and God will show you what it means.
- (30) I don't claim to have more wisdom than anyone else, but I'll reveal to you the secret of your dream so you won't kill the other guys.
- (31) You saw a great, bright, and excellently terrible image.
- (32) Head of fine gold, breast and arms of silver, belly and thighs of brass.
- (33) Legs of iron, feet partly iron, partly clay.
- (34) You saw a stone was cut out without hands that struck the image on his iron and clay feet, breaking them to pieces.
- (35-44) This is the dream and what it means: And in the days of these kings will the God of heaven set up a kingdom which will never be destroyed; and the kingdom will not be left to other people, but, it will break in pieces and consume all these kingdoms, and it will stand forever.
- (45) Forasmuch as you saw the stone was cut out of a mountain without hands, and that it broke in pieces the iron, brass, clay, silver, and gold, and the great God has made known to the king what will come to pass someday; and the dream is certain, and the interpretation of it is equally sure.
- (46) Then King 'nezzar fell on his face and worshipped Dan.
- (47) Look Dan, your God is a God of Gods, and a Lord of kings, a revealer of secrets.
- (48) The king made Dan a ruler over the whole province of Babylon, and chief of the governors over all the wise men.
- (49) And Dan got Shadrach, Meshach, and Abednego hired to oversee the affairs of the province of Babylon, and Dan got to sit in the King's gate.

Neat, eh?

Remember Shadrach, Meshach, and Abednego? I guess it does pay to know somebody in the right places, even when it's "cool" in the furnace!

Now, why would Jesus even think of including a reference to this story in his rebuke to those who listened to His parable? Here's the bottom line of the dream.

Kingdoms, good and bad, strong and weak, honorable and despicable, will come and go. None of them have a hope in the Middle East of everlasting success. This is why God said He'd establish a kingdom that will never be destroyed, nor will it be left in the hands of people. Moreover, it will break into little pieces and will consume every other kingdom, and it will stand forever.

Dan told 'neezar that just as sure as he saw a stone (somehow cut out of a mountain without human hands) wipe out the image in his dream, God would wipe out and crush every other kingdom, and establish a kingdom beyond the expectations of anyone, and it would be eternal to boot! There was no doubt about the dream. Nor was there to be any disputing the interpretation either.

The advice of Jesus?

Earthly kings and kingdoms will come and go. The heavenly King, and His kingdom, will come and never go!

So here we have this eloquent parable of the wicked renters. The tapestry is woven with the beauty, strength, and integrity of each of the prophecies introduced by Isaiah and Daniel. The relevance of prophecy would indeed be fulfilled, and in very short order for those who heard Jesus tell this parable I might add.

What's so amazing to me is the statement of the religious leaders in attendance after Jesus told them the owner would wipe out the wicked tenants and place the care and keeping of the vineyard in someone else's hands. Keep in mind they figured out quite quickly Jesus was more than likely talking about them.

What did they say? "God forbid!"

On the contrary, God did not forbid the crushing defeat, He guaranteed it!

In fact, a stone, rejected by others who'd attempt to build the sanctuary with self-righteousness, would become the pivotal support of the sanctuary of God's presence. This is surely the work of the Lord, and it's a marvelous thing in my eyes. This was a day the Lord created all by Himself and I'll rejoice and be glad in it!

In fact, a stone, a foundation of the sanctuary of God's kingdom for me, has become a stumbling stone to those who persist in the never-ending struggle on the path of self-righteousness.

In fact, a stone, precious for sure, a foundation laid in Zion has become for me the security of life itself, a refuge from anxiety and alarm, a liberation from the stagnation, brokenness, and bondage to the refuge of lies of self-righteousness.

In fact, a stone, similar to the one used to wipe out the image in the 'neezar's dream, has crushed to pieces the good, the bad, and the ugly kingdoms of this world's invention. What has risen in their place is the eternal, indestructible sanctuary of the kingdom of God!

You see, once again, this parable is far from being about you and me. It's not about "us" folks. Contrary to the central truth, proposed by many scholars, the time of God's patience will not run out some time in the future, nor is His judgment to be rolled out in some future cataclysmic event. God informed us through the prophets the time of liberation would occur the moment a stone, rejected still by most today, would become the cornerstone of the sanctuary of God's kingdom.

Jesus in this parable was debunking the traditional view of the status quo. He was actually pointing out to those who should have had some understanding exactly how futile self-righteousness really is.

We are "not" stewards of the kingdom of God! It is not a responsibility we bear to support the kingdom. Why? God found out we made a useless foundation, so He found a stone, a precious stone, a sure stone, an everlasting stone!

Furthermore, we do not have a human responsibility to "tend" the garden and "bear" fruit. Bearing fruit was never our responsibility, never will be. God bore all the fruit He needed on the scarred hands and bruised back of a "stone" which smote the kingdoms of this world into oblivion

The parable certainly is a revelation of the trust God places in humankind and our application of judgment. The truth is He didn't trust us at all so He applied His own judgment of us on Jesus on our behalf!

Unfortunately, this parable's been used mercilessly as a whipping tool to keep passengers in their assigned, regimented seats. I used to buy into the lifestyle, quite willing to pay the ticket on those flights of fancy. I've come to recognize it did nothing but instill fear and trepidation into me. I was always afraid the plane would crash and somehow I wouldn't survive, even though I had all my bags packed safely in the cargo hold, and I was tucked securely in my seat belt with oxygen mask and lifejacket stored close by.

MAN, I'M STONED !   PARABLE OF HUSBANDMEN

I don't live like that anymore.

You see, God set up a vineyard for me to enjoy with a foundation stone beyond compare. He built a hedge about the sanctuary to protect and comfort me. Height, depth, width, principalities, powers, death, tribulations-none of these, and more, can ever affect me adversely. God has become for me a tall tower of refuge and strength.

I never liked this parable all that much before, however, I've really come to enjoy the parable. Seriously. To me it's become a positive reinforcement of God's sovereign love, grace, and mercy. Taken as a whole, in context, I've come to understand and appreciate why Jesus would take such a curious story to paint a picture of the kingdom of God. It actually makes perfect sense to me. I dig it.

A stone!

My, oh my! If ever there was a person who needed to get stoned it was me! Why did it ever take so long for me to get the picture? Who'd have thunk it would come down to this? Some of you might think I'm a tad stoned! Well, I'm more than proud to agree.

Man, I'm stoned!

32. CRUNCHING CHICKLETS!

THE PARABLE OF THE WEDDING OF THE KING'S SON
Matt 22:1-15

Here's a real tasty treat for you to chew on. It's about a king who throws a wedding party for his son and nobody shows. Remember I said the host was a King! Oh my! I doubt you've spent a whole lot of time on this parable, and most of you have never read it. If you've heard one sermon about it in your lifetime then consider yourself among the few who have.

Hold onto your eyelids. It's eye-popping scary, at least this is what the traditional approach would have you believe. Of course, I'll give you a different perspective in a bit. Please accept my humble interpretation. Don't feel I'm threatened if you choose to read it in your own favorite version along side. If fact, I think it'd be a good idea to read your version as you wade through mine.

Jesus wasn't through with the chief priests and elders just yet 'cause He had more parables up His sleeves.

"Ya wanna know what the kingdom of heaven's like? Well, it's like a certain king, a king who'd been planning to throw a whoppin' big wedding party for his son. The wedding invitations had already been sent out. Just to be on the safe side the king, on the day of the ceremony, decided to send out His servants to remind the invitees the festivities were about to begin."

"One respondent said, 'Sorry dude, can't make it.'"

"Another said, 'Sorry bud, just can't make it.'"

"Ditto, ditto, ditto. Everyone either forgot or had made other plans for the day. The servants returned to the king with the bad news."

"The King was more than a touch perplexed. 'O.K., get back out there. Visit them all again. Tell them I've prepared a feast, I've had the oxen and fattened calves killed, the coals are pipin' hot on the bar-b, the eye's of rib steak are just waitin' to get happy, the wedding's about to start, so, come now!'"

"Unfortunately, the servants didn't get any better response this go 'round. Folks simply carried on with their lives. One farmer dude went home to his take care of his chickens, ducks, and pigs, another went to the office to take care of his unfinished business. Other folks scared and abused the living daylights out of the king's servants, and some of them were even killed!"

"When the king heard what happened he was ticked. Since he was a king you could say he was royally ticked. He assembled his armies and sent them out to destroy the murderers and burn their city to the ground. Then he told the servants, 'Hey, the wedding's on again, but those who've received invitations weren't worthy. So, go out onto the freeways and tell as many folks as you can find to come to the marriage and reception.'"

"Off they went to the highways in search of wanna-be wedding crashers. They gathered as many do-gooders and no-good-doers as they could find, enough in fact to furnish the entire wedding celebration with guests."

"When the king came in to see the guests he came upon a man who wasn't wearing the appropriate wedding attire. The king inquired, 'Hey, how come you made it into the wedding without a tux?' Well, the stunned guest was speechless to say the least."

"Then the king said to the servants, 'Put cuffs on this guy's wrists, locks on his ankles, and get him out of here. Chuck him way out where the sun don't shine, where all he'll hear is folks crying and crunching their teeth. Look, many are called, but few are chosen.'"

Upon hearing this little story the Pharisees took off and had a little pow wow. Man, they were ripped. All they could talk about was how they could trap Jesus because of what He was teaching.

Now, aren't you thrilled Matt recorded this little beauty? Alrighty then. If you've been paying attention to the context you'd have noticed this little incident occurs, in Matt's recording, immediately at the conclusion of what I would call the "parable of the stone," or as you might prefer, the "parable of the wicked tenants." If the Pharisees, chief priests, and elders weren't bent out of shape by the stoning Jesus talked about, they were in for another direct hit with this one. Jesus was more than likely quite charmed to let them have it some more.

This parable is sometimes referred to as the "parable of the rejected invitation." Just imagine the scope of understanding that would arise from that title. Some scholars even suggest verses 1-10 comprise one parable while verses 11-14 contain a second parable, closely aligned of course, and yet, with a different message. This second parable is often called the "parable of the wedding garment."

There's also some discussion as to whether Matt's account is the same as the account of Luke (14:16-24). It's suggested both Matt and Luke added and deleted information to suit their particular audiences. Some even question whether Matt even wrote everything generally accorded to his pen. Oh well.

Take verse 7 as an example. Many scholars suggest these aren't the words of Jesus at all. What? How can this be? Well, Matt didn't write his little "book" until at least 80 A.D., a good 10 years after Rome wiped Jerusalem off the map, so to speak. Therefore, according to these scholars, Matt took it upon himself to justify the wrath of God upon those who rejected Him. Why Matt would equate the evil empire of Rome with God is anybody's guess.

Well, before I give my two cents worth, let's take a brief look at the traditional points of view.

Central Truth:

The time to accept the invitation of God to become a part of His kingdom is not to be put off. Procrastination is the surest way to achieve a negative judgment and the resultant punishment. An abuse of privilege results in condemnation. A lack of spiritual preparation will result in rejection.

Traditional Interpretations:

- King=God; Son=Jesus; First bidding=to Jews; Servants=prophets & preachers; Second bidding=to Gentiles.
- The parable is an indictment against the Jews. They were chosen, they declined the honor, they were wiped out, and the honor given to others.
- Jews blew it, so, Gentiles are in.
- The open invitation to a feast of joy is not something anyone should refuse. To do so, in spite of the most normally valid reasons of attending to family or business, is to do so at tremendous peril.

234

- God will wipe out those who haven't clothed themselves in the new purity of righteousness.
- This parable is a warning to Gentiles that, although they'll be allowed into the kingdom, they'd better shape up before they get there.
- Few are chosen in comparison to the many who are called.

Practical Applications:

- Those who slight God commit a greater insult than those who openly oppose Him.
- Those who neglect the opportunity to become a Christian may become a victim of their own folly.
- The willingness to honor the King's son (Jesus) is a noble offense.
- The way a person comes to a task is a demonstration of the spirit in their heart. Wearing the right garments is far less important than wearing the right spirit.
- Things that make men deaf to the invitation of Jesus are not necessarily bad in themselves. One of the great dangers in life is that good things can come between us and Jesus.
- It reminds us that God's invitation is the invitation of grace.

Well now, isn't this interesting.

The Greek word for parable is "parabolay," literally "thrown along side." Another thing I've discovered in my studies is that it's commonly acknowledged parables are used to illustrate existing truth, as opposed to a means of conveying new truth. Jesus often took the liberty to rattle the cages of understanding held by the religious establishment of the day. As I examine the context of the teachings of Jesus I've outlined in a previous chapter I'm convinced Jesus was doing two things with this parable.

First of all, He was shining a light on the status quo concepts espoused by the religious establishment. He was illuminating and exposing, for what it was, the self-righteous nature of what was commonly understood and taught. Indeed, He was illustrating existing truth as the religious leaders understood it. This is precisely the reason Jesus was such a threat to them.

Secondly, He was actually laying the groundwork for a new and living way He was soon to introduce with the sacrificial gift of His very life. Jesus knew why He was on earth. His mission was to expose the very reason God sent Him-we simply were not going to gain the righteous acceptance of God without His intervention.

Jesus threw this parable "along side" the many other stories He'd been using to enlighten those who gathered around Him. There's little doubt in my mind the chief priests, elders, scribes, and Pharisees understood a whole lot less than we generously give them credit for. To be sure, they were very familiar with the scriptures and traditional rabbinical interpretations of them, however, they were quite unprepared for the message Jesus was laying on them.

I think it's necessary for us to revisit the parable for a moment before I press on with my understanding.

A king wanted to throw a wedding party for his princely son and a beautiful princess-to-be. Invitations were sent out to discriminating guests. Preparations for the delightful event are wrapped up so the king, anxious to show off, sent servants out to remind the guests of their obligation to attend.

"Party's on!"

Oh no. Folks have made other plans. One chap is on his way back to the ranch. One guy actually prefers to go to work. The rest of the invited guests apparently are a tad less excited about the expected commitment. What'd they do? Hey, they beat up some of the servants up, and then, they even killed some of them. Balls, or what?

Ouch.

The king puts the wedding on hold, calls up the troops, puts an A.P.B. out for the murderers, kills them, and then, adding insult to injury, burns their city to the ground. The king gets another wedding ceremony in gear. He finds more servants and gives them the scoop. "Look, those last folks I invited weren't worth the trouble. Go out to the highways and byways and invite whoever you can find." Servants hit the roads, literally. Good or bad. Whatever. Whoever. They filled the joint. Party's just a happenin'.

Oh. Oh (second parable-supposedly).

King makes his grand entrance. Off to the side the King sees this wedding crasher without his doodads on.

"How'd you make it in here without a tux?"

Reply?

Silence must be golden.

Not!

"What, cat got your tongue? Hey guards, 'cuff this guy and get him out of here. Let 'im weep. Make sure his chicklets chatter with the other folks. Lots of folks are called but few are chosen."

Common sense would have us believing the king's a little bit of a loose cannon. He's not only a poor planner, he's can't execute the plan worth a hoot. When things don't go his way he wipes out those who oppose his intentions. Not only that, he burns down the city where they lived. (Now, if they're dead, why burn down the homes where they lived? Just wondering.)

To top it off, the king gets upset when some poor soul has the nerve to show up without the proper attire, casting him out to where even sheep can't get to sleep by counting other sheep, and barking out a mad man's proclamation that many folks get called but few are chosen.

Plum goofy!

EXACTLY!!!

Don't you get it? Goofy!

This is exactly what Jesus is trying to explain to the religious think tank. He was painting a picture for them of the incredible limitation of their understanding. Existing truth? No kidding. This is exactly where these folks were in their understanding. The traditional approach to the interpretation of this parable is uniquely parallel to the understanding of the Pharisees to whom Jesus directed His teaching.

Look, the only thing self-righteous people can see is themselves. It's no surprise to me Jesus would use a story like this to show these cats just how tangled up they were. They correctly assumed Jesus was showing them up. The reality is that the religious leaders had painted God, not to mention themselves, into a box. It was a convenient little box.

Mess with God and He'll squish you like a bug! Show a bit of procrastination and you'll be a no show at the party. There'll always be someone else who'll be willing to show up for the dance if you've got your priorities a tad out of whack. Don't dare show up without your dancing shoes either. Forget your tux and you'll find yourself on the outside without a hope of even looking through the stained glass windows at rows of tables filled with obedient little diners.

Matt told us what the Pharisees thought of Jesus' little tale. They saw themselves implicitly in His depiction of a marriage in their imaginary kingdom of heaven.

How did they respond?

They couldn't handle it. They took off. Where to? Did they leave to conspire to kill Jesus? Did they leave to warn their followers they were sailing on a sinking ship?

NOT!

They huddled together to conspire as to how they could trap Jesus. They could hardly believe their ears. There must have been a certain amount of confusion concerning what they had just heard. Surely Jesus didn't really mean this kingdom of heaven describing the wrath of an angry, spiteful God was all they had to look forward to.

I'm convinced what Jesus revealed about the understanding of the Pharisees was truly true. It is an accurate description of the condition of mankind's plight before one miraculous, history-changing event-the cross!

Yes, the system of self-righteous was indeed in play before the cross. The favor and acceptance of God was dependent upon a system of laws, rules, and regulations that provided the conditions of merit. Few of the many who were called actually got chosen for their sense and sensibility. What an amazing picture of hopelessness Jesus painted with this parable.

Fortunately for me, the events of one wicked weekend altered the balance of my eternity. My seat at a table at the banquet of banquets is secure and I'm in with bells on. The party to celebrate the joy of the kingdom of God is on baby!

My chicklets aren't headed for the crunching chambers. Oh no, they're smilin' and chompin' their way around the buffet table, enjoyin' every bite!

33. **WOE !**

<u>THE PARABLE OF THE TEN VIRGINS</u>
Matthew 25:1-13

We just gotta do some more context stuff. I love context. There's so much significant stuff between Matthew 22:15 and this parable in chapter 25 it would be a grave injustice on my part to not even gloss over it quickly. So here goes. Hang in there.

After a time out the Pharisees return to try to stump the star contestant concerning whether or not they should be paying their taxes to Caesar. How lame! Jesus rebuffed them with a flip of the coin.

"If Caesar's face is on the coin, then pay your taxes to Caesar. Oh yeah, and give tribute to God for what He's due too."

The Sadducees show up the next day to creatively set a trap for a worthy adversary concerning the resurrection, one of their pet doctrines. Not! They didn't even believe in a resurrection.

Here's the scoop.

A woman gets widowed by her husband, and then she becomes a hand-me-down bride to his brother, and so on, and so on, and so on, and so on, and so on, and so on. Yep, 7 times she gets passed down the pike. Perhaps that's why they're called turnpikes. Anyway, the first husband had a bunch of brothers it seems. Hey, families were much larger back then. Oh no, the lady dies of exhaustion. Who wouldn't?

The question-de-jour? Whose wife would she be in the resurrection?

Jesus wasn't about to let this lame, goofy hypothetical illustration go without a response.

"Who cares?"

Don't you just love it? And then in one of the most poignant statements about this topic Jesus drops this bomb.

"God isn't the God of the dead, but of the living!"

Oh, the Pharisees loved it when they heard about that discussion. Jesus surely had put one over on the Sadducees. Now it was again their turn. They decided to let loose one of their lawyers into the fray.

"Hey Jesus, what's the greatest commandment?"

Jesus, with probably the most often quoted answer of all time replied, "Love God with all your heart, soul, and mind, and love your neighbor like you love yourself."

Now Jesus turns the table. "What do you think of Jesus, and whose son do you think He is?"

"David's' son!" came the single reply from all the Pharisees in the crowd.

"Well," Jesus says, "the scriptures say Dave called Jesus 'Lord,' so, if Dave called Him 'Dad,' how could Jesus be Dave's son?"

Go figure. Nobody had an answer for that one.

Then we have perhaps one of the most damning pieces of literature ever written. Jesus was talking to folks of all stripes, in addition to His disciples. Jesus blew a gasket. He released a tirade you ought to read. In Matthew chapter 23 you'll find the most stinging indictment of self-righteousness you'll ever come across, anywhere!

- 23:13 WOE!
- 23:14 WOE!
- 23:15 WOE!
- 23:16 WOE!
- 23:23 WOE!
- 23:25 WOE!
- 23:27 WOE!
- 23:29 WOE!

Hypocrites! Fools! Blind guides! Whitewashed sepulchers! And that's not all. Read it. It's amazing how Jesus goes on and on.

- 23:13 "You shut up the kingdom of heaven against men!"
- 23:25 "...full of extortion and excess..."
- 23:32 "...you fill up the measure of your fathers..."
- 23:34-39 "I sent you prophets, wise men, scribes. You killed some of them. Why? So all the righteous blood shed upon the earth would come upon you...Look, I'm telling you, all these things will come upon this generation...O Jerusalem, I'd love to have gathered you like a hen gathers her chicks but you wouldn't let me...so, you won't get to see me for who I am until you say 'Blessed is he who comes in the name of the Lord.'"

Incredible, eh? Could Jesus have drawn a better picture for all of us? It was a warning to those who literally saw Jesus yet didn't even recognize Him for who He really was-the Son of God, the spotless Lamb who'd come to wipe away the sin of the "whole world" with the shedding of His blood, within their very lifetime no less!

Jesus then leaves one area of the Temple 'cause the disciples wanted to give Him a little tour. As they looked over the Temple site Jesus informed them there wouldn't be a stone left standing of the magnificent structure.

Ouch. I wonder what the disciples thought when they heard that little timbit of information. On the Mount of Olives later that day the disciples started to question Jesus concerning the timing of this calamity.

Some more "woes."

Jesus lays on them some wonderful descriptions of the glorious day soon coming to alter all of history. He tells them to take a hint from the fig tree. When the young branches start leafing you know summer time is here. Similarly there were signs the kingdom of God was at hand.

And then this:

- "Here's the bottom-line guys: This generation won't pass away before all these things will come to pass! Look, heaven and earth will pass away but you can take what I'm telling you to the bank! It's a done deal" (Matt 24:34)!
- What does Jesus tell His disciples to do?
- "Just watch. It'll happen before your very eyes! You may not know the hour but it will happen" (Matt 24:42)!
- Jesus puts folks on notice. If a nice guy would know when a thief would come and rob his home he'd stand guard. So be ready 'cause the Son of man will come when you don't think He will (24:43,44).
- Good on the servant who's ready when his master returns home from holidays, no good on those who aren't prepared (24:45-51).

All of this context just to set up this next parable. Here we read the delightful tale of ten virgins-five stupid, five smart. Here's my version.

"Then...

Sorry, got to stop right here. When is "then"?

I'm serious. This is so important. If you don't understand when "then" is, you'll miss the whole point of the parable. Jesus has been talking about a time before the Son of man comes to do what He's been sent to do.

Who's the Son of Man? I think we'll agree it is Jesus.

What did He come for? He came to save the whole world.

When did He do it? On the cross more than just a few years ago.

You see, most folks still think He's got to come back someday in the future to finish God's business. In my humble opinion, if Jesus didn't come to do what He was sent to do on the cross, and out of the tomb, we're all in deep doo-doo.

So, continuing on with this theme of un-expectancy Jesus tells this little story of what expectancy ought to be like before the son of Man completed His work here on earth. Remember, He's said it would happen in their lifetime, before their very eyes.

Perhaps let's start again.

"Then will the kingdom of God be likened to ten virgins who took their lanterns and went to meet the bride's groom-to-be. Five of them were pretty bright (perhaps pretty and bright), and five of them a few sandwiches less than you'd need to have a picnic (perhaps pretty as well but less bright). The five stupid virgins took their lanterns but neglected to take extra oil along, while the wise five took some extra oil in oilcans along with their lanterns."

"The virgins grew tired waiting for the slowpoke bridegroom so they all took a nap. About midnight someone heard a commotion outside and went to warn the sleepy head virgins."

"Hey, get up! The bridegroom is coming. Go outside and meet him."

"All ten virgins got up with a startled look on their faces and began the process of relighting their lanterns. Of course the stupid virgins begged the wise five, 'Give us some of your oil, cause our lanterns are empty.'"

"The wise five said, 'No way! There won't be enough for us and enough for you as well. Go over to Mo-Mart and buy your own oil.'"

"Off went the stupid five to do some oil shopping. And while they were gone guess who showed up? The bridegroom. Riiiiiggggghhht! Guess who got to go into the wedding ceremony with the bridegroom? The five wise virgins. Riiiiiggghhht!"

"And the door was bolted shut behind them. Not too long after the five stupid virgins came scrambling up the sidewalk and started banging on the door. 'Hey guys, let us in!' But the Master of the house shouted back, 'You wedding crashers can get lost, I have no idea who you are!'"

"Keep your eyes open folks, 'cause you just don't know the day or hour when the Son of Man will show up to finish His work here."

Yes, folks indeed got married in the time of Jesus as well. Don't kid yourself for they knew how to party too. I'd bet they'd rack themselves pretty high up on the scale of celebratory excitement when it came to the marriage ceremony. Marriage was a significant thread in the fabric of their society.

Marriages today are often entered into with rose-colored glasses, somewhat skeptical about the terms of endearment and how long the "feelings" will last. Many folks of substance wouldn't think of entering into a marriage covenant without a legally prepared document to cement their relationship. We call it a "pre-nup" 'cause the cement is often more like quick sand! Often there's either too much to lose for one entrant to the game, while on the other hand, there may be a whole lot to gain for the other willing contestant.

Well, they did it a little different back then. It's not that they didn't have marriage contracts. Au contraire. I think they actually entered into these contracts with a whole lot more permanency built in to them.

Having some knowledge of the cultural context of the marriage contract is certainly of benefit in gaining a deeper insight into the message Jesus was trying to convey in this parable, even though the wedding is not really the significant issue in the story.

There were three main ingredients to a marriage contract in the Jewish culture Jesus was witness to which are quite different from what occurs today.

If you've ever seen the phenomenal movie called the "Fiddler on the Roof" you no doubt will remember with some amusement the wonderful scenes depicting the tradition of marriage in the Jewish heritage.

The eldest daughter wished to marry a miracle sewing machine guy rather than the butcher dude of her father's choosing. The second daughter chose to enter into an "agreement" with a foreigner of her own faith who was bent on revolutionizing the world. A third daughter threw a bomb upon the all-important tradition by falling in love "outside" the faith. Then the family was scattered with the rest of the townsfolk to America and elsewhere, and who knows what became of the last two daughters. What a great show. The tension between tradition and love could not be expressed in a more charming way.

Anyway, the first ingredient of the marriage contract was the engagement. This part of the deal is most unpalatable for western society today. The bride and groom had nothing to do with this part! You got it. Dad and Mom (mostly dad) of a girl and Dad and Mom (mostly dad) of a boy arranged the contract. The two were usually paired up, often with the help of a matchmaker, long before the kids were even close to hitting puberty. Love wasn't even a glint in the eye let alone an entrenched desire of the heart for the engaging youngsters.

The second stage of the contract was initiated when the young couple reached the ripe old age of marriage-ability. The "betrothal" was celebrated with a ceremony accompanied by a great deal of feasting and festivity. Those folks really could throw a party. Since a dowry payment was made to the father of the bride at this time the contract to marry was absolutely binding and could be broken only by death or divorce. Remember now, betrothal didn't equate with either cohabitation or hanky-panky!

Stage 1 – engagement

Stage 2 – betrothal

Stage 3 – marriage

The marriage contract achieved its conclusion approximately a year after the betrothal. Finally, they could literally get it on, whether they wanted to or not! Hey, getting married did have its benefits. You could even get out of going to church for a week or so. Talk about a party. It could last up to a week.

By now I'll bet your wondering where all these smart and stupid virgins fit in. Well, this passage has been called the "parable of the ten virgins."

For the status quo of the religious establishment it has to be considered one of the classics because it empowers the power mongers with the control they crave so much. It's become for them a hammer to pound upon the slothful and a sword to wield against those who choose to procrastinate.

One of the tragedies of time is the loss of perspective and context. Virginity, in the modern concept, is somewhat skewed and soiled. Oh to be sure, most of us understand what a virgin is, however, the sanctity of it's significance has been lost in a society bent on laissez-faire and que sera, que sera (let it be and whatever).

Anyway, the fact we have virgins in the story isn't really all that important in the scheme of things either. Why? Because virginity isn't the issue, thus, it would be far more beneficial to our understanding if we'd simply call them bridesmaids. This explains why I'd rather entitle it the "parable of the ten bridesmaids."

They were most likely young women who were close friends of the bride attending to her special needs at this very momentous occasion, hence, bridesmaids. The fact they were virgins is probably due to the fact they, like the bride, had not engaged in sexual activity yet.

According to sources close to me, 10 was the number of folks required to be present at any office or ceremony, such as at the benedictions accompanying the marriage ceremonies. Hence, 10 bridesmaids (virgins).

O.K. Here's the scene.

The bride's bunkered up at her parents' house waiting for her beloved to come and scoop her up. Keeping her company are her 10 best friends (virgin bridesmaids), primping and pooffing, soothing and bubbling, giggling and tearing up with excitement. Now I'm sure these chicks would have done their share of pre-partying at their little bridal shower too.

Eagerly they all await the arrival of the man of the hour. When he might show would be anybody's guess. I wouldn't doubt if the groom and his buddies were having a bit of a stag goin' on at some local establishment, or a friendly game on the links.

Seems the women folk partied out a bit too soon. One by one their lamps started burning out just as their eyelids became heavy with slumber. Where was that bridegroom anyhow? The bride, no doubt, was hoping he wasn't going to be a no-show as she dosed off into a power nap.

Come midnight, who shows up but dude husband-to-be with his rather noisy entourage? Their clamor startles the slumbering spies who were supposed to be keeping an eye out for the bride, her bridesmaids (10 virgins) and her family.

"Hurry up! Get up! He's coming! He's almost here! He's almost here!"

Can you just imagine the scene of at least 11 screaming women trying to wipe the smudge out of their eyes long enough to get their mascara back on line, their lipstick reset to glitter, and their hairdos back into shape! Wow! They must have been flying around the house like scared jack rabbits.

"Oh, the lamps!"

One of the objects of interest in the parable is the lamp these bridesmaids had at their disposal. They truly were lamps as opposed to torches, although they served a similar purpose. They're referred to as "lappid" in Talmudic writings, and as either "lampad" or "lampadas" in the Aramaic form of the Greek word.

The lamp consisted of a round receptacle for either a composition of pitch or oil for a wick, most commonly olive oil. This receptacle was placed in a hollow cup or deep saucer (Beth Shiqqua) fastened by a pointed end into a long wooden pole, allowing it to be hoisted high into the air. It was customary, according to Jewish authorities, for at least ten of such lamps to be carried in a bridal procession, hence a role for the 10 bridesmaids (virgins). No doubt the bridesmaids (virgins) showed up at the shower with these lamps knowing full well it was going to be a long night. They'd be used to light up the backyard patio and then as the street lights on the trip down honeymoon lane.

Oh, Oh! Jerusalem. We have a problem!

In the hustle and bustle the bridesmaids first swung into action to shed some light on the situation. The problem was that only 5 of the 10 lamps would light up. Obviously some bodies forgot to bring some extra oil.

Let's call them the dumb 5. The 5 bright lights (that's funny, eh? Bright lights!) got their receptacles refilled and relit their lamps ready with time to spare, prepared to hit the road with the rest of the processional. The dumb 5 begged the wise 5 for some oil.

"No way!" "Tough titty!" Oh, that must have stung, especially coming from the other girls who thought they were friends.

"Go up to Moe Mart and pick some up. They're open late."

The dumb 5 had little choice other than to take the chance the wedding party would still be there when they'd get back. Off they went in search of more oil.

One of the highest of highlights of the marriage event was the processional. The happy couple didn't just walk down an aisle of red carpet fettered with white and pink daisy petals to a waiting limo for the drive to an airport where they'd take off for a fabulous honeymoon on some enchanted island in the sun. Oh no. The honeymoon procession meandered through the narrow streets from the home of the bride's parents to the happy couple's new pad. Hey, the whole village usually got into the act.

"Everyone from 6 to 60 will follow the marriage drum." At least that's how one popular Jewish saying went.

The groom and bride were no doubt in a hurry. Who could blame them? The processional took off, confetti and streamers scattered everywhere, singing and shouting interrupting an otherwise placid little bedroom community with lamps a blazin'. The noisy band of merry-makers continued unabashed in their celebration. Soon the groom lifted his bride over the threshold, the folks wired for a whale of a time had filtered inside, and the door was closed. Party's on!

Along came the dumb 5! They got their oil all right. Unfortunately, they missed the processional. And now nobody would answer the door they were pounding on. After a great deal of persistence the door finally opened up. Who greeted them but the groom, the lord of his castle.

"Get lost! The party's already happenin.' I have no idea who you are and the party's already booked full."

Yikes! It sure didn't take Jesus a thousand words to paint a picture like it does me, eh? As you can well imagine interpreters have a field day with this one. Let me take a shot at highlighting some of the traditional approaches of interpretation.

Central Truth:

The Lord's return may be imminent, however, it may come when you least expect it. Therefore, the purpose of this parable is to impress upon believers the need for vigilance and preparedness.

Traditional Interpretations:

- The parable sent a message to the Jews, who were prepared throughout the centuries for a special

relationship with God, and yet, when the time came to receive the Son they weren't ready.
- For the disciples it was a warning to prepare for the coming destruction of Jerusalem and a call to have a ready witness.
- For the church of today it's a parable to encourage believers to prepare for the Lord's return and a plea for spiritual preparedness.
- The day the door will be shut for good is fast approaching. In fact, it could happen any day now, probably during our generation.

Practical Application:
- Seize opportunities when they show up.
- Character is revealed during times of crisis.
- Certain things like faith and character can't be borrowed. You'd better have an ample supply on hand.
- Be careful not to miss opportunities to witness and bring others into the fold.
- Don't leave it to chance you'll have enough time to squeak in at the very last moment.
- We're on the preparation committee not on the time and place committee.

Be assured when He was speaking this parable to the disciples, among others, Jesus knew full well how much they understood. Furthermore, He was cognizant of the fact preparation was their responsibility.

I'm convinced Jesus was in a bit of a bind. On one hand, it was important He continue His assault on the system of self-righteousness that was still at play. On the other hand, He knew full well a system of grace would soon revolutionize history. Jesus found it somewhat difficult to help folks understand how a plan they couldn't even comprehend would come to fruition.

I still can't believe how long it's taken me to come around to understanding the bigger picture. Before the cross, the way I see it now, the ball was indeed still in our court. Before the cross the requirements of the legal system of self-righteousness was the only game in town.

At the cross, the way I see it now, the game took a radical change as God took control of the ball and tossed it into the court of courts.

Jesus no doubt used this little tale to illustrate preparedness for those whose eternal future actually depended upon it at the time He spoke the parable. The perilous nature of self-righteousness could not have been pictured any better.

Virginity wasn't the issue. Falling asleep on the job wasn't the issue. Knowing the groom wasn't the issue. The issue wasn't even the fact the 5 wise virgin bridesmaids were too selfish to share the wealth with their 5 less than bright fellow virgin bridesmaids.

No, the issue was running out of oil and not having a backup plan. There were 5 dumb virgin bridesmaids and 5 on the ball virgin bridesmaids. The ones who were prepared got to enjoy the party.

What's the moral of the story according to the status quo?

You snooze-you lose.

Let me tell you, this may work for everything that has a consequence here on earth, but where it no longer works is in regards to the consequence of your eternal abode.

Why?

The cross!

It's almost humorous to me to find scholars suggesting Matt himself added the final phrase into the story just to point out the fact the Parousia was still an event in the future. Hey, "You just never know when the Son of God might just show up, so, watch out!"

Why have so many scholars not picked up on the fact that the Parousia did happen when it happened? And all of this after Jesus had spent a chapter or so in Matt's account describing in amazing detail the feat of the coming of the Son of Man. Jesus told them all they'd get to see everything unfold right before their very eyes (23:36). Hey, Matt saw it happen before His very eyes.

What gives? In fact, it happened right in front of him and he still didn't get it. I guess it's no wonder so many today still haven't clued in.

The traditional central truth suggests the return of the Lord is imminent and it may come when we least expect it. As far as I am concerned the Lord can come back whenever He jolly well wants to. Jesus has come once already to do the will of our Father and He has accomplished everything He intended to accomplish.

He is not going to come again to judge this world. He will not come again to die for the sins of the world. Been here! Done that!

There's nothing I need to "do" to prepare for His return. There's nothing that can scare me into being ever vigilant. I'm not afraid at all if He should come back tonight. My eternal destiny has been prepared for me. I didn't have a thing to do with it. Someone, a whole lot more powerful and proficient than I, built my mansion upon a corner stone that the builders of the systems of self-righteousness have rejected.

May I impress upon you the effect of the cross was to bar the door open, not to close it! It was not to present a major detraction by forcing upon the masses a more serious system of self-righteousness. Folks, the door is not about to close anytime soon. The door has never been more wide open.

Paul wrote over and over again that Jesus wasn't going to come and die all over again. To him the whole notion of another coming for a judgment was a nonstarter. If Jesus is going to come again, and I've already said He can come whenever He wants to, it will be to take His bride off to some glorious everlasting honeymoon.

I'm convinced God, through the blood of Jesus, has prepared His bride just the way He wants her. She is spotless, pure, radiant, and a blessed bride of His choosing. The One we all owe a huge ovation to is none other than God Himself and His precious Son who gave up a King's ransom to acquire the joy and privilege of the bride's eternal company.

Jesus employed this parable to illustrate in a particularly disturbing fashion the results of the status quo. The parable is a severe depiction of the abject failure and dismal ineptitude of the system of self-righteousness we've come to love and adore so much. We've grabbed onto the myth of our own ability and are spreading the crap around like we have the best news going.

Well, I've got some news for you. The best news of all is that you've been purchased and redeemed by the blood of the Lamb. That's it!

Are you still a bride in waiting?

Let me be perhaps the very first person to ever tell you the groom has already picked you up. The processional has already taken place and you've been carried over the threshold of the mansion of God's blessing.

Party's on folks! It's time to celebrate life!

34. BLACK AND WHITE !

THE PARABLE OF THE TALENTS
Matthew 25:14-30

Matt continues his assault on the record book of the last week of Jesus' life here on earth, the remembrance of events takes us to the Mount of Olives where Jesus is enlightening the disciples, religious leaders, and interested others. We'll pick it up at verse 14 of chapter 25, where Jesus continues to scare the colorful togas off folks who've been content to maintain the status quo for far too long.

"...For the kingdom of God is like a man preparing to travel to a far off foreign country. He convened a business meeting with his servants to delegate authority and responsibilities to oversee the operation of his business while he'd be away. To one of his servants he gave 5 shares, to another 2, and to another he gave 1 share. He appropriated these shares of stock to each of the servants based upon his assessment of their abilities to deal with the task at hand. Then he hit the road."

"Now, the one who'd received the 5 shares creatively worked his portfolio in the marketplace 'til he actually had gained another 5 shares. Similarly, the one who'd received 2 shares doubled the amount entrusted to him. But, the one who'd received 1 share dug a hole in the garden and hid his master's money in it, presuming to protect it."

"Eventually, when the master returned, he called together his servants one at a time to find out how things went while he was away."

"5 talent guy: 'Master, you gave me 5 shares to take care of. Well, here's the 5 you gave me, and, check it out, here's 5 more I've gained for you.'"

"Master: 'My. My. Well done you good and faithful servant. You've been faithful over a few things so I'm going to give you the responsibility to govern over many things. Come on in and enjoy my company.'"

"2 talent guy: 'Master, you gave me 2 shares. Lookie here, I've gained an additional 2 shares for you.'"

251

"Master: 'My. My. Well done you good and faithful servant. You've been faithful over a few things so I'm going to give you the responsibility to govern over many things. Come on in and enjoy my company.'"

"1 talent guy: 'Master, I knew you were a pretty hard businessman. You've harvested where you haven't even planted, and you've gathered in profit seemingly without investment. I was afraid to lose any of your investment so I went and hid the share out in the garden. So, here's the talent you gave me to look after.'"

"Master: 'My. My. You are an ignorant, lazy servant. If you presumed I harvest where I don't plant profit without investing you should have at least taken my money to the bank and received some interest.'"

"The master gave instructions to take the talent away from the irresponsible servant and assign it to the one who now had the 10 shares. Why? Because those who have something will be given abundantly more, but, those who have nothing will end with even less! Furthermore, the master ordered the unprofitable servant cast out into the darkness where crying and teeth grinding were the only things left to do."

For the record, a "talent" in the time of Jesus wasn't an ability to sing or play a musical instrument. Nor was it some special gifting to play golf, tennis, or hockey, or special business acumen of creating fame and fortune. It was, however, a weight of something as opposed to being a coin or denomination. Its value depended on the commodity like copper, gold, or silver, the most common being silver. A "drachma" was a unit of silver coinage in Greece weighing in at about 4.3 grams. A talent was equal to approximately 6,000 drachmas. The Roman equivalent was known as the "denarius."

Do the math. We're not talking about chunk change here. Jesus wasn't underestimating at all the value or significance of the owner's generosity and expectation.

In my version of Matt's account above you'll notice I've used the word "shares" instead of the word "talent." I've employed this term simply as a point of reference from common knowledge today of mutual funds, stocks, and bonds.

The big cheese in this particular tale put into the care and keeping of some of his employees some shares in his company with the expectation they'd help grow his fortunes. Sounds like a sound business plan to me.

You might also find it curious to discover many slaves were given the opportunity to freely exchange in the world of business. The owners would surely expect a return on their investment, whether through a yearly fixed tax, or as a percentage of the profits earned by their servants. No doubt there was a tacit understanding the servants would be rewarded in some fashion for their business smarts, as well as reprimand for negligence, as was the case in this parable.

Hey, this almost reminds me of a reality show in which folks were fired when they didn't perform to the level of expectation of the big guy with the hair apparent. I doubt very much the inventor and producer of the popular show even knew there was a Biblical model.

As has been my pattern, allow me to give you a brief synopsis of the traditional approach to this particular parable.

Central Truth:

God has imparted to each of us certain resources. We have a responsibility, as stewards, to appropriate these resources wisely. Too often we fall into the temptation to minimize the trust that God has placed within each of us as servants.

Traditional Interpretations:

- The impending judgment and tones of expectancy are evident as the end drew near for the ministry of Jesus. His message has a variety of significance and implication for a variety of folks.
  1. Jews: The parable speaks of the necessity for Israel to be faithful to God and make Him known.
  2. Disciples: The parable discloses an urgency of His appeal to service. Preparing them for His coming departure Jesus paints a picture of the rewards for faithful service, namely, more responsibility.
  3. The church: The parable is wise counsel for active Christian service in light of the impending return of Jesus. Rather than

degenerating into idleness this parable is an
inspiration to crank it up a notch or two.
- Since God is a loving heavenly Father, as opposed to an
austere, disassociated taskmaster, all conduct gone
astray is based upon a wrong view of God. The
awareness of His loving kindness towards us should
inspire us to become His earnest servants.
- The dispersal of gifts and abilities is the responsibility
of God. What we do with it is our responsibility.

Practical Application:
- Jealousy has no part in the life of a Christian.
- Accountability is measured according to ability/gifting.
- Neglecting work entrusted to a person is to neglect the
opportunities of widening the sphere of influence
towards others. Faithful service widens opportunity.
- The reward of work well done is more work.
- The reward of work undone is unemployment.
- The one left out in the cold is the one who won't try.
- God doesn't want extraordinary people who can do
extraordinary things nearly as much as He wants
ordinary people who do ordinary things extraordinarily
well.

Jesus said the kingdom of God "is like a man who left others in
charge of his affairs when he took off to deal with issues elsewhere on
the planet. He came back to discover varying degrees of success, as
well as abject failure. Jesus was actually giving us an insight into the
kingdom of God that only He could see. Folks, the parable isn't about
us, it's actually about God, and about His incredible history of dealing
with His people.

By now you know I'm a strong advocate of context. In my
opinion, this entire section of Matthew's account is a set up for God's
ultimate plan of redemptive action for His creation. Prior to this
parable in Matthew 24 is a message of the successes and failures of
human achievement. The parable in the first verses of Matthew 25
illustrate for us the levels of preparedness of folks for an uncertain,
impending date with a groom. This particular parable treats us to the
justice of a system based upon our success or failure under the plan of
self-righteousness.

If you're scared spitless by now perhaps you'd better not read from verse 31 to 46 of chapter 25. If someone asks you for a drink of water, a shirt, a sleeping bag, a prison door key, well, all I can say is you'd better take your hands out of your pocket and get busy if you're inclined to think what you do make a whiff of a difference to God. Scary stuff.

Context! Hey, there's more.

The last week of Jesus' life on our planet gets underway. According to Matt, some cute chick with an immortal memorial washes the feet of Jesus with some of that incredible Angel perfumed body lotion. The brief scent of the expensive toiletry sends the disciples into freak-out mode. One goes so far as to betray Him. I could tell you more but I think you've heard the history lesson from there.

Back in the day sheep were generally white, goats commonly black. It wasn't too hard to tell the difference. Well, I truly believe this parable is a prime example of the kingdom of God as Jesus saw it. It was pretty much a case of black and white as far as God was concerned too. When He took off to some other part of His creation to deal with other issues He left folks with the challenge of carrying on without Him.

Black & white. Some handled the responsibility, some didn't. Some handled the pressure, some didn't.

Did Jesus paint for us an accurate picture of our responsibility? Absolutely!

Did He not give to us in this parable a violent warning concerning our responsibility in achieving the acceptance of a taskmaster? Absolutely!

Our standing in the sight of God was indeed to be measured according to "our" faithfulness. Black and white, like sheep and goats. We were either one or the other. Our fate, based on our accomplishments, was to be either life in eternal bliss, or life in eternal agony.

And here's the rub for me given the rest of the story of the cross and the resurrection. If God were happy with this system why would He waste His time on a pointless plan to send Jesus to wipe the system of self-righteousness out?

You see, folks could never measure up! The reality is that not one single person has the ability, capability, resourcefulness, creativity, giftedness, talent, strength, perseverance, determination, resolve, fortitude, finances, etc., etc., etc. to make it into the good book of God.

Allow me to put it another way. If the system of self-righteousness could make us holy, righteous, and pure in God's eyes, then what was Jesus doing here? God knew we were in deep doo-doo. Without His intervention we'd all end up in the toilet!

Why? Well, it just so happened there was not one righteous person among us. No, not even one!

Why? Because every last one of us came up short of the glory of God.

Fortunately for us, God unilaterally chose not to use His magic wand to dispense upon folks His justice based upon the performance of different qualitative and quantitative sets of talents and abilities. I'd lose all respect for God if this were not true. I can no longer fathom a God, with the kind of grace I've come to appreciate, who'd allow the system of self-righteousness to continue after the cross.

Accepting the notion we'd better "get with the program" and do something with the gifts and talents given to us by God is a frightful thing. Again, please don't think I'm advocating a total lack of responsibility in life.

I only have to look at my family to recognize the different characteristics, talents, and abilities. Each one is encouraged to maximize their particular gifting. However, failure is not only tolerated, it's regarded an acceptable, educational tool for life. Each one in my family is being taught success or failure in any endeavor will never affect the quality or quantity of my love for them. Being the best they can be is very noble. Losing sucks! One thing will never change. Not one of them will ever stop being a member of my family, or from receiving everything I have to offer them.

God is no less of a parent than I! It's beyond the scope of my understanding to accept God could, in good conscience, turf someone who doesn't employ all the talent and ability they can muster to the max. God doesn't get turned on with extraordinary folks who do extraordinarily well any more than He does by ordinary folks who do extraordinary things well.

As scary as this might sound to you, what you do never makes much of an impression on God. Jesus came to show us God had a plan, a new and living way. To be sure, Jesus came to paint for us a picture of our inability, and this parable is perhaps a prime example. However, He came to give us a glimpse of grace in the flesh. What would make the difference?

What can I say? The cross has made the difference for me. No longer is my eternal future left up to me.

The measuring stick is no longer the appropriation of my effort. The measurement of my acceptability is no longer based upon my faith and faithfulness. It's no longer dependent upon my belief, upon how much I put in the offering plate, upon how fortunate I am in my business life, nor is it dependent upon my success as a husband and father.

I'm acceptable in God's sight because of only one thing, the blood of Jesus! I get to eat at the buffet of God's pleasure because of His grace. I get to dwell in the warmth of His love because of His mercy.

Let me address the notion of gifting and our responsibility, lest you think I'm slipping a bit too far off my rocker. Never assume I'm promoting inactivity or a "do-nothing" mentality. On the contrary, I'd elevate the whole idea of service and accountability more than even traditionalists would. Really. I'm a firm believer in a servant mentality. Works are a good thing. It's just that good works will not alter God's view and opinion of you.

God doesn't judge you according to your work so don't judge God according to His work!

His view and opinion of you is blood etched in stone, in fact, "the" stone.

Good works take on a whole new meaning when viewed in this light. That's what this whole concept is all about. It's all about attitude. Good works are now an opportunity and privilege, stricken forever from the obligation to perform.

This parable, perhaps the last Jesus ever spoke, is about a master who left on a mission and left the franchise in the care and keeping of folks whose level of achievement was all over the map. A system of judgment with reward and punishment was warranted and justified. Reward and punishment were indeed meted out.

But, viewed in context it is a remarkable illustration of just why God sent Jesus to do what He was about to do at the conclusion of that last tumultuous week. While the system of justice and retribution in this world may be based upon achievement, God saw to it that His eternal justice was brought to bear for "one and all," "once and for all," upon the cross and through the resurrection.

Jesus indeed paid it all.

He took the brunt of what I deserved, forever placing me in a different perspective in the eyes of God. It was the performance of Jesus and His good work that lifted me out of the pit of performance-based self-righteousness I for so long struggled with.

Black and white!

Let there be no mistake. The differences between the system of self-righteousness and the system of grace are as different as black and white. However, the sheer brilliance of the plan of God for His kingdom is that there is no longer a difference between black and white, sheep and goats. Different colors. Different animals.

As we like to say in our family, "sames but different."

Red and yellow, black and white, "all" are precious in His sight. Jesus loves all the children of the world.

His children are we "all!"

Indeed.

35. LET'S WRAP THIS UP

CONCLUSION

In the beginning of this book I introduced you to the concept of wanting "more" out of life. Hey, this idea is hardly new. One only has to look at the explosion of self-help, health and wellness titles on the bookshelves of the major reading establishments to realize the tremendous humanic struggle to find that the purpose and meaning of our existence rages on.

I proudly and freely admit that I now find myself in a constant state of discovery. I'm so thrilled my horizons are ever expanding. The little piece of sky I was content to idolize for so long is no longer satisfying. A number of years ago I made the conscious decision to open the door and take a hike. Literally and figuratively! The risk I took has paid off in spades.

I am, without a doubt, the greatest beneficiary of this particular study of the parables of Jesus. The revelation of the nature of God's heart for His kingdom has had a major impact on my understanding of life. The parables not only harbor foundational truths about God, they reveal who I am in His sight. Just as they illuminate the nature of God's kingdom, they shine a beacon upon the "why's?" and "wherefore's?" of my little candlestick.

There are two words I'd chose to expose the "more" I've come to appreciate as the skies of possibilities and the landscapes of reality cast their impressions upon my exciting curb of the universe.

The first word is "liberty."

I can hardly begin to explain to you the freedom I've experienced over the past number of years. Perhaps the biggest sense of relief has been from the stench of entitlement. The sense of entitlement is merely a symptom of the plague of self-righteousness that has wreaked unspeakable havoc upon humanity for far too long. I had to come to the shocking realization that the Pharisees and Sadducees Jesus encountered didn't have a patent on self-righteousness. I'd been a pay-as-you-go traveler on the train of religion for decades. I'm not even sorry to disappoint you, but I've been off that track for quite some time now.

The parables have reminded me once again that what I "do" matters little in the scheme of things.

LET'S WRAP THIS UP

The thing which matters is what God has done! His grace has blessed me with what I could never have deserved, and His mercy has protected me from what I so richly deserved.

I've been liberated from the debilitating ruin of theological positions such as the doctrine of sin and the fateful consequences of it. I'm free of the enticing skill of determining the eternal fate of others. I'm no longer bound to the production of "works," nor caught in the peril of doubt and hopelessness.

No, the parables have once again opened my eyes to the truth of God's intention to save and bless His kingdom. The fact I've come to understand the "all-inclusiveness" of His kingdom has been liberating beyond compare.

The central theme of almost every parable He told was not merely a revelation of the human condition, but so much more, it's a revelation of the heart condition of God towards the human condition. Over and over again Jesus painted poignant pictures of His Father's unfailing love for His children and of His reclamation "work," the ultimate being the sacrificial parable of His only precious Son.

Folks, it was God's "works" that counted, not mine! When the impact of this truth hits you between the blinkers watch out! It's liberating to the max.

The second word I'd use to describe the "more" I've come to enjoy is "abundance." I'm way past being just blessed! Knowing I'm a child of the King, and a citizen of the Kingdom of God, should be enough to satisfy me, but that's only the cutting edge. The abundance I experience doesn't consist merely in the tangibles of life it's the intangible stuff that rings my bell. The world is at my fingertips. The parables are a majestic tapestry of God's heart to share Himself, in all of His totality, with me.

Contrary to popular belief, I'm not simply the magnitude of my memories. I'm certainly not merely the collective wisdom (however staggering) of my mental capacity. I'm not even the majestic nature of my physical specimen, nor the fluid uniqueness of my charming character and personality. I should also say that I am certainly not only the sum of my creative genius! I'm more than all these put together. I'm nothing less than a precious child of God!

The knowledge of it completes me. The knowledge of this incredible truth makes everything I do worthwhile. It validates my heart and intention for others. It gives purpose and meaning to my existence. It inspires me to live in the "now."

LET'S WRAP THIS UP

I'm so thrilled with the luxury of being exposed to such good stuff out there to enlarge my understanding. I'm so thankful to the collective expressions of wisdom that enlighten me as I move along my journey of discovery. If I had told you a few years ago I'd be reading and enjoying books covering a whole range of subjects such as quantum physics, and more amazingly, understanding them, I'd have thought I was taking some serious loony pills. Now, with Donna way out in front of me, I'm reading contemporary possibility thinking authors like Jack Canfield, Bob Proctor, David Gikandy, and Eckhart Tolle, finding myself challenged and stimulated beyond belief. Their books don't even have pictures! Who'd have thunk it!

Folks, the theme song really tells it like it is. The poet wisely questions, "Why settle for just a piece of sky?"

Well, the more I know the more I realize I don't know. The more pages I read the more I discover there are so many more books to help me fall asleep at night. The more phenomenal Royal Caribbean cruise ships I travel on, the more Royal Caribbean cruise vacations I want to luxuriate on. The more places I travel to, the more places I yet want to enjoy. The more people I come to know, the more wonderful folks I want still to meet. On and on it goes. Abundance.

Folks, let me tell you there's absolutely nothing wrong with wanting more! I'm not in the least bit embarrassed or ashamed to promote and encourage others to get out of the sandbox they find so addictive and comfortable. The experience of discovery will revolutionize your life as it has mine.

Thanks for the honor and privilege of allowing me to share my journey with you. I trust this study of the parables of God's revelation will provoke you to spread your wings to experience the liberty and abundance He created for you.

The ticket to your world of dreams has been purchased with the blood of the ultimate parable, Jesus. He rose to new life once, and for "all," to make it possible to live an eternal, enjoyable life.

"Papa, watch me fly!"

Hope you enjoy your flight of discovery as much as I am.

All the best...

ABOUT THE AUTHOR

Roger Rapske and his wife Donna currently reside in Sequoia Ridge at Coyote Creek, a wonderful oasis in beautiful British Columbia, Canada. They share their love of life in the abundance and liberty of God's blessings with their phenomenally creative children Richard and Mandilyn, daughter-in-law Sharla, and two very precious grandchildren, Ryan and Keira.

Roger is an avid putzer, sports junkie, non-earth-muffin food addict (he likes his junk food), a very blessed husband, proud father, and grateful grandpa. He loves to create things, from the challenge of being an author to the artistic pursuits of calligraphy, doodling, needlework, stained glass work, intarsia, unique picture framing and matting, wood-working and constructing wooden projects from architectural drawings.

Roger has gained a wealth of experience and insight from years spent in the industries of religion and business. He holds a Bachelor of Theology Degree from North American Baptist College and has served in various capacities in a number of different church situations. He has spent over 35 years in the automotive industry, holding virtually every position possible in a car dealership, from owing a Volkswagen dealership to driving a parts truck (perhaps his favorite job of all). Following a stint at retirement he currently works as a customization co-ordinator at a major automotive dealership.

Roger's other contribution to the literary world is a provocative, major theological treatise, a translation and commentary . based upon the writings of the most prolific contributor to the New Testament entitled, "But…an unauthorized autobiography of the Apostle Paul."

The author will consider invitations for speaking engagements and can be contacted at threescoops@shaw.ca

262

 www.trafford.com

North America & international
toll-free: 1 888 232 4444 (USA & Canada)
phone: 250 383 6864 ♦ fax: 812 355 4082